# Luther and the Mystics

# Luther and the Mystics

A re-examination of Luther's spiritual experience and his relationship to the mystics

## Bengt R. Hoffman

AUGSBURG PUBLISHING HOUSE
Minneapolis, Minnesota

LUTHER AND THE MYSTICS

# Contents

## PART IV: CONCLUSION

To
Pearl

# Abbreviations

CM — *The Church, Mysticism, Sanctification and the Natural,* ed. Ivar Asheim, Philadelphia, 1967.

LW — *Luther's Works,* eds. H. T. Lehmann and J. Pelikan, St. Louis and Philadelphia, 1955-

RGG — *Die Religion in Geschichte und Gegenwart,* Wittenberg, 1957.

W — *D. Martin Luthers Werke,* Kritische Gesamtausgabe, Weimar edition, vols. 1-58, 1883-

WB — *D. Martin Luthers Werke,* Kritische Gesamtausgabe, Weimar edition, Briefwechsel, vols. 1-14, 1930-1970.

WT — *D. Martin Luthers Werke,* Kritische Gesamtausgabe, Weimar edition, Tischreden, vols. 1-6, 1912-1921.

# Preface

It may seem surprising that an interest in the problems of ethical decision-making and a teaching task in ethics can issue in a treatment of mystical theology. However, the close relationship between the moral and the mystical has become increasingly evident to me. This realization is in part an outcome of critical observations. "Rational decision-making" in much contemporary Christian ethics tends to disregard the unique source of power available to the Christian and to depend almost exclusively on criteria provided by the social sciences. The result is that Christian moral responsibility is discussed within the framework of the belief that existence precedes essence. It seems to me that this dependence obscures the Christian ground of moral responsibility which alone inspires cross-bearing and cannot be limited to purely rational considerations. From strict observational scientific vantage points theology as a science has the dubious distinction of being either a prayed theology or nothing. The enterprise of ethical analysis in Christian theology is similarly related to the life of Christian duty which surpasses rational decision-making and seeks inspiration and strength in the essence which precedes existence. It is therefore erroneous to say that Christian ethics is no different from ethics in general. True, we can agree with Martin Luther that "a Christian uses the world in such a way that there is no difference between him

9

and an ungodly man." But we must also agree with him when
he adds: "Yet there is the greatest possible difference. I do
indeed live in the flesh but I do not live on the basis of my own
self. What you hear me speak proceeds from another source."
This happens when we are "touched by the Holy Spirit." In
this sense Christians, writes Luther, are at the center of
God's work in the world. No one can shoulder the Christian
moral commitment without incessant recourse to the mystical
surd behind the ordinary logic of things (*LW* 26; 171-172.
*LW* 24; 79).

The background to these critical observations is a positive
realization which has stolen into my thoughts about the Christian revelation ever since my first acquaintance with the
healthy necessity of historical and linguistic criticism during
my initiation into theology at Swedish universities, in Lutheran parish work, ecumenical service and studies at Yale. It
became increasingly clear that Christian thought and life
wells forth not only from *promise* of the consummation of all
things in Christ at the end of time, but also from *presence*
here and now. The "knowledge in Christ" comes to us from
sources beyond the commonsensical and the linear-logical.
Christ is indeed with us as he promised, engendering a new
"knowledge" and a trust beyond the purely reasonable. If
theological thought about the Christ revelation borrows all its
tools from scientific materialism it loses its sense for supernatural symbol and power.

In Martin Luther's writings I found intriguing references
to "mystical theology" and to experience of "the mystical
Christ." My consultation of secondary literature led to the
discovery that many scholarly queries into Luther's world of
thought ignore or minimize such utterances. A few scholars
maintain that Luther's kinship with mystics was essential,
not accidental. Their works helped me greatly as I turned to
a more sustained study of the primary sources, Luther's own
words. But these scholars are, of course, not responsible for
my choice of point of entry, namely a scrutiny of the neglect

of Luther's spirituality in goodly portions of widely used interpretative literature.

Material edited by Luther's friends and followers may at times reflect views which appear to be at variance with Luther's basic thought. As I have occasion to point out in Chapter 7, footnote 40, and in Chapter 10, footnote 14, quotations culled from works whose authenticity has been in part questioned, fit into themes which can be found throughout Luther's production.

I owe debts of gratitude to helpful librarians at the University of Uppsala, to research workers at the Institut für Spätmittelalter und Reformation at the University of Tübingen, and to Professor Donald Matthews, Librarian at the Lutheran Theological Seminary at Gettysburg. I thank Jerome Abraham, Gettysburg seminarian, and John Siegmund, M.Div., for their assistance in work on footnotes and indexes. Pearl, my wife, not only typed drafts but also helped greatly in the revision process. The dedication page carries her name on this account but also for the deeper reason that she is a co-pilgrim in the concerns raised by this book.

Wherever there is general agreement between *Luther's Works* and my own renderings, the former have been quoted for the benefit of the American student of Luther's thought. At points where my perception of the original in some measure differs from *Luther's Works*, my translation has been used. The relevant footnote carries an indication to that effect.

In cases where no English translation currently exists, the translation in the text is mine. In this category fall some renderings from the Latin where my understanding of the text has been aided by access to German translations.

BENGT HOFFMAN

# Introduction

*Imputation and experience—an integral tension in Martin Luther's theology.*

Martin Luther placed a limit on Christian mysticism by his emphasis on "the external word." Theological interpretations of Luther which put prime emphasis on externality certainly have a wealth of material to work with. In his battle against Roman *Werkheiligkeit*, the piety of works, against mystical salvation schemes that did not have Christ at the center, and against the almost "discarnate" forms of enthusiastic Reformation piety, Luther employed terms reflecting his desire to anchor the gospel firmly in history and in Holy Writ. He used expressions like "righteousness outside us," "Christ for us" and, as noted, "the external word," which point away from the human person to something objective, and he underlined the eschatological character of sanctification. This objective and eschatological vocabulary is the summation of Luther's attempts to bring out the imputative character of faith. Since righteousness is imputed the individual Christian has done nothing about it himself. The Christian is advised to take hold of the promise of forgiveness given in the word but think nothing of the movements of his soul which, because they fluctuate, are not reliable guides to God.

However, we find in Luther's thought another category of terms mirroring personal experience and an awareness of non-rational forces active in faith. These terms convey Luther's persuasion that precisely the external in sign and word reaches and is meant for the internal, for "heart" and "feeling." The imputation of God's righteousness is in fact unavailing without the indwelling of Christ which can be experienced "with mystical eyes," in Luther's words.

Luther alluded to the area of the personal and non-rational through the following phraseology, to take a few examples: "the kingdom in us," "the *unio mystica,*" "the mystical Christ," *gemitus,* the anguish, the pain of standing before God without even the merit of knowing what to say, and *raptus,* the transporting bliss of God's presence. The words "feel" and "experience" appeared frequently in Luther's terminology when he described the inner, personal side of God's redemptive work. The general frame of reference for this other side of Luther's world is "mysticism."

## The meaning of mysticism

It should be quite clear from the outset that Martin Luther never dealt with mysticism as a uniform body of belief. It is perhaps one of the major difficulties in the discourses on Luther's relationship to mysticism that the term in question is frequently used as a general notion about whose content there is supposed to be universal agreement. No such agreement exists. Without attempting a formulation which would remove our lack of a definitive definition, let us first of all determine that if the term "mysticism" is to be applied to Luther at all it must be understood to have reference to the non-rational experience-side of faith which played an important role in his theology. In his own way Luther came close to various descriptions of mystical experience. Mysticism has been pictured as "a conscious direct contact of the soul with Transcendental Reality" (Sharpe), "the establishment of conscious relation with the Absolute" (Underhill), "the soul's possible union in this life with Absolute Reality" (Rufus Jones), "the experimental perception of God's presence and being" (Pattison), "the most divine knowledge of God which takes place in the union which is above intelligence, when the intellect is united to the superlucent rays" (Dionysius the Areopagite), "as by the hands of angels we both feel the being of God and attribute to angelic ministration whatever similitude in which the feeling was conveyed" (Bernard of Clairvaux).

Mysticism in the forms thus described seems to deny that knowledge is limited to the range of physical sensation and psychological common sense. Sense impressions, the process of intellection, the gradual unfolding of the content of normal consciousness are not to provide the final corrals for man's quest of God. The foundation for the mystical method is not in logic but in life. By experience the mystic is persuaded that the seeking person can know in a way in which knowledge is not attainable by sensate experience alone. Through prayer and meditation the mystical seeker is in union with his Lord and apprehends the reality or some of the reality of that lordship.

As suggested, Martin Luther was evidently acquainted with the personal experiential spirituality of which mystics speak. But mysticism as a conceptual system to be accepted or rejected was of little interest to him. He spoke of the mystical as the inner side of the external creed, personally appropriated and felt, and this to him was not a system called mysticism but rather mystical theology. It is notable that when Luther tried his hand at something resembling a definition of the mystical approach he borrowed it from a so-called mystic, Bernard of Clairvaux. "Mystical theology," wrote Luther, is of the "experimental" and "experiential" order. That is to say, mystical theology is experience of God. Luther's use of the word "mystical" emerges from his elaboration of the treasures hidden in Christ. Wisdom and love are hidden in the suffering and dying Christ, he wrote. Hidden? Yes, for those treasures are visible "to mystical and spiritual eyes." [1] Mystical theology, then, is the inner, spiritual side of the Christian faith on Luther's accounting.

## The question of methodology

I will attempt to analyze various theological approaches to the mystical elements in Luther's theology and lift out some aspects of his thought reflecting mystical spiritual experience. The main methodological procedure is thereby given: some major theological interpretations will be examined with respect to their understanding of the mystical in Luther; the place of particular preconceptions in such accounts will be the object of investigation; in the process Luther's statements indicating a central concern with the mystical will be examined for a deeper significance than has generally been accorded to them.

But inside this general approach one particular methodological question must be considered. Martin Luther did not, as indicated, devote much energy to definitions of mysticism but rather conceived of the mystical side of faith as the "experimental" and "experiential" apprehension of God and related this experience very closely to God's gift of righteousness through faith in Christ. Hence the method of approach to our first concern in the field of mysticism, medieval mysticism, becomes important. In the literature on the subject we encounter a systematic method which both Protestants and Roman Catholics apply from strict dogmatic starting points: in Protestant scholarship a framework which excludes the indwelling of Christ and concentrates on the imputative Christ-deed; in Roman Catholic research a graduation theory of acquired and infused grace. Secondly, some of the writers concerned look at the area of investigation from a primarily phenomenological angle. This is to say, they endeavor to evince the phenomenological overlapping discernible between medieval mystics and Luther. Thirdly, we note a predominantly generic method which arranges the different mystical authors of some interest to Luther in categories of general systematic intention.

The reason why the first method, the dogmatic one, is not viable for the purpose we have set ourselves, will be explicated as the thesis and its background are discussed later in this Introduction. Concerning the second method, the phenomenological one, it will be applied with some necessary modifications. A search for phenomena of mystical import common to mystics and Luther immediately encounters the fact that "mysticism" may signify so many varied religious postures that the common denominator tends to lose its meaning. The method in question will consequently be used in constant rapport with Luther's central tenet, justification by faith. The third method, the generic one, seems to grow in part out of Luther's own suggestions. It will be combined with the phenomenological approach in the present account. This will be done, however, with due recognition of the fact that categorization of medieval mystics does not do justice to every individual mystic. Luther at one point quoted the same mystic favorably, and, at another point, disapprovingly. In neither case should adoption or rejection of a total system be implied. As in the case of the phenomenological method, the generic approach will be employed with Luther's thought of justification in mind.

## On rationalism

Two terms, "rationalism" and "intellectualism," will appear rather frequently on the following pages, hence a brief discourse on their usage should be helpful.

The two terms, rationalism and intellectualism, are employed to indicate a reliance on the testimonies of the senses and a corollary use of logic as it emanates from the world of empirical, natural observation. As far as our subject is concerned rationalism and intellectualism in this sense are not always helpful as they tend to expunge phenomena not amenable to the logical process. Rationalism in fact often becomes an antipode of affirmations of the miraculous. The rationalistic mind would maintain that revelations of deity should be capable of adequate rational attributes, lest theology become wholly vacuous. The objection of the rationalist to the paranormal is that a language about it would not "make sense."

The objection is certainly valid inasmuch as language conveys concepts and no other medium possesses this faculty as long as telepathic communication has not become a common pneumatogram. Yet, the rational-linguistic attributes only predicate and qualify, they do not comprehend their subject. Comprehension requires an assistance which rational assertions cannot provide. This assistance is given by a faculty in man which exceeds his reason. Man has his moments of religion which divulge an a priori drive toward the beyond. In contradistinction to much rationalistic thought I assume that man is a *homo religiosus*.

Rudolf Otto who devoted much reflection to the tension between rationalism and the "inward cognition" that recognizes miraculous occurrences, claimed that the difference between rationalism and its opposite, affirmation of the miraculous, is not that the former denies the latter, the miraculous. Rationalists often produce rational theories to explain miracles and anti-rationalists are often unconcerned about the controversy concerning miracles. The difference, Otto averred, is rather in the mental attitude. Does the attitude permit the rational to preponderate over or even exclude the non-rational or, does the non-rational assume tyrannical power over the rational? In our definition of rationalism the place of the non-rational in religion is next to non-existent. The symbols of forces beyond the causal chain are given intellectualistic and rationalistic interpretations. This bias to rationalization is evident in many interpretations of Martin Luther's theology.

## The thesis and its background

The thesis of the present study is that *Martin Luther's faith-consciousness was significantly molded by mystical experience and that western dependence on rationalism has obscured or eclipsed this mystical light*. This is to say that the rational attributes of trustworthiness and loving care ascribed to God and the corresponding realities of faith and trustfulness found in man, are shot through with non-rational intimations, experiences of fascinating, awe-inspiring and bliss-giving presence.

Luther's language about God residing in the heart of the believer was not only figurative. It was based on actual experience. The rational terms for God-man union were underpinned by mystical knowledge.

As indicated, there are barriers built into western intellectual thought structures which render it difficult to grasp the intimate connection between the conceptual-doctrinal and the experiential in Luther's legacy. I see this difficulty as a threefold censorship to which much western scholarship has been subjected, mostly unawares. The three tendencies toward constriction will hopefully become manifest as the account proceeds. I will, however, call attention to them in this Introduction in order to alert the reader to my leanings and also to have the censoring notions assembled in one context.

First, numerous interpretations of Luther's mystical nomenclature are influenced by a desire to emphasize at each essential doctrinal locus a fundamental theological-logical contradistinction between Protestantism and Roman Catholicism. The mystical is not judged germane to non-Roman notions of faith and salvation and hence ruled out of serious consideration.

Second, Melanchthonian intellectualism tended to interpret Luther in logical-conceptual categories. Hence Luther's mystical utterances received and receive rather short shrift in what has been called "the Lutheran school." Words like "holiness" and "God's wrath" were interpreted from a moral point of view, as law chastising man before the receipt of grace, not as symbols for the experience of God's presence.[2]

Third, theology's servitude under a Newtonian scientific philosophy largely ruled out a significant recognition of supernatural or transrational elements in Luther's thinking. Within a mindset dominated by causality mechanistically understood, it becomes difficult to reckon seriously with the possibility that Luther experienced faith, under word and sacrament, much the same way as some mystics whom he cherished.

Some elaboration on the last point is in order, not least because contemporary western culture finds itself in an unparalleled encounter between the intellectualistic style of Renaissance man and a new mystical mode, including realization of mind's power over matter and appreciation of the miraculous.[3] It is the glory of Renaissance man to have essayed the conquest of our world through the development of intellection. The machine has been the instrument of this conquest. But the dream of eventual total mastery has also been applied to man's being, his natural instincts and his intuitive intimations. In neither instance would it be appropriate to point accusing fingers. The world has gained by the Renaissance approach and technology is here to stay. Yet, the Renaissance ideal denigrates the non-intellectual components of man, instincts, feelings and intuitive intimations, by assuming that they must become entirely subservient to the intellect. The Renaissance ideal is a world, including the inner world of man, wholly harnessed by human reason. The unusually strong contemporary interest in things mystical should be seen in part as a protest against this ideal. Increasing numbers find—most of them without formulating the finding in words—intellectualism's blueprint of the future inadequate. This inadequacy is twofold. Persons of the Renaissance tradition will usually not accept "the primitive," including the religious drive, as an ideal part of man and certainly not as a bona fide part of modern man. Moreover, Renaissance man rejects, in the name of the clear daylight of reason, any suggestions about impulses from beyond the empirical world.

Much theological inquiry into the meaning of divine revelation has been and still is wrought up in the presuppositions of Renaissance man. In theological reflection the conceptual and the doctrinal, the confidence that faith can be exhaustively comprised in rational concepts, prevailed and prevail over the devotional, inexpressible and non-rational impulses that accompany the God-man relationship. This culturally conditioned limitation on the part of much theological research hampers a fuller understanding of Martin Luther's world of thought. For an exclusive intellectualization of the message of our prophets always threatens to deemphasize the non-rational, mystical source of their message.

On the other hand, it should be made clear that stress on the supra-rational in Luther's life and thought is not tantamount to advocacy of irrationalism. The accentuation will simply say that a concept of deity frequently fails where the feeling of deity remains as an osmosis. The feeling of paranormal presence is always a part of true faith, in varying degrees. Such a feeling is not to be equated with subjective emotion. I share Rudolf Otto's opinion that religious awe should not have its focus on a psychological process but rather on an object, the God of mystery. Yet, the subjective affect belongs intrinsically to the picture.

An inquiry into Luther's mystical inclinations may be interpreted as an attempt to theologize about a matter which has already been declared impervious to conceptualization. But reasoning about the experiences of faith must remain a priority. Rudolf Otto's words on this issue are still apposite. Theology's task, he wrote, is to "deepen the Christian conception of God by permeating it with its non-rational elements." [4]

## Three approaches

Luther's relationship to the mystics, i.e., those to whom religion was experience of God, has been the object of systematic treatment in theological circles ever since the Reformer departed this world. One has sensed that the question is a crucial one. I will follow some of this discussion and divide different judgments and appraisals of Luther's way with mystics into three major avenues: traditional-confessional theology, liberal and neo-orthodox theology, and pneumatic theology. While these rubrics may appear inadequate or even arbitrary from some points of view, it should be remembered that they are not intended as definite categories or titles for total systematic schemes. The group headings have been formulated with respect to one single point, the attitude towards mystics and mysticism. This problem in its turn revolves around a theologian's theory of knowledge, that is to say, how he reckons with the rational.

There is one form of reckoning with the rational which could be termed theological supernaturalism. Much confessional orthodoxy falls in this category. Its treatment of mystical elements in Martin Luther's thought makes this especially clear. Confessional orthodoxy represents a kind of rationalism which repristinates Luther's ideas in the molds of the Lutheran schoolmen. Although Protestant theology was primarily anti-Catholic it almost unwittingly repaired to rationalistic-scholastic ruts much like those of its opponents.

The second grouping, here termed liberal-neo-orthodox, discussed (and discusses) mysticism and mysticism in Luther's thinking largely guided by a theory of knowledge derived from natural science and historical criticism. The rationalism of this category is the common sense attributed to "modern man." Scientific wariness of supernatural presupposition is a characteristic of this theological rationalism. Its communication of Luther's theology of faith to the common sense of "modern man" resorts to an empirical frame of reference which has little room for the mystical. This lack of space for the mystical becomes more acute in cases where the theologian combines with his empiricism a Protestant persuasion that mysticism is inferior theology because it is Roman Catholic theology.

Finally, the third bracket, the pneumatic interpreters, embraces scholars who have deliberately approached Martin Luther's world with concessions to non-rational elements in religious experience and theologizing related to that experience. Like the representatives of the two previous groups they do not necessarily see eye to eye on all major theological loci. Yet, with respect to Luther's understanding of mystical theology their interpretations coincide in essence.

# PART I

# Theological
# Interpretations
# of
# Luther's Faith

# CHAPTER 1

# Traditional Confessional Views

The spirit of scholasticism is present in Lutheran orthodoxy. In order to defend itself against the Roman assaults, against Calvinistic teachings and against spiritualistic aberrations in their own midst, the Lutheran Protestants made an intellectualized system out of Martin Luther's writings. The rediscovery of the meaning of God's righteousness and man's justification was incorporated into a system of tight formulations. The same kind of defense mechanism against tendencies of religious dissipation that was set in motion by medieval scholasticism now appeared on Protestant ground. Minds of great intellectual discernment formulated the order of salvation inherent in the new experience. The Lutheran revolution was codified in confessions and dogmatic treatises. The rationalism which had been rejected when it appeared in scholastic garb on Roman soil stole into the world of the Reformation.

In order to recover the pristine truth of the Christian beginnings the Protestant Orthodox tended to look at the word of the Bible as inerrant in the external, verbal, mechanical sense. Perhaps they forgot that Martin Luther himself had spoken of the Word as dynamic Christ-presence, where the external sound and symbol became a potent message, radiating God and God-in-Christ. In a rational, logical manner they chiselled out guidelines for the Christian revelation and life.

That revelation and that life, however, are grounded in

something which is non-rational. When one intellectualizes in orderly fashion about something which is at its root non-rational, the "repristination," the recovery of the original, the pristine in the Christ drama and the wordings about it, may well lose the pristine inner glow in the process. Any defensive situation, any polemical stance may lead to a sharpening of formulations and a reliance on the intellect which obscures the immediate experience which lay at the root of the original testimonies. Lutheran "repristination theology," however admirable and understandable, suffers from a lack of sense for the unpredictability and adventure which are part of the life of the Holy Spirit. In fact, Lutheran orthodoxy has always had considerable trouble making theological sense of the third article of the Apostolic Creed. The Holy Spirit seems enshrined in sacramental positivism. The step forward to evangelical freedom in this way turns into a step backward to the sacramental positivism of the Roman church which was a target for Lutheran orthodoxy's verbal surface attacks.

Thus the systematizers of Lutheran theology belonging to the repristination school displayed little or no awareness of Luther's kinship with mystical experience. This kinship does not fit their range of apperception. In the minds of the Lutheran schoolmen mysticism was tantamount to the kind of "spiritualism" which they knew had Luther's deep disapproval. Fortified by such high disapproval they overlooked Luther's allusions to mystical experience as part of theological faith. They did so guided by a desire to maintain *ordo salutis* as an objective account of the nature of faith. The suggestion that Luther showed affinity with subjective mystics did not agree with Orthodoxy's summary of biblical revelation.

One of the most prominent early Lutheran compendia on evangelical Lutheran loci is *Abraham Calovius'* (1612-1686) *Hypomnemata*. Calovius made no direct reference to the mystical life nor to Martin Luther's acquaintance with mystical writing. But his general attitude to the uncertainties of spiritual immediacy and intimacy, which are correlates of mystical apprehension, can be perceived in his rejection of the third use of the law. For, although in essential regards equally rationalistic in their expositions of doctrine, Lutheran and Calvinistic orthodoxy diverged substantially concerning the significance of commands for a Christian life.

Calovius argued as follows. Lutheran doctrine speaks of a civil use of the law and a religious use of the law. Through civil law God keeps men within necessary bounds. The religious use of the law concerns the chastising effect of interdictions and moral obligations. The religious use is a prelude to salvation—by chastising us it reminds us of our innate sinfulness. But the Calvinistic teaching introduces a third use of the law which is described as dutiful obedience, as holding a promise of growing awareness of God and as serving as a vehicle of sanctification. Now, Calovius objected, by depicting sanctification in this manner the Calvinists had constructed a false foundation. They had, said Calovius, created a foundation with building blocks from the sphere of *man* whereas the real basis for Christian living is "universal propositions" about *God.*

These universal propositions, Calovius continued, revolve around the belief or scriptural fact that God has mercy on *all* and that Christ has achieved remission of sins and salvation for *all.* Faith must be derived from dogmatic universals. Faith cannot be private, as the Calvinist doctrine on the third use of the law wrongly suggests. Faith, Calovius maintained, is public, not private, for Christ delivered *all.*[1]

There are two strikes against mystical theology implied in the notion of faith as public, universal propositions as opposed to private experience. First, the confessional *compendium* now under discussion conceived of theology as a congeries of "propositions."[2] That is to say, we deal with expressions in which the predicate affirms or denies something about the subject and purports to do so in a final manner. The biblical message has in this view been exhaustively encased in a number of categorical cognitive statements. Because mysticism, and especially the mystical forms within Luther's purview, did not suffer the intellectualistic ways of Roman scholasticism, it is safe to assume that the same animus would prevail between the mystics and Protestant scholastics, the repristination theologians.[3] Conversely, inasmuch as Lutheran schoolman Calovius resorted exclusively to rationality in submitting the body of doctrinal loci he did in fact rule out a non-rational, mystical element in faith. Propositional orthodox theology in Calovian vintage was bound to the conceptual in a fashion which excluded the mystical.

Secondly, since much mysticism speaks of experience and immediate contact with the Godhead it falls into the category which Calovius shunned as "privatism" in religion. Jesus' words about his revealing certain truths to the lowly and humble and concealing them from the exalted and strong carry little meaning for repristination theology. The "propositions" are said to be public not only in the sense that they are valid for all but also in the sense that they are approachable and attainable by all.

Lutheran orthodoxy frequently arrived at its dogmatic assertions in confutation of Calvinistic doctrine.[4] This is also the case in a voluminous work on apologetics, *Grundtlicher Beweis*, written by the Wittenberg faculty more than one hundred years after Luther's death. The book in question asserted: "The faith that leads to blessedness is such a trust in God that I, a poor sinner, condemned by the law, know, trust and am assured by the word of the gospel that God wishes to forgive me all my sins and this from his sheer grace for the sake of Jesus Christ and confer on me my Lord Jesus Christ's righteousness so that I thereby become righteous and eternally blessed." What man is told in the word of the gospel must consequently be appropriated. God's promises must be trusted and the individual reader should include himself in their general assurance.[5] The dogmatic treatise was quite explicit in its judgment concerning personal experience. Nothing in me, a sinner, gives me the right to "include myself in a special promise." There is in the word of the gospel no *verbum singulare*, no special address to the individual. Rather, "the *verbum universale*, the general promise which goes for all, should be placed as the foundation." Jesus provides "a precious general merit." Through faith in him we receive forgiveness of sins, righteousness and blessedness, not as a personal gift but as an appropriation of a universal offer.[6]

As evidenced by *Grundtlicher Beweis* the Wittenberg faculty, around the middle of the 17th century, was of course well aware that many Christians insisted that a certain internalization and personalization must be part of, even considered an integral element of, salvation. The orthodox schoolmen were quite explicit in their refutation of such a doctrine. Those who conceived of the Christian faith in terms of an individual address from the word of God or a felt inner testimony were pronounced heretics.[7] Although no direct reference was made to Martin Luther—such references are remarkably rare in Lutheran orthodox writings—it was obviously Luther's emphasis on "the outer word" and "Christ for us" which obtained exclusive attention. Faith was represented as an appropriation of Christ's righteousness and the appropriation consisted of a repetition of the assertion that "Jesus Christ died for me." "The signs" of faith, especially the practice of divine feeling and good works, were judged of no avail without such appropriation as objective assurance and only heresy could claim essential dignity for them.[8]

Hence the other side of Luther's view of faith, the experience side, the mystical aspect, remained unrecognized in *Grundtlicher Beweis*. In the same fashion as Calovian dogmatics, faith in the voluminous Wittenberg treatise was largely equated with the conceptual appropriation of the doctrine about faith.[9]

To move from the works of Lutheran orthodoxy in the 17th century to the same kind of writings in the 19th century is like transferring from one apartment to another and finding identical furnishings. In the meantime pietism and Newtonian science had appeared on the scene and traditional orthodoxy was no doubt compelled to register their appearance. Yet the doctrinal formulas have changed very little. *Heinrich Schmid's*

well-known and much used work on Christian dogmatics
bears out this observation. Schmid prefaced his exposition
by placing a definite limit on his use of viable dogmaticians.
Hollatius, he wrote, must be the last expounder of true Christianity considered in the book. However, Schmid continued,
even Hollatius should be handled with some care for he au-
thored his works at a time when great uncertainty had set in
concerning orthodox theology. Schmid found Baumgarten
even more influenced by questionable ideas, especially the
notions of pietism. Schmid chose not to discuss this statement
in detail, that is to say whether pietism was, as he phrased
it, "deviation from Lutheran principles." But he really left
his readers in no doubt whatever as to where he stood. He
noted that pietism had exerted a corroding influence on the
"uncolored purity" of right doctrine. Schmid was as confident
at the middle of the 19th century as his mentors had been
one hundred and two hundred years previously that there was
no substance to the allegation that Lutheran dogmatics had
grown old and tired. "The old dogmatics," he asserted, "is not
antiquated and shall never become antiquated." [10]

From Schmid's work, which is in part an anthology of Lutheran schoolmen through the centuries, Gerhard, Calovius,
Hutter, Quenstedt, Hollatius and the credal documents, the
Augsburg Confession and the Formula of Concord, two terms
will be lifted out with bearing upon the mystical tradition,
*unio mystica* and *illuminatio*. As far as *unio mystica* is concerned Heinrich Schmid thought that the term could be safely
adopted by orthodox Lutheran theology provided it was part
and parcel of justification by faith as "forgiveness of sins"
and regeneration as "the faculty of faith." Justification by
faith and regeneration on Schmid's accounting produced "the
abiding of God in special fashion in the justified or reborn."
In this sense, Schmid opined, a Lutheran theologian may well
speak of "the substance of God" uniting with "the substance
of man." However, unification could take place only in the
believer. Under some circumstances this assertion might be
made also by a pietist and Schmid doubtless betrayed that he

had grappled with pietism as none of his fathers in the faith. But he repaired to solid conceptual ground as he continued that the mystical union was not *substantialis* nor was it *personalis*. The reader was promptly returned to the realm of rational appropriation even with respect to *unio mystica*.[11]

Let us digress and examine some of Lutheran orthodoxy's uses of the mystical-sounding term *unio mystica*. Lutheran orthodoxy has always had a way of employing the term which in a helpful manner highlights the issue of the mystical in Luther's legacy. Since Schmid recorded dicta by mentors enjoying orthodox imprimatur it matters little that we take Quenstedt as our guide, a dogmatician *en vogue* 150 years before Schmid but approvingly used by the latter. Quenstedt wrote in 1685, "Christ and the believers remain separate persons in the mystical union." Quenstedt was anxious to underline the separation for he thought that the passage in John 17:22 so demanded. When Jesus said, "The glory which thou hast given me I have given to them, that they may be one even as we are one," he must in Quenstedt's view have meant union with built-in separation. Quenstedt emphasized that the connecting word is "even" which means "similarly." The mystical union was more in the nature of an analogue. It was therefore heretical to argue that the human person changed into the divine person in *unio mystica*. It was by no means a matter of confluence of God and man in one substance or one person. Thus *unio mystica* in Lutheran orthodoxy was molded by a concern for the objective doctrine of a revelatory deed done for men and appropriated by them without any essential regard for "the harmony and concert of the affects." *Unio mystica* had become part of a largely conceptual order of salvation. The construction put upon the mystical notion in question was such that it had little room for the language and experience of the medieval mystics with whom Martin Luther was in spiritual contact.[12]

The second word of mystical import to be examined in Schmid's work is *illuminatio*, stage number two in the spiritual life of mystics (the other stages being purification and union) but not treated by Schmid with any reference to the mystical order of exercise and experience. Illumination could never be immediate, according to Schmid. At this point he obviously echoed Luther's warnings against enthusiasts who, abandoning external signs, claimed to contact the uncreated word. Schmid found supporting evidence in a passage from 2 Peter which reads, "We heard this voice borne from heaven, for we were with him on the holy mountain." The point here would be that the disciples were not given a direct illumination. The light dawned in their hearts only because Jesus mediated it.

In like manner the word of God mediates illumination, said Schmid. This word is "the prophetic word," he wrote, and as prophetic word it is *verbum Dei auditum,* the aural word communicated by Scripture. Direct communication with the Godhead was not part of God's promise. The word can be read calmly and rationally. Therefore "ecstasy" which is sometimes said to accompany illumination must be rejected by sound doctrine. Wrote Schmid: "God does not promise in his word to illuminate anyone through ecstasy." One may find people holding these erroneous notions in the camp which is what Schmid brands an "antithesis" to sound Christian teaching, namely "Platonists, quakers and mystics." In the last analysis, this Lutheran 19th century dogmatician declared, ecstasy could be tolerated as an excusable heresy.

But the "rapture" which was occasionally introduced in descriptions of spiritual illumination Schmid condemned out of hand. "Rapture" was worse than *ecstasis,* he thought, for "it adds violence." To Schmid and his fellow scholastics among the Lutherans the experience which Luther and some mystics specified as *raptus,* the experience of being swept into God's arms, was too much of a human attempt to take the kingdom by human force. *Illuminatio,* then, was simply the mediated teaching of the word of God, not the feeling of God's entry into the soul after purification.[13]

A quarter century after Schmid, *Ernst Luthardt* in a dogmatics *Kompendium* quoted Luther as saying that Wessel, the

Dutch mystic, and he, Martin Luther, seemed to think so much alike that "my opponents could get the idea that Luther fetched everything from Wessel." Luthardt obviously felt it incumbent upon him to extricate Martin Luther from the suspicion of having an essential rapport with a mystic and consequently commented that appearances are deceiving. Luther and Wessel were indeed worlds apart, he asserted.[14] In fact, Luthardt continued, mysticism and Lutheran faith are contrasts. Looking at the mystic's threefold way to God, purification, illumination and union, as a dogmatic chart on a par with the orthodox order of salvation and comparing it with the rational orthodox *ordo salutis,* Luthardt found the mystical alternative wanting. Purification had been placed at the wrong juncture, he said. He averred that "mysticism speaks of the threefold way: purification, illumination and the mystical union. Our orthodox doctors held that illumination had to precede purification." In wordings which would seem to be far removed from Martin Luther's experience Luthardt declared that *knowledge* is more important than *will* in Christian faith.[15] In other words, man had to be enlightened by correct doctrine before it was possible to speak of a cleansing process. A rationalism not dissimilar to the use of reason in Roman scholasticism had emerged. The difference was one of accent rather than a disparity in kind. Instead of reason applied to tradition and natural law in Roman fashion there was with Luthardt a method of intellection applied to Scripture and eventuating in dogmatic code words which automatically expunged mystical theology.

The best contemporary example of repristination theology's posture with regard to mysticism is *Pieper* and *Mueller's Christliche Dogmatik.* This book has served many generations of students at the Lutheran Church–Missouri Synod seminary in St. Louis. Like other works by orthodox Lutheran scholars it does not discuss mysticism directly, a fact which invites the suggestion that orthodox Lutheranism has taken for granted that mysticism and Luther's theology have nothing to do with one another. One can speak of an *argumentum de silentio,* an argument against mysticism inherent in the very silence about it.

Discussing Schleiermacher's theology Pieper-Mueller contend that theological certainty remains unattainable as long as a theological system, like that of Schleiermacher, revolves around the subjective human "I." Theological certainty, Pieper-Mueller maintain, is communicated through "the Holy Spirit in the Word." According to these authors certainty lodged in a person's self or his "I," "is not Christian." Documentation for this anti-Schleiermacherian pronouncement is sought in Luther's pamphlet addressed to the King of England. It was in this pamphlet that Luther, under the pressure of an argument in favor of doctrinal licentiousness, came out squarely on the side of doctrine against man-made salvation schemes.[16] The implication for mystical theology—for which, incidentally, Schleiermacher had little understanding—is that it cannot find room in a theological faith since it is subjective.

The Pieper-Mueller work offers another piece of documentation from Luther in support of its anti-subjective thesis. Luther is cited as likening the word of God unto a strong tree. It is buffeted by winds but it stands. Our human nature, on the other hand, is not steadfast. Knocked around by temptations of hatred, envy and the ruses of the devil our nature will fall without the Word to lean on.[17] The Pieper-Mueller work now asserts that the Christian life must be grounded in the objective certainty afforded by scriptural pronouncements about God-in-Christ and shun all inclinations to watch for and rely upon any positive changes in the soul. This means, if I have rightly understood, that the question of *truth*, which is a rational one, predominates over the question of *trust*, which is a volitional and emotional one. "The recognition of truth," write the authors, is based on "Christ's word." This is, they suggest, precisely what "modern theology," from Schleiermacher and Ritschl to Barth and Aulén, has failed to make clear. Modern theology speaks, the authors aver, of the certainty of faith in terms which have been cut to the measuring rods of the world. Modern theology, they hold, has therefore left the real faith.[18] The strong tree of biblical certainty has been abandoned for a reliance on human aspirations. None of the authors thus criticized have displayed much interest in a mystical current with Luther. Yet, their silence on the matter is an argument in itself. For the judgment in *Christliche Dogmatik* concerning the subjective and the private in man's religious quest would strike equally hard at any attempt to ascribe significance to Luther's mystical vocabulary.

A further probe into the thought pattern of *Christliche Dogmatik* by Pieper and Mueller leads us to the conclusion that its process of ratiocination actually prevents a deeper understanding for the place of the mystical in Luther's faith or faith in general. The book's main argument regarding the subjective and affective is based on an almost exclusively intellective foundation. This is particularly evident in the book's discussion of Christian certainty. Christian certainty is said to be based on presumably inerrant statements in the Bible. These statements must be appropriated but this appropriation must not be linked to a spiritual-psychological process within man's soul. The transference of the gospel from word to man takes place on a purely dogmatic-rational level, as a reasoned acceptance of biblical formulations of truth. Luther's emphasis on "the external word" and "Christ for you" has become the sole theological message of the Reformation. By the very nature of its rationalization method the theological work under review can have no receiver for the elements of Luther's mystical theology. The book's silence on Reformation concerns about mysticism, which has been the object of our query, thus becomes understandable. There is no receiver for the emissions of the mystical life.

In summary, repristination theology in the Lutheran tradition is dependent on a method of ratiocination which tends to render the biblical message as objective truths, objective in the sense that they are considered objects to be accepted on the level of intellect, not on the level of consciousness. A dogmatic system is then presented to the church and the world with formulations almost in the nature of the formulas of applied science. Religious experience inspired by non-rational forces is disregarded. Mysticism and mystical theology are looked upon as heretical suggestions and because they embrace non-rational areas of inspiration, like charismatic events, Lutheran orthodoxy does not register them for it possesses no receptacle for a proper treatment of them in a theological context. To the Lutheran schoolmen God is conceivable in the sense that his salvatory activity as depicted in Scripture can be rationally grasped. By constructions of the intellect they propose to exhaust the mystery of God-in-Christ.

Three deficiencies with respect to the mystical are discernible in Lutheran orthodoxy through the centuries up to the present time.

*First,* it is not sensitive to the mystical experience since mystical experience is conscious of incomprehensible realms, whereas Lutheran orthodoxy confines itself to rendering revelation dogmatically comprehensible.

*Second,* Lutheran orthodoxy is consequently not interested in undertaking a differentiation with respect to various forms of mysticism. Martin Luther's interest in this matter has accordingly escaped Lutheran orthodoxy.

*Third,* as a result of the foregoing, Lutheran orthodoxy has failed to discover any significance in the mystical terminology appearing in Martin Luther's theology of faith.

The mystical vocabulary in Luther's theology will be discussed at some length in the latter part of the present investigation but it will also be touched upon in the subsequent section dealing with liberal and neo-orthodox theology's understanding of references to the mystical in Luther's thought.

# CHAPTER 2

# Liberal
# and Neo-Orthodox Views

In order to probe further into the nature of Luther's contact with and understanding of mystics and mystical theology we now enter an area of enquiry where the impact of cultural change and scientific knowledge has been much stronger than in Lutheran orthodoxy. Liberal and neo-orthodox theologies, despite their polemical relationship, share a desire, not so apparent in Lutheran orthodoxy, to relate to culture, as well as a commitment to rational judgment which renders difficult an adequate evaluation of the non-rational contribution to the rational.[1]

Since it would seem that Martin Luther did acknowledge precisely the place of the non-rational in theological persuasion one might ask what are the particular methods in liberal and neo-orthodox thought systems which seem to impede the insight or preclude a recognition. The suggestion growing out of the following examination is twofold. Luther's view concerning mystical experience has been obscured by the method of generalizing mysticism and by the method of applying culturally conditioned preconceptions to the material.

## A. Mysticism generalized

Theological reflection which has been influenced by *Albrecht Ritschl* (1822-1889) as well as by the methodological yardsticks of natural science in the 19th and the beginning of the 20th century appears to have employed the term "mysticism" as an undifferentiated, indivisible totality. We shall be referring to this notion as mysticism *en bloc*. Mysticism *en bloc* means that the impression is created that the reality behind the term does not contain significant diversity.

One reason for the persistent appearance of "mysticism" as a generalized category is no doubt lack of scholarly attention to the area. Until rather recently Protestant studies of Luther in his relationship to mysticism have been few and mainly focused on the post-Reformation phenomenon of enthusiastic mysticism. Another reason could well be the tendency to take over, without independent investigation, magisterial verdicts from the pens of respected scholars. Judgments on mysticism have in this way been transmitted from generation to generation without further basic work at the sources. A third reason for the generalized use of the term mysticism is clearly the Protestant predilection for absolute categories as distinctions are hammered out between evangelical and Catholic truth. For instance, Protestants have absolutized the dichotomy speculation-faith as one peculiarly apposite to the Roman Catholic-Protestant controversy. Mysticism is frequently classed as speculation and invariably placed in the non-evangelical camp. Another example of the absolutizing tendency is discernible in the controversy about man's continuity with God or his discontinuity. Liberal and neo-orthodox theological reflection assigns mysticism *in toto* and *as such* to the former—and Catholic—bracket.

Ritschl was once described as a theologian who, despite his basic methodology, aroused an interest in mysticism. It has been said that his "idea of the uniqueness of the Christian experience" proved untenable and therefore opened an avenue to the world of the mystics.[2] Be that as it may, Ritschl's direct treatment of mysticism was in itself no invitation to mysticism. He drew a sharp demarcation line between what he termed "the Catholic-mystical" and the "evangelical-Lutheran."[3] He tended to treat mysticism, first, as a totality with uniform basic thrusts, and second, as a phenomenon which basically militates against evangelical Lutheran concepts.

*Karl Holl* (1866-1926) can perhaps not be readily classified in the category "liberal-positive." [4] But as a writer on mysticism and its influence on Luther he no doubt partly qualified for the classification. Holl contraposed biblical Protestantism and mysticism. In the process he dealt with mysticism as one block, the characteristics of which he assumed to be equally typical for any and all forms of mystical behavior.

According to Holl, mysticism discovered deep within man a kinship with God, the divine spark, and converted these religious discoveries into autonomous values.[5] All mysticism is in Holl's view "a subtle search for enjoyment." In all mystical circles suffering is accepted as a pleasure.[6] The goal of a Christian life was therefore one thing for Martin Luther and a totally different thing for the mystics. Mysticism represented, Holl wrote, a human urge for happiness whereas Martin Luther placed personal responsibility in the center.[7]

In later additions to the original Luther study Holl made an interesting, qualifying note on the structure of mysticism. He had observed a difference between Romanic and German mysticism. His final conclusion, however, coincided with his earlier assertion: there are no fundamental distinctions, for all mysticism is grounded in a philosophical notion of God.[8] Returning to the problem later in the account now quoted Holl conceded that German mysticism "goes deeper into sin-consciousness" than other forms of mysticism but even on second thought he could not agree that this sin-consciousness was akin to Luther's. The German mystics, Holl wrote, supposed that sin was "only an untoward thing." Tauler, for instance, spoke of inner freedom, *Gelassenheit,* in a way that would let sin just "float by", not allowing it to "concern the inner man." [9] Therefore, despite the nuances that had come into Holl's purview, this prominent student of Luther's world of thought was unable to conclude that mystical theologies preceding Luther spoke of religious experience in the same vein as the Reformer.

Since Holl has played an important part in molding the image of Martin Luther for the modern world, a few additional illustrations of his method of generalization about mysticism may be in order. One of them concerns Luther's term for despair about salvation and the sense of being assaulted by demonic power, *Anfechtung*. With respect to *Anfechtung*, Holl declared, there was an absolute distinction between Luther and the world of mystics.[10]

In claiming that *Anfechtung* was a unique Luther experience and perhaps a special insight of the Reformation, Holl neglected the fact that few, if any in Luther's spiritual entourage on the Protestant side, knew what *Anfechtung* meant. Holl also appears to have been unaware of a remark once made by Luther about one particular mystic who in Luther's view had experienced *Anfechtung*. The mystic was Gerson and Luther said about him in a table conversation that, although there were quite a few who knew the meaning of bodily and fleshly *Anfechtung*, Gerson "was the only one who wrote about spiritual *Anfechtung*. Therefore he alone can comfort and build up consciences." Holl's idea that mysticism as such can have no room for *Anfechtung* becomes less tenable in the light of this remark by Luther.[11]

With respect to Luther's notion on *Anfechtung* Karl Holl was guided by his concept of mysticism as a blockword with unequivocal basic content under all circumstances. In the process he placed the notion of *Anfechtung* among Reformation teachings maintaining that mysticism by its nature was unaware of the reality in question. However, Holl's generalization does not do justice to the fact that Luther himself acknowledged his affinity with mystic Gerson regarding the experience of spiritual *Anfechtung*. Holl's generalization of mysticism led him to assume, erroneously it would seem, that an absolute distinction prevailed between a person who knows *Anfechtung* and the mystics.

Mysticism's concept of the world was analyzed by Holl with the aid of the generalized picture he had of mystical theology. Holl took for granted that mysticism *en bloc* had absorbed the Platonic tendency to approach the world as a shadow. Therefore Christianity and mysticism could be contraposed, Christianity taking the positive stance in regard to the world and mysticism the negative. To prove his point Holl introduced Luther's concept of God's wrath. Mysticism, he said, regards the world as a shadow, hence has no concept of God's wrath. In Holl's reading two antipodal world pictures vie for supremacy in the discourse on wrath, one emerging from evangelical Christianity, the other from mysticism.[12]

The question of Reformation theology's realism and mysticism's idealism with regard to the world assumes a greater degree of complexity on closer examination. Martin Luther, who did look at the world as a real place where God's wrath was abroad, also knew that in one sense it was a shadow. He maintained that upon arrival on the other side of death we humans shall know this to be so. Then, he wrote, "we perceive that the whole world is dead." That is to say, the living world is rather the invisible one which will once be visible with the aid of faculties of sight other than the ones we now possess.[13] Conversely, mystic Johann Tauler, who did experience the determinate world as a very fleeting thing, also recognized its deep significance. "If I were not a priest," said Tauler, "I would consider it a great thing to be able to make shoes and I would like to make them better than everything else." Tauler saw the importance of work in the world. "Man ought to perform good, useful work," he wrote.[14] Tauler experienced God's wrath through the awareness of his own incapacity before God. For it is precisely God's greatness and our pettiness that create the notion of wrath in us.[15] It would seem that Holl again employed his concept of a mysticism *en bloc* in order to create absolute polarity between an evangelical-reformation view of the world and a mystical view. But the actual mental attitudes involved on either side do not seem to warrant the judgment.

We are still concerned with the generalization of mysticism and its effect on the interpretation of Luther's relationship to the mystical and turn now to another important question,

namely, the problem of man's kinship with or alienation from
God. The pivotal point here is the matter of fear of God. If
there is no fear of God in a person's heart, so the argument
goes, one can assume that he takes a link with God for granted.
If there is fear of God the agent knows that God is the wholly
other. Karl Holl suggested, on the basis of a not at all improb-
able characterization of mysticism, that it presupposes "an
indestructible bridge" from man to God "in the innermost of
man." Such an idea was tantamount to a derogation of the
Christian experience of godly fear, according to Holl. Consequently mysticism proved anew that it was the antipode to
Christianity. The idea of an indestructible bridge was incomprehensible to Luther himself, Holl pointed out.[16]

Holl's dictum that mysticism knows no fear of God mainly
because it arrogates a certain kinship with God loses some of
its pungency when we are confronted with mystical assertions
about encounter with the divine as in part implying fear and
trembling. Johann Tauler, one of the mystics who enjoyed
Luther's confidence, declared that the righteous have gone
through the fear of God and he spoke of the tremendous distance between man and God, a distance so great that the very
word God should indeed be pronounced with fearful trembling.[17]

As far as the problem of "kinship" with God is concerned,
Holl presumably construed every suggestion about an eternal
ground of the soul as a mystical attempt to assume an inner
presence of an unobstructed bridge to salvation and divinization. Yet not all mystics fall into this generalized category.
Tauler, for one, told his listeners that no one would be able
to look into the ultimate ground of his being as long as he
had accumulated obstacles in the way. This ground would
mean nothing to him unless he repented. The obstacle may be
minute, Tauler warned, but it will have the same effect as
large ones, namely to keep us away from contact with the
soul's ground. The soul is then darkened and cannot reflect
God.[18] Commenting on these words of Tauler's Martin Luther
wrote that man possesses an innate ground or a material from

God. The material must be indestructible for it is from God. God is the sculptor working with the material.[19] The Frankfurter, anonymous author of *Theologia Germanica,* a book edited and published by Luther, had similar pronouncements about "the ground." To his mind man had the dual capacity of looking into time and eternity. But the fact that man has the capacity to look into eternity did not mean that he could accord essence to himself. In so doing he would perish.[20]

The conclusion to be drawn from the above discussion on God-fear and God-kinship is that Karl Holl's generalized view of mysticism prevented him from recognizing the ambiguity of the problem. Both Luther and some mystics evidently knew about the realities of fear of God as well as of a ground which man has in common with God. The theological question to pose would be the question of emphasis,not the question of either-or. If the methodological tool applied is mysticism *en bloc* the enquiry moves too far away from reality.

We have previously discussed mysticism's relationship to the world. A portion of this problem is the correlation between the mystical and the ethical. Karl Holl touched upon this subject and since his treatment provides a further opportunity to observe his use of a mysticism *en bloc* notion it will now be given some attention. Briefly Holl thought mysticism was not concerned with duty and moral striving. From the point of view of ethics Holl characterized mysticism as "play." In contradistinction to the alleged lack of moral concern among mystics Holl spoke of Martin Luther as having contributed an "unremitting earnestness." From the ethical vantage point Holl pitted two contradictory postures against one another.[21]

Holl's contention that mystics lean toward lack of moral seriousness in their teachings does not rhyme with Johann Tauler's emphasis on "the humblest deed" as an outflow of life in God or *Theologia Germanica's* reminder to the effect that living in Christ does not consist of detailed moral commandments, yet life in Christ inspires man "to remain in the best." [22] This is to say, the moral life according to those mystics whom Luther cherished most, is the life derived from life in God. The mystic's persuasion on this score is not far from Luther's understanding when in a sermon on John 14:12 he spoke about the works cut out for Christians, their moral responsibilities and the practical moral assistance to the world which only Christians can offer. Why only Christians? Because their moral life is derived from life in Christ.[23] It would appear that the danger of applying a generalized notion of mysticism becomes apparent also with regard to the interconnection between the moral and the mystical.

In our examination of mysticism as an *en bloc* idea in Holl's Luther analysis note should furthermore be taken of the fact that Holl characterized mysticism's notion of the Godhead as "pantheism." Luther, Holl argued, represented the antithetical stance, a Christocentric, personalized faith.[24]

If pantheism is defined as the belief or doctrine that God is not a personality but that all laws, forces and manifestations of the self-existent universe are God, there is no doubt some mysticism which fits the description. Affirmations from the writings of, say, Dionysius the Areopagite and Meister Eckhart may conceivably be pantheistic in the sense here indicated. But in the sermons of Tauler and the tract of the Frankfurter it would be difficult to substantiate Holl's generalization. Tauler suggested that God be addressed as a person and the Frankfurter spoke of God's "selfdom." [25]

It must be concluded that Holl's proposition concerning an antithetical relationship between, on the one hand, a pervasive pantheism in all mystical documents, and, on the other, a Christocentric, personalized faith in Luther's thought, proves to be inadequate. Again, the reason seems to be a mysticism *en bloc* notion.

Holl's schema of antithetical reflection prompted him to suggest that all Catholic thought—scholastic, monastic and mystical—included indifference to the created world and a preponderance of possessive love. On Holl's view the other side of the spectrum belonged to Martin Luther who introduced "a much higher demand." [26]

This is not the place to discuss the validity of Holl's judgment that indifference to the created world and possessive love inherent in spiritual aspiration are pervasive peculiarities in Roman Catholic life or that, conversely, commitment to the created world and non-possessive faith would be the earmarks of Protestant existence. Holl did imply such a bisection and it does raise questions. What concerns us, however, is the suggestion that mysticism was a coherent, monolithic, Roman Catholic philosophy, which consistently poses the right questions in the wrong way, namely from anthropological rather than theological points of entry. Not only was mysticism on Holl's accounting a uniform body of thought closed to divergent interpretations but this mysticism *en bloc* was also interwoven with an even larger block, including scholasticism and monasticism. Two critical observations should be made in this connection. First, a considerable number of mystics would have to be removed from the company to which they were thus assigned. Both scholasticism and monasticism had ardent critics among mystics.[27] The conspectus in Catholic thought, taken for granted by Holl, was no doubt less than absolute. The very fact that medieval mystics did speak out against some forms of establishment emasculates the theory that mysticism is an unequivocal body of thought and practice. Secondly, the six Luther passages to which Holl referred in support of his thesis that indifference and possessive love are the hallmarks of scholasticism, monasticism and mysticism, do not contain any direct mention of mysticism or mystics.[28]

A similar tendency to generalize mysticism as representing total uniformity and similar attempts to demonstrate an absolute theological polarity between mysticism and Martin Luther's theology appeared in *Erich Seeberg's* (1888-1945) analysis of the Reformer's thought.

More clearly than Holl, Seeberg perceived the peril of generalizing mysticism so that as a linguistic symbol it comes to stand for an unambiguous aggregate of concentric notions with different mystics throughout the history of the church. Seeberg paid attention to the fact that Luther acknowledged a certain spiritual kinship with some mystics and he pointed to the apparent affinity between Luther's theology and mystical reflection with respect to personal experience of the divine, experience of cross and suffering in Christ's discipleship, and a feeling of God's awesome hiddenness. It is furthermore worthy of note that Seeberg surmised that Luther's rejection of sacramental positivism ultimately had its genesis in his kinship with mystics.[29]

With good discernment for the strategy best suited to his intent Seeberg selected Tauler among the mystics as the prime object of critical enquiry. In the tradition of Holl, Seeberg alluded to the mystical, Taulerian "ground of the soul" as the "finest and frailest bridge between man and God."[30] Moreover, when Tauler spoke of an *imitatio* of Christ he did not think of ethical tasks alone but conceived of *imitatio* "mystically," i.e., in terms of a formation of Christ in man. The idea of the formation of Christ in man, Seeberg maintained, was in turn derived from metaphysical reasoning rooted in a Platonic concept of supersensible prototypes.[31] Seeberg reached the conclusion that the mystic, even Tauler, represented a basically philosophical notion which should be counterposed by Luther's solidly Christian insight.

As noted in the discussion of Holl's Luther study it seems inadequate to isolate from the rest of Tauler's body of reflection the idea which Seeberg termed "a metaphysical kinship between God and man in Tauler." Tauler knew, as already suggested, the essential truth of justification. In other words, Seeberg spiritualized Tauler's theology at the expense of the existential. Conversely, Seeberg tended to de-spiritualize Luther's thought at the expense of the celestial, claiming that "Luther perceived the entire man as flesh, even his spirit, even the soul-spark."[32]

Having conceded that Luther at some points was in concord with mysticism—God as experience, life with God as cross and suffering, the ineffable majesty of God as hidden, a spiritualized view of the sacraments—Erich Seeberg proceeded to enumerate "the differences" which he regarded as "more important" than the unitive traits. The over-all difference was, said

Seeberg, simply the purported fact that Luther did not subscribe to "the traditional mystical theology." The traditional mystical theology was the theology which, according to Seeberg, "in the essence has taken its cue from the Areopagite." [33] This assertion implied that all mysticism would endow man himself with theological significance beyond the limits set by the gospel. The assertion further implied that all mysticism offered "the three roads," aimed at relinquishing of self and aspired to "the mystical union." On the other hand, none of these notions was present in Luther's thought on Seeberg's reading. Mysticism *en bloc* was of such a nature that no essential affinity could exist between it and Luther's theology.

In relation to some important dogmatic problems Seeberg spelled out his view of the alleged polarity between mysticism and Luther. One of these problems concerned the method of spiritual endeavor. Seeberg's argument ran as follows. Mysticism proposes to attain union with the Godhead by dint of technical means, that is to say, certain strict routines of meditation, prayer and liturgy. "Mysticism is artificial sublimation, artifice and technique." To Luther such "methodism" of attainment was wholly foreign. In fact, his Reformation revolved to a great extent around freedom from such "methodism." "Luther's theology for the life of each man" is sound, concrete and non-technical.[34] Seeberg consequently pitted against each other a notion which purportedly reflects man's self-liberation and a notion which reckons with receipt of grace, without methodical preparation on man's part.

Seeberg's polarization of mysticism and Luther on the matter of devotional method, apart from reflecting a generalized view of mysticism, may not survive a scrutiny of Luther's opinion on the matter. Rudolf Otto has pointed out that Luther placed considerable weight on "method" in Christian devotional life. In a tract of 1535 entitled *How to Pray*, Luther insisted on methodical meditation. Luther's goal for such meditation was the immersion of the soul in the Spirit.[35]

In his treatment of another theological issue, the problem of dualism versus monism, Erich Seeberg maintained the same

absolute distinction between the pervasive theological fallacy of mysticism and the theological correctness of Luther's
thought. Luther's position was depicted as one of dualism
between the creature and the Creator. But "for the Anabaptists and in mysticism" the solution to the man-God problem
is "monistic." [36]

Again, only with assistance of a generalization can this
dispensation method prevail. No doubt Luther rather consistently experienced the reality of "dualism" in his personal
search for a gracious God. On the other hand, Seeberg's mysticism *en bloc* prevented him from seeing that the mystical
experience of *gemītus* reduced man to a point where he was
nothing and God all. Not all mystics saw this, but some did.
It was therefore only with the aid of a theoretical generalization that Seeberg could insist that mysticism "knows nothing
of the profound tension in the depth of our existence without
which we cannot live." [37]

Albeit less dependent than Holl on rigid universals, Seeberg did operate with generalizations of mysticism which hide
the significance of Luther's expressions of kinship with some
mystics.

*Emanuel Hirsch* (1888-    ) in his examination of Reformation theology adjudged Luther's contribution as the beginning
of a process of purification and demythologization. He considered the late Middle Ages a period of vague religiosity and
saw the advent of Luther as a necessary reaction against "the
theological and ecclesiastical contamination" of a waning
era.[38] Mysticism was, Hirsch reasoned, an element in the general opacity of the religious situation. He characterized mysticism *en bloc* as "opaque" or "dusky." [39] He found Martin
Luther's "renewal of piety" significantly expressed in Luther's own hymn, "Aus tiefer Not schrei ich zu Dir" (From
deepest want I cry to Thee). In Hirsch's opinion mysticism
denoted the contrary; it represented an unwarranted human
confidence and, consequently, could be dealt with only as a
counter-pole to true evangelical Christianity. Thus Hirsch
placed, on the one side, the "ecstatic and enthusiastic God-

passion" of mysticism and, on the other side Martin Luther who, by his concentration on the genuine and original in religion, underlined the difference between the essential and the non-essential and kept clear of the ecstatic and the enthusiastic.[40] The genuinely evangelical was, Hirsch thought, non-ecstatic, as evidenced by the fact that "Jesus was calm," and further underscored by Luther whose encounters with ecstatic and introspective mysticism had become warning signs to him since he was in the monastery.[41] Hirsch's mysticism *en bloc* showed mysticism as a subevangelical phenomenon which has nothing essential in common with the simplicity, purity and directness of Martin Luther's recovery of Pauline Christianity. The animus of Roman Catholic life was demand and petition. The animus of Protestantism was receipt of a gift.[42] As noted, mysticism fell entirely in the former camp.

Another generalization connected with the problem of mysticism was the following. Hirsch was convinced that Luther, after initial devotion to mystical practice, had totally abandoned mysticism. Hirsch phrased his persuasion in this manner: "Originally Luther had practiced the religious resignation of Romanic mysticism. . . . Around 1513, meditating on Romans 1:17, he rediscovered the Pauline gospel." [43] It would seem that Hirsch did not consider the possibility that Luther's "practice of resignation" represented a religious perception which remained with him as an outflow of "the inner faith." With mysticism *en bloc* controlling Hirsch's concepts as a primary generalization, the second generalization lies close at hand, namely, the notion that mysticism with Luther belonged entirely to the past after a certain year or experience. The generalization in question is based upon the somewhat mechanistic belief that ideas cannot exist outside the logical hierarchy where they originated. When one hierarchical structure goes all individual ideas belonging to it also have to go. By this reckoning it may sound plausible to say that mystical theology was at a given time entirely supplanted with Reformation theology. In the case of Luther's relationship with mystical theology the picture seemed to be more complex than that.

Hirsch followed the example of others in his theological generation. He analyzed Luther's connection with medieval mystics guided by a generalized notion of mysticism. The medieval mystics *en bloc* typified theologically non-essential matters such as ecstasy and enthusiasm; hence their concern was regarded as contrary to the Reformation. For Hirsch it would presumably have availed little to look for differentiation among mystics in order to determine who was closer to or more distant from Luther. By the theological nature of things any kind of mystical theology belonged in the wrong logical-theological framework according to Hirsch.

To *Heinrich Bornkamm* (1905-   ) the two major deficiencies of mysticism are the absence of a theological locus for guilt and the teaching about obliteration of I-consciousness. The result of these inadequacies is, Bornkamm alleged, that a true mystic cannot live in true community and not to be able or willing to live in a true community is of course a symptom of basic malfunction.[44] From a Protestant point of view "the immediacy of mysticism" must be termed an "untruth." To Bornkamm contact between God and man is not direct.[45] The generalizations about mysticism—no guilt-theology, no true community — were then pitted against Luther's theology. Bornkamm pointed out that he performed this duty as "a theological historian." With the coming of Luther guilt received its proper place. The self was restored to its theological function within the divine economy of justification. The historically transmitted faith replaced the purported immediacy of spiritual experience. These generalized contrapositions were, Bornkamm felt, pedagogically essential. The Protestant cause benefitted from pronouncements of this clarifying nature. "Protestantism," he declared, "must wage a hard and determined border war against each attempt to persuade it to stage a reformation from within mysticism's spirit. . . . The difference is one of essence." [46]

Four considerations will be selected that illumine Bornkamm's use of a mysticism *en bloc* as it related to Luther. First, Bornkamm's concept of "faith" presumably prompted employment of the mysticism-*en-bloc* idea. Bornkamm's concept of "faith" in his work on Protestantism and mysticism was predominantly historical. Whatever else can be said about faith, Bornkamm's proposition rendered it first and foremost a phenomenon in and of history and, as such, faith was based on "objective" events through which God speaks *indirectly.* The obverse supposition would be that of mysticism which is depicted as a-historical and claims *direct,* immediate contact with God. Bornkamm heard all of mysticism say only the latter, actually or potentially. To support his notion of total distinction between faith with Luther and faith with a mystic Bornkamm needed his generalization of mysticism.

The critical objection to the method thus applied, would be that it is not clear what "indirect" and "direct" mean. If "direct" connotes an attempt to attain salvation without the media, word and Christ, Tauler, for one, did not answer the description. Central to his mysticism was the persuasion that Christ is the way and the truth.[47] When faith comes it is not man's doing, according to Tauler, but something God wants to do with man once man has said, "Lord depart from me for I am a sinner." [48] In Luther's thought faith was *both* "historical faith" *and* "true faith." [49] The latter involved "immediate," "direct" feeling. Faith makes out of the Christian and Christ *one* person, and this can be immediately felt and experienced, Luther said.[50] Bornkamm's generalization of mysticism with respect to faith appears to accord neither with the indications of historical anchorage for faith in Taulerian theology nor with the suggestions from Luther that faith is also immediate experience.

Secondly, Bornkamm censured mysticism *in toto* for extinction of "I"-consciousness. When Tauler said that man, lost in God, is "almost annihilated" ("zunichte"), it has to be seen in the context of Tauler's total experience. For Tauler also said that a person who has been "engulfed" in God "finds himself in Him." In God men may become "masters of their own self." But preceding this new birth of the self a seeker has to go through the hell of becoming nothing.[51] We have to ask ourselves what "obliteration" or "extinction" of the "I" means. Do we have in mind an actual-psychological death of consciousness or a religious-theological change of consciousness? The suggestion that mysticism would advocate the former is not borne out by Tauler's thoughts about the self. Because "extinction" is consequently conceived religiously, is there in this regard much difference between Luther and the mystic Tauler? Finally, if obliteration of the "I" carries the religious meaning it has with this one mystic alone, Bornkamm's generalization of mysticism regarding the obliteration theme has lost its validity.

Thirdly, in his use of contraposition to achieve conceptual clarity, Bornkamm seems to have been influenced by a not uncommon predilection among German theologians of older vintage. There is a tendency to view Luther as a hero of Germanic virility in contradistinction to the mystics, considered to be somewhat ungermanic, more feminine, vague and weak.[52] This idea is then, as it were, transplanted onto theological soil. Luther, a blunt and virile prophet, represents a posture of realistic theological straightforwardness. Mysticism, Luther's alleged theological foe, represents more plausible, circuitous, vacuous theological manners. Again, a generalization of mysticism serves the purpose of pitting systems of truth against each other.

Fourthly, Bornkamm presumably saw mysticism largely in the context of the Reformer's battle with the *Schwärmer* and generalized about mysticism accordingly. He conceivably evaluated medieval mysticism with the aid of Luther's violent reaction against the docetic aberrations of *Schwärmertum*.[53] Immersion-in-God mysticism and spiritualistic mysticism are perhaps rejected as legitimate parts of a Christian body of thought—and made to stand for all of mysticism—because Luther repudiated them in his battle against the Zwickau prophets. If that was the case, the generalization obviously loses its usefulness. The question as to why nothing mystical, on Bornkamm's accounting, can have anything to do with true reformation will be a matter for separate discussion revolving around the role of presupposition on the subject of Luther and the mystics.

*Gerhard Ebeling* (1912-   ) has reached the following major conclusions on mysticism and Luther's relation to mystical theology. The employment of mystical terms in Luther's writings is a matter of just that, terms, and not a question of essence. We arrive in *medias res* by focusing attention on Ebeling's treatment of Luther's spiritual relationship to Tauler. Although examining Tauler's impact on Luther's gospel interpretation, Ebeling deliberately avoided a discussion of "the range of Tauler's influence." He pointed to "the enthusiastic judgments by which Luther refers to German mysticism, as he understood it." Tauler's influence, Ebeling continued, found "an unconsciously objective limit" in Luther's world. Not only that, it "also found a temporal limit in Luther's development." Luther, said Ebeling, "withdrew from his admiration of the German theologian [*Theologia Germanica*] and Tauler already in 1520." Since then Luther never quoted nor recommended either of them.[54]

Two notions implied in the above deliberations with bearing on the generalization issue will be lifted out here. First we will consider the depth of Tauler's kinship with and the duration of Tauler's influence on Luther. Ebeling let it be understood that the kinship and the influence were more limited than might be supposed. Although ostensibly leaving the question open, Ebeling nevertheless proffered an indirect claim. He suggested, as noted, that Luther was guided by a built-in, objective, presumably dogmatic "limit" with respect to Tauler's influence. Moreover, Ebeling alleged, a "temporal limit" also existed which effectively curtailed Tauler's impact on Luther. This is to say, Ebeling proposed that it is possible to chronologically-statistically determine the end of Tauler's sway over Luther's life. This is tantamount to claiming that mysticism ceased at a certain temporal juncture in Luther's thinking.[55]

Guided by his generalized view of mysticism as an antipode of neoplatonic, speculative theology Ebeling here seems to seek corroboration in an *argumentum ad tempus et mathematicas* for the truth of his generalization. However, the danger of grounding a theological assertion—"Luther and mysticism are divided in essence"—on linguistic statistics is clearly shown in this case. Another thorough investigator of Luther's attitude to mysticism has produced figures that refute the above assertion, claiming that there are in Luther's writings "from 1515 to 1544, 26 references to Tauler," *nota bene* references of a positive character.[56]

The depth of Tauler's kinship with Luther can obviously not be ascertained with reference to statistical information. If anything such information points in the opposite direction from the one suggested by Ebeling.

The second consideration bearing on the issue of a generalized notion of mysticism concerns Luther's assessment of his debt to German mysticism and Ebeling's view of the position. Martin Luther had a high regard for German mysticism, often even an enthusiastic one. At some points he gave his approval to other mystical writing as well. But, as noted, Ebeling cautions that this was mysticism "as he [Luther] understood it." Mysticism as Luther understood it was one thing, mysticism as "later critical considerations" have interpreted it was another. This is to say, Luther's spontaneous assessment might have to be revised by more deliberate later assessors of his assessment.

Among systematizers of Luther's thought the idea is not uncommon that Luther did not always know his own theology best but that later systematizers might see it more clearly.[57] No doubt changing cultural conditions render qualifying explanations necessary concerning Luther's statements of cultural and social import as well as some matters of purely dogmatic-conceptual character. Yet in the case before us we deal with a subject involving spiritual sensitivity and internal judgment. When a generalized picture of mysticism has led to the necessity of dispossessing Luther of such inner, spiritual intuition, it must have been overapplied. For we deal here with more than a conceptual-logical reality such as a notion of mysticism *en bloc.* When Luther admitted kinship with mystics it was a matter of intuitive inner recognition on a spiritual level, beyond the pale of conceptualization. Luther's spiritual sensorium should have priority with respect to his professions of inner affinity. His judgment of some mystics may not suit our conceptions, yet to become an assessor of a prophet's assessment of his spiritual debts is a precarious undertaking.

In addition to the two prominent considerations discussed above (the depth and duration of the Luther-Tauler link and the evaluation of Luther's verdict about mystical theology) some further attention will now be given to a few of Luther's comments on biblical passages as well as Ebeling's interpretations of these comments. The latter again brings to mind the problem of a generalized notion of mysticism. The following subjects will be discussed: equation of scholasticism and mysticism, alleged repudiations of all mysticism by Luther, and finally, the meaning of "false religion" in Ebeling's interpretation of Luther's usage of the term.

Luther often emphasized that scholasticism's pretension to meet God by thought alone is contemptible. He, Luther, had experienced, in rare moments, the horror of an unprotected encounter with God.[58] Ebeling, explicating, hears Luther say that fallacious knowledge about God, reason's knowledge, is plainly "the speculative, mystical theology of neoplatonism." [59]

Presumably implied in Ebeling's exegesis is the judgment, noted also with other writers, that speculative scholasticism and experiential mysticism are co-extensive or concentric. In the passages consulted by Ebeling and referred to as documentation, no dictum appears to warrant the equation of conceptual speculation and mysticism.[60] Yet a generalized idea of mysticism seems to call for this construction.

Did Luther repudiate all mysticism? In 1515-1516 he reminded his listeners and readers that Christ has given man access to God and only through Christ the Lord does man

receive justification by faith, remission of sins and so access
to God.[61] He then proceeded to warn his listeners of the danger
of seeking religious experience outside Christ and the Word.
He did so while elaborating Paul's admonition in Romans 5:2,
"Through him we have obtained access to this grace in which
we stand, and we rejoice in our hope of sharing the glory of
God." Ebeling paraphrased the comments by Luther as follows: "The knowledge about God which reason ("die Vernunft") possesses, is the speculative, mystical theology of neoplatonism, which teaches a method of penetrating the inner
dark spaces and of hearing the uncreated word and of im-
mersing oneself therein." [62]

One observes that Ebeling, in his paraphrase, interpreted
Luther as having spoken of *all* mystical knowledge. However,
a closer examination of the Luther passage reveals that Luther was alluding to the mysticism of Dionysius the Areopagite, not to a general category called speculative, mystical neoplatonism. Dionysius represented the kind of human religious
endeavor which did not fit into Luther's experience and theology. Expounding on Luther's judgment J. Ficker remarked in
the *Weimarausgabe* regarding the Reformer's warning not to
seek religious experience outside Christ: " . . . that is to say,
the *mystica theologia* of the Areopagite. The subsequent
verses have reference to this book with respect to content,
also partly with respect to individual terms." The impression
left by Ebeling is, on the contrary, that no specific mystic is
involved but that the clause implies a universal rejection of
mysticism as tantamount to "the speculative mystical theology
of neoplatonism." [63] For the reference "neoplatonism" does
not immediately guide the attention to Dionysius, a neoplaton-
ist, since the pervasive thrust of Ebeling's accounts of mysticism seems to be precisely its neoplatonic flair.

A third example of the invisible presence of a generalized
concept of mysticism in some of Ebeling's analyses of Luther
dicta deals with Galatians 4:8: "Formerly when you did not
know God, you were in bondage to beings that by nature are
no gods." Luther elucidated: *Religio falsa* is the kind of reli-

gion which endeavors to find a *deus clemens,* a gracious God, by works of various sorts. Only knowledge of Christ can protect from such worship of self. "Thus everyone who strays from the knowledge of Christ unfailingly plunges into idolatry." In *this* regard *religiones, observationes* become false.[64] Paraphrasing these remarks Ebeling suggested that they purport to show that "all the ways of religion and worldly wisdom" are "the God-knowledge of reason." [65] The question is, did Luther intend to say that all religions are false or that reason's God-knowledge is under all circumstances useless? Have "all the ways of religion" been condemned in a statement to the effect that the knowledge of Christ is the cure for idolatry? Mystical theology would, however, fall into the category of false religion on Ebeling's view, for it is according to him "God-knowledge of reason." A generalization of mysticism has barred mystical knowledge from being anything but "worldly wisdom."

A more radical kind of generalization of the mystical way, even in its putatively Christian forms, has been propounded by neo-orthodox theologian *Karl Barth* (1886-1968). He ruled out the possibility of spiritual internalization as part of salvation. The New Testament passages on death as man's entry into life "have nothing to do with a mysticism of physical or spiritual dying." [66] In Barth's opinion the Christian *kerygma,* the message from God to man, does not betoken union with Christ in a mystical fashion. Mystical unity with God is no more than "a deepening of human self-consciousness," Barth held. He repeated a common criticism of Christian mysticism when asserting that mystical theology privatizes Christian faith instead of letting it remain what it is, public.[67] Already in early Christian times, said Barth, mysticism was "a privately practicing foreign body." [68] Mysticism, in whatever form, is anthropology and disguised cosmology.[69] Barth did not doubt that mysticism is the opposite pole of the Christian faith. "The Christian faith," he wrote, "is the day which heralded the passing of the mystical night." Mysticism offers experiences, true, but who assures us that these do not emerge from "spirits totally other than the Holy Spirit"?[70] Barth shared the categorical opinion of many theologians, whose presuppositions for theological system-building may be at variance with his own, that mysticism *in toto* (including forms that claim Christian allegiance) calculates with an independent "ground" within man, a "being" of a somewhat autonomous nature. On behalf of the *kerygma* Barth announced a contrary judgment. Christ's deed, so his theology went, annuls man's "being." Man is nothing, looked at as "being." Barth disagreed with his reformed co-theologian, Calvin, on this score. Calvin spoke of *insitio in Christum*, a grafting into Christ, and a *coniunctio*, a process of uniting in friendship and love with Christ. Even more incisively Barth differed with mystic Angelus Silesius' utterance that Christ might be born a thousand times in Bethlehem, yet were he not permitted to be born in the soul, that soul would be eternally lost.[71] However, Barth conceded that one may well speak positively about mysticism from a theological point of view provided the proper perspective were preserved. After all, St. Paul referred to a Christ-presence involving experiences of an emotional and intuitive nature. Barth allowed for Pauline mysticism; it was, he wrote, "a mysticism which observes the distance." To observe the distance is to interpret man from Christ. Mysticism generally chose the opposite approach; it interpreted Christ from man. The "manward" was, wrote Barth, erroneously emphasized by mysticism, pietism, Schleiermacher and monasticism.[72] Although Barth was unable to agree with Martin Luther's gospel interpretation at important junctures, the Swiss theologian's view on mysticism would coincide at least with the antipodal thinking about faith versus mysticism often ascribed to Luther. This becomes apparent on reading Barth's interpretation of the words "overcome by the world" in 1 John 5:4. Barth averred that the passage does not deal with "that mystical emptying . . . an artificially anticipated death." Justification is not man's "task." "God has not created man to the art of such emptying."[73] Humanly speaking, the mystical urge might be a legitimate enjoyment and a manifestation of human love of God.[74] But Christ's deed takes everything connected with man's being away and that is the decisive point. Theologically speaking, man is totally depraved and the only term that describes his natural relation to God is discontinuity. To Barth mysticism must be in error since it reckons with continuity of some sort. Whether or not mysticism should be examined for diversity is of minor interest against the background of that theological persuasion. The very fact that "the ground of being," "the soul's longing" or "the image of God" are spoken of in a positive vein by the mystics rules them out for positive consideration in a work on church dogmatics. Mysticism *en bloc* is a foreign body, Barth insisted.

Is the movement from man to God exhaustively human as Barth appeared to think? Can we accept Barth's assumption that man's "religion" has no room for any of God's salvatory work? Is not the longing to which much mystical theology gives expression also in part God's longing? Although Barth's generalization of mysticism is unavoidable and logical given Barth's conception of theology's role, is it possible to excise personal internalization from faith? The *kerygma* is by its very nature both objective and subjective. Since Barth was persuaded that personal experience in faith was theologically insignificant he would have had difficulty understanding Luther's suggestion that mystical theology is experience of God.

What concerned *Reinhold Niebuhr* (1891-1971) most intensively in connection with the problem of mysticism was its approach to individuality. Niebuhr had gained the impression that "mysticism regards individuality as evil." He was certain that "all mystic philosophies . . . lose the very individuality . . . they emphasize." The deepest reason for the purported hankering after liberation from individuality is that mysticism invariably thinks of sin as involved in physical necessity.[75] From a treatise on nature mysticism Reinhold Niebuhr received his picture of the nature of mysticism. Meister Eckhart may have been Niebuhr's prototype for mysticism *en bloc*.[76] Reinhold Niebuhr made little distinction between the impersonal mysticism of the unfathomable and the

personal mysticism of Christ-allegiance. Niebuhr's generalized image of mysticism, with predominantly Eckhartian
overtones, contained the following sampling of ideas which,
according to Niebuhr, characterizes *all* mysticism: the death
of individuality, fear of action for fear of sinning, indifference to history, the notion that the Holy Spirit is a mere extension of the human spirit.[77] In traditional style Reinhold
Niebuhr then counterposed what he termed "the heresy of
mysticism" and genuine Christianity, which he termed historical, biblical and prophetic.[78]

Niebuhr shared with theological liberals who preceded him
a common persuasion that mystical theology could not be
integrated with Christian reflection. He differed from them in
his treatment of Luther himself. The theologians of the historical-critical school had said about Luther that mysticism
did not substantially belong in his thought. Reinhold Niebuhr,
on the contrary, accused Luther of "mystical doctrines of
passivity." After having made a traditional distinction between, on the one hand, unacceptable, non-biblical mysticism
and, on the other, biblical faith, Niebuhr assigned Luther to
an area closer to the former than the latter. Reinhold Niebuhr
clearly availed himself of a generalized concept of mysticism,
with hardly a borderline between nature mysticism and personality mysticism. The result was an indirect repudiation—
understandable on the part of a social ethicist who witnessed
much Lutheran socio-ethical quietism—of the inward, personal
element in faith.

In *conclusion*, the generalization of the concept of Christian
mysticism as exclusively manward and subjective, in contradistinction to the mainstream of Protestant theology depicted
as Godward and objective, has had a distorting effect on inquiries into Luther's relationship to medieval mystics. Three
results are discernible in this process.

1. The generalized view of Christian mysticism accords
little significance to the suggestion that basic theological dif-

ferences exist in Christian mysticism and that Luther saw the importance of differentiation.

2. The generalized view of Christian mysticism encourages an oversimplified polarity-thinking according to which mystical theology, described as unbiblical and unevangelical, is pitted against biblical faith (whether historical-critically interpreted or from a neo-orthodox angle) as historically sound and evangelical.

3. The generalized view of Christian mysticism bolsters the tendency to deemphasize as insignificant certain indications that Luther regarded his affinity with some mystical thinkers as essential.

The idea that Christian mysticism or all mysticism revolves around *one* leading basic concept or represents *one* main thrust has enabled the generalizer of the meaning of mysticism to relegate mystical theology "as such" to an alien, unevangelical or heretical system of thought.[79] The widespread acceptance of this approach is, I would suggest, rooted in the persistence of an exclusively logical-ideological method of apprehending biblical reality and subsequent Christ-related religious experience.

## B. The power of preconception

We said above that liberal and neo-orthodox theologies often operate on the notion of presumed integrality of mysticism and without much attention to its diverse forms. It was noted that the generalizations may in part be substitutes for individual investigation, also that standard judgments on mystics and mysticism are presumably transmitted from one generation of theologians to another as supposedly final and incontestable. But we have, moreover, had reason to suggest that the use of generalizations serves the purpose of contraposing the Roman Catholic body of beliefs and the evangelical Lutheran scheme of salvation. In other words, mysticism *en bloc* is employed to support the argument that an essential, all-

pervasive difference between Catholic and Protestant-Lutheran thought is detectable at every important doctrinal point.
Generalizing about mysticism thus serves the purpose of uni-
versalizing an historical rift within the church.

In our continuing examination of theological method as it relates to mystical theology with Luther, it is now suggested that
liberal and neo-orthodox theologies often come to the problem of Luther and mysticism with certain standing preconceptions, a given *Vorverständnis*, which obscure the meaning
and importance of the mystical approach in Luther's life and
thought. This *Vorverständnis* emerges from the very cultural
atmosphere and scientific climate which these theologies wish
to address in apologetic or kerygmatic moods. Some of the
same thinkers who were consulted on the matter of integrality
and generalization will also provide illustrations in the present
context. Harnack will be added at the beginning and Ozment
at the end. They stand in different cultures and eras, yet
evince the pervasiveness of some preconceptions through the
generations.

*Adolf Harnack* (1851-1930), a disciple of Ritschl's, thought
that the essence of the gospel was "the naive eternal life in
the midst of time." Culture was the unfolding of individuality
and freedom. The process had only one safeguard, the gospel,
foundation for "all ethical culture." Harnack saw history as
a three stage event: "progress" from the Old Testament to
the gospel, a fall from the gospel to Greek metaphysics and,
through Luther, an "evolution" or "development" to disposition ethics.[1] In Harnack's judgment Jesus' preaching consisted
of three truths: first, the message of the kingdom of God as
a reality close at hand or as future salvation; secondly, the
message about Jesus' deeds and thoughts; thirdly, the new
righteousness or the new law. Harnack adopted the attitude
of his mentor, Ritschl, respecting the links between mysticism
and the rest of Catholicism. Mysticism was "the Catholic version of individual piety." Thus Harnack took the same stance
regarding mysticism as the theologians chosen to illustrate the
generalization tendency. Harnack referred to "wide-ranging

examinations . . . in order to classify the mystics." He considered the inquiries useless. "The differences are essentially irrelevant. Mysticism is always the same. The differences never concern its essence." [2]

Against this background Harnack then described Luther as a person of sober common sense who naturally found mysticism wholly unsatisfactory. Later, through his religious experience, Luther formulated a theology which is a total refutation of mysticism's way of life. Harnack claimed that "Luther hardly experienced the movement of the mystic between rapture and fear for he was too stern with himself." [3] In contradistinction to the mystics "who always landed in elevated feelings but seldom attained a pervasive feeling of peace" and soon arrived at "psychological self-destruction," Martin Luther displayed "an active piety" which brought him "a steadier, more blissful certainty." "Through a cheerful faith he became a hero," Harnack declared. True, Luther may have learned "from the old mystics, but what they only sought he found." [4] What Luther found about Christ was, according to Harnack, first and foremost that he is "the historical Christ." Catholic piety spoke of a kind of mystical presence which lodged Christ's closeness also in good works, Harnack explained. In opposition to this sort of piety Luther spoke of "a gracious God in faith." In his approach to faith Luther was firm and cheerful ("kräftig und freudig")[5] According to Luther there was, Harnack thought, no mystery or enigma in the awakening of faith through the Holy Spirit.[6]

The emphasis on the historical and the robustly commonsensical in Luther's faith led Harnack to assert that Luther was vastly separated from mystical beliefs "by the totally non-mystical persuasion that trust in God for Christ's sake is the proper content of religion, not to be outdone by any speculation. Trust in God's truth and Christ's deed was rooted in one thing . . . *per crucem Christi*, through the cross of Christ." [7] To Harnack it was important to exclude from his Luther interpretation any suggestion that Luther's life in Christ was in any sense "immediate." Harnack regarded the mystics' way of speaking of *imitatio Christi* dangerous and wholly alien to Luther's way of thinking. Imitation theology can, after all, "not seldom drift into becoming a Christ," he wrote.[8] Harnack looked at faith, and consequently also Luther's faith, as mediated, not as immediately experienced. Christ and the Christian faith are historical. History mediates Christ and the Christian faith. Therefore, Harnack reasoned, theological ramparts had to be erected against the onslaught of the unpredictable and emotion-oriented movement of mysticism. Remain in the historical, this was Harnack's advice. How can one remain in the historical when you unleash all the powers of the imagination and declare them to be the organ for union with the Godhead?[9]

Harnack's preconception which governed his appraisal of Luther's thought was shaped by adherence to the commonsensical. In a Ritschlian vein he developed an immanental, this-worldly conception of the gospel. He could therefore say that "neither mystical contemplation nor ascetic life style are included in the gospel."[10] Adhering to a basically commonsensical notion of the salvation story Harnack endeavored to accommodate Luther within its boundaries. Because, to him, the gospel was a non-mystical message, Luther was hailed as a basically commonsensical man. Did not an essential portion of Luther's legacy get lost in the process? In his lecture on Psalm 116, for instance, Luther dealt with religious ecstasy as the meaning of faith. Another word for it, said Luther, would be *raptus*, rapture, a word from the mystical vocabulary. He knew not only rapture in God but also the forlorn sighing of despair called *gemitus*. When the Psalmist exclaims, "I said in my *excessu*," Luther commented that *excessus* can mean both rapture and fear and he proceeded to offer a table of definitions of states of mind which, he was aware, cannot be adequately defined since their genesis is in realities which are not commonsensical.[11] Such and similar Luther dicta cannot be ascribed to common sense but rather convey an impression radically opposed to the one Harnack intended to give. On account of his preconception he was no doubt unable to cope with the non-rational overtones in Luther's descriptions of faith.

Another side of the philosophy of common sense which we detect in Harnack's Luther image is the question of "immediacy" in faith. On Harnack's theological view, apologetically related to the scientific reason of the 19th century, Martin Luther could not have anything in common with those who accorded some theological dignity to religious imagination and immediate experience. Apologetic theology claimed Christ as the fountainhead, yet, molded in part by those whom it addressed, the empirical skeptics, apologetic theology dared not announce that Christ is near in a mystical, immediate way. Luther insisted that Christ's presence could be felt. Harnack read, yet did not read, words to this effect. Scientific reason, the yardsticks of natural science, provided the building material for his preconception that nothing invisible can be said to be "immediately" present. For that would be tantamount to destroying "the historical" and open up for uncontrollable "powers of imagination." [12]

We have noted that *Karl Holl* has been cited as a scholar who rendered Luther more modern and consistent than he was. Holl depicted Luther as a man whose conscience and conscious thought—it is important to take cognizance of the terms— were always awake and alert. Luther's conscience and conscious thought eventually produced a liberating conceptual solution to a great spiritual dilemma, Holl seemed to conclude. In states of spiritual confusion most people take their refuge in "visions or miracles that would guarantee . . . grace," Holl suggested. Luther did not desire visions for he did not cherish any sidesteps ("Seitensprünge"), Holl proposed, with a perhaps less felicitous analogical overtone. In Holl's account Luther sometimes emerged as a man who consciously guarded himself against feeling and intuition. We find with Holl a primarily cognitive, reflective Luther.[13] Rather than being inspired from on high Luther, in Holl's understanding, sets his conscience and his conscious thought in motion and arrives at a solution. After profound theological deliberation the Reformer emerges with the theological key. The transcendent and the mystical intimations in Luther's struggle are absent in Holl's account of Luther. The illumination depicted by Holl was a conceptual illumination. A new kind of "knowledge" had been added to the store of life's knowledge. The new knowledge was not emotional-spiritual, said Holl, but entered the life stream as an idea long hidden under layers of false Catholic anthropology and now revived. St. Paul mediated this idea, the concept of justification by faith.[14]

Thus Karl Holl's interpretation of Luther was borne by a preconception which conceptualism had molded. This is to say, the Reformer emerged as an intellectual problem solver on a high level. The intellectual came first, intuitive experience and spiritual kinship with souls having the same experiences came second. The belief in theological thought as an enterprise dealing with mere concept pervaded Holl's work. As an interpreter of Luther, Holl registered transmitted ideas and saw the process he recorded as a concatenation of evolving or recovered thoughts. It was difficult for him to treat the claims of spiritual presence as starting points for rational assessment. In defense of Luther's originality Holl was prompted by his conceptualism to say that "Luther is not under the extraneous influence" of mysticism.[15] The implication was that intellectual ideas lie at the root of the Reformation, mysticism representing another and unfortunately heretical set of ideas. The illumination which changed the direction of Luther's life was a conceptual illumination by Holl's standards. The new intellectual insight was seen as mediated to him by St. Paul. Justification by faith was "a thought that became his salvation." [16] Luther, said Holl, "founded" a new relationship with God, i.e., a conceptual scheme. In his conceptualism Holl would have found no "sense" in the allegation that non-rational intimations are the source of theology and that the feeling remains where the concept fails, that interpenetration of rational and non-rational is the secret of theological thought.[17]

A corollary to Holl's rationalistic presupposition was his

inability to find a place for "the inner life" in his assessment of Luther's theology. To the world of conceptual concatenation religion becomes a series of rational assertions. A skeptical scientific society does not accept intimation, intuition and feeling, elements of the mystical way, as objects for rational inquiry. Hence a theological preconception that is formed precisely by the values of a rationalistic community minimizes the importance of feeling and experience connected with the new relationship to the divine. Luther's "inner life" was of little interest to Holl's appraisal. His intention was to register concepts as they faded or egressed. The "inner life" belonged to a private domain which was not a legitimate area for an analytical theologian. The analysis or registration of concepts concerned a gospel which was public; it included concepts accessible to all. Time and again Holl presented the mystic as a man bent on having God for his private possession. Luther was contrasted as a man basing his certainty on the word which is available to all.[18] With respect to the place of "the inner life" in theological reflection Holl, a person of liberal theological persuasion, joined the company of Lutheran orthodoxy. The preconceptions of both liberals and the orthodox held no brief for the suggestion that Christ lives in the believer in a private, subjective, felt, psychologically decipherable manner.

The preconceptions serving Holl thus rendered Martin Luther as a man who saw the conceptual issues with prophetic clarity. The felt presence and power of the divine grace found no room in the inn.

With respect to mysticism *en bloc,* we noted *Erich Seeberg's* suggestion that Luther placed little value on method in devotional life. We also registered evidence to the contrary. What Seeberg desired to show was that Luther basically rejected mystical theology which, by its very nature, would develop technical assistance toward increased spiritual awareness. The illustration in question assumes added significance in our present context. For in bending the material slightly to support his contention Seeberg exposed a preconception which prevented him from recognizing the issue involved in the puzzling presence of mystical terminology in Luther's thinking. It was incumbent upon Seeberg to show that Luther's theology limited man's adoration of God to methodical fulfillment of vocational duties, thereby parrying the mystical invitation to further God-awareness by methodical practice of devotion. The preconception governing this reading of Luther and implicit in the tendency to overspiritualize mysticism and despiritualize Luther, was the intellectualistic notion that knowledge emanating from a non-rational realm can have no bearing upon the rational undertaking of theology. Consequently, the fact that Luther did place great emphasis on the ordered and regular practice of meditation and prayer could not appear in a Seeberg account. The fact could have been deliberately omitted with reference to its insignificance in the light of Luther's total concept of the Christian life. In any event, an intellectualistic preconception dominated Seeberg's enquiry.[19]

The encyclopedia *Die Religion in Geschichte und Gegenwart* partly characterizes *Emanuel Hirsch* by claiming that Holl's writings have meant much to him and that Hirsch brought Martin Luther into concert with historical criticism.[20] Hirsch's preconceptions as a Luther scholar were to a great extent formed by Holl's thought and intense historical criticism. He emphasized the personal in Luther's faith and Luther's belief that God is present in the soul of the individual seeker. Hirsch averred that the common *tradition* of church and faith meant little to Luther. The outward signs were always closely related to an *individual* breakthrough, to communion with the eternal God. Hirsch also heard Luther say that sustaining this individual breakthrough is a hidden event, an occurrence between God who makes himself present and the individual soul. Luther "knew this with trembling." Hirsch thus acknowledged the private, personal and subjective element in faith. He went as far as saying that "not the orthodox teachers but Spener, Francke, Zinzendorf and Schleiermacher . . . are . . . his true disciples." According to

Hirsch these leaders had all experienced the breakthrough by reaching beyond *Kirchenglaube,* church faith, to a personal experience of the God who addresses the heart in wrath and grace. Hirsch believed that Luther had "a transdogmatic measuring rod for the manifestation of the gospel via the medium of conceptual thought." [21]

Thus far Hirsch appeared to have underscored the internal nature of Luther's faith much more unhesitatingly than his mentor Holl. The existential character of Luther's experience and the personal realization of God's grace and presence seemed to receive their due in Hirsch's analysis of Luther's theology. Hirsch's preoccupation with Kierkegaard no doubt furthered his sensitivity on the issue of divine presence. But having directed his attention to what he regarded as the kernel of Luther's renewal Emanuel Hirsch turned to the task of demythologizing Luther, guided no doubt by a desire to render the central Reformation message more attainable to modern man. Luther became the object of the queries of historical criticism. The criteria of modern historical science and critical biblical scholarship were applied as tests. Hirsch found that Luther's innermost concern adequately coincided with the results of critical research. In his explanation of the first article of the Apostolic Creed Luther was, said Hirsch, already on his way from myth and metaphysics toward a "transdogmatic faith." The wordings of Luther's explanation may, Hirsch wrote, appear "simple and common. Yet the seriousness of personal actualization makes the difference clear between unadulterated strong faith and all the unclear ecclesiastical contaminations." [22]

Hirsch elaborated on his use of the term "contaminations" by drawing attention to Luther's angelology. As his elaboration aids us in gaining a better understanding of the role of Hirsch's preconceptions an exposition and discussion of the matter will be useful. Hirsch interpreted Luther's angelology as follows. Christ as servant can only be discerned by faith. The angels, shining beings serving God, do not stand in the way of such faith. But angels may belong to man's temptations. When they bring the message about Jesus' birth they do not guarantee that Jesus was a virgin's son or that he was a son of God descended from heaven. Those are holy mysteries, actualized, meaningful only to faith. Martin Luther did not believe in Jesus on the basis of the dogma of God becoming man, nor on the basis of the history of the virgin birth. What are these, then? "They are helpful thoughts." But faith in Jesus and in the gospel must not be submerged in an external lore of miracle.[23]

So much for Hirsch's summary of Luther's view on angels. Since Hirsch did not attach references to angelological comments in Luther's writings we shall have to select material on our own which may or may not have been the basis of Hirsch's paraphrase. But before an exposition of such documentation let us focus on preconceptions that appear in the account just submitted. First, Hirsch suggested that Luther did not believe in Jesus on the basis of the dogma of God becoming man. This was presumably, on Hirsch's part, a demarcation against traditional orthodox beliefs. Secondly, Hirsch termed what he called the lore of miracle—belief in angels as transmitters of divine communication, the story of the virgin birth—helpful thoughts and nothing more. This was presumably an attempt to delimit the evangelical from the mystical or the occult.

On the first point Hirsch tended to intellectualize in existentialistic fashion Luther's belief that the central dogma is a necessary external sign without which the spiritual life falls apart. Luther's stance on this score emerged with special clarity in his booklet against the King of England. It appears that an existentialistic framework, in other words a rather recent system of philosophical reflection, was applied by Hirsch to interpret the place of dogma in Luther's thought. The emphasis on existential actualization through faith renders the external historical symbols of God's incarnation more or less unessential. The dogma of incarnation was in this way transposed into a process of inner actualization. Hirsch placed a philosophical construction on Luther's dogma of incarnational externality. He thereby vitiated Luther's view of the external incarnation according to which the external signs of God's action in Christ are indispensable to faith.

Secondly, on the problem of paranormal lore, Hirsch's psychologized angelology revealed a preconception molded by rationalism. At this point a Luther statement on angels will be a helpful reference as background to Hirsch's understanding of what Luther said on the matter. Luther's "Sermon on the angels" of 1535 seems a significant area of enquiry. In this tract we read among other things: "One says there are no spirits. If we rightly believed that they do exist we would not live in such [false] security." Unbeknown to them "people become obsessed" by dark angels. But "the good angels" are mightier.

> One may become an apostate from God to angels. . . .
> We read in Scripture that angels do not desire to be
> worshipped. But we are permitted to pray as follows:
> Dear God, you know what the enemy has in mind,
> send your holy angels. For as a child is entrusted in
> the care of its parents, so we are under the angels'
> protection and entrusted to them.

The links with the unseen are real. "Envy, pride, unchastity" debase the minds so that they become vehicles for obsession. But in all this we should know that "the dear good angels are much wiser than the wicked angels." [24]

A comparison between Hirsch's summary of Luther's angelology and Luther's sermon on the angels shows that Hirsch "modernized" Luther's view and the modernization has deprived Luther's belief of its divinatory imagination, to apply a cognomen from Barth's terminology. Luther would maintain that the angelic is the extension of faith. He saw the angels as supernatural helpers in Christ's work. The fact that they are not normally observable within our existence would, one might suppose, not have caused Luther a great deal of worry. He assumed all the time that faith itself moved in an "invisible" realm. In this invisible realm there are invisible entities conveying power to men through faith. The connection between the visible and the invisible also includes the possibility of obsession by dark angels. Angels should not and do not wish to be worshipped. God in Christ is the ruler. Thus Luther affirmed the biblical accounts of an angelic reality, not because these accounts had to be believed as credal cognition but because they were in line with faith and in concert with Christ. On the other hand, Hirsch's version of Luther's angelology, in contrast to Luther's sermon on angels, lays bare a rationalism which has to immanentalize and anthropologize before it can theologize. Hirsch claimed that Luther would consign the angels to the realm of helpful thought, not to a living reality. The paranormal in the precincts of revelation and faith are assigned to external lore of no intrinsic significance by Hirsch on Luther's behalf. But Luther, on the contrary, assumed a constant living communication between the determinate world and the invisible world productive of miracle. Hirsch suggested that he heard Luther say that Christology had eclipsed angelology. But Luther rather said that, notwithstanding their rejection of candidacy for the role of worship objects, the angels as submanagers of invisible spheres are essential for the operation of the visible ones. All in all, Hirsch's reading of Luther on the matter of angels lays bare a preconception which excises supernatural intimations and presents a Luther who would be more acceptable in a rationalistic climate.

We shall digress at this point for some further discussion of the wider issue raised in connection with Hirsch's presentation of Luther's angelology. For it bears on the modern skepticism about or rejection of "religious supernaturalism," a sentiment and a repudiation in which Hirsch no doubt shared and which must have helped shape his preconceptions. The unspoken but plainly discernible presupposition behind Hirsch's version of Luther's angelology is that the Bible and Christian thinkers up to the scientific age were dependent on a pre-Newtonian world picture and the idea of a sacralized universe, including invisible hierarchies of supernatural beings. Subsequently the modern world view has found such notions to be metaphysical in the sense that they cannot be empirically verified, hence they belong to the area of superstition, hallucination or at best "helpful thought." The task of theology then becomes to concentrate on those sides of the gospel, and gospel interpreters like Luther, that are universal and in keeping with the development of human knowledge and the state of modern thought. Mystical theological insight has found such assertions by modern rationalism both helpful and harmful. They have been helpful for they point up the need of constant theological application to man's changing situation and lend weight to the incarnational character of Christian life. It must be conceded that much of Luther's gospel application was formed by a culture and a society in part founded on concepts which man has outgrown. But the assertions of rationalism have been harmful in the sense that they assume a solipsism of human existence which expunges its supernatural homing aspects. Modern rationalism in the theological field (Hase, D. F. Strauss, Bultmann and, in their steps, Hirsch) has in the tradition of all rationalism approached the biblical stories of paranormal or supernatural import with the idea that they represent supernatural *concepts* not in keeping with natural *concepts*. Yet the stories beckon to the beginning and the continuation and they suggest the source of sustenance without which life is lost. Pure conceptualization shies away from the feeling that non-rational forces are at work. But implied in the revelation of God in Christ are supernormal elements which modern thought cannot remove without vitiating the meaning of revelation. The paranormal in faith's relation to God belongs to the story of God's incarnation. When Luther took the angels seriously, as parts of the invisible where faith moves, he was not simply under the spell of medieval lore but was rather, as Karl Barth has said, "in the theme of Christian faith." The angels, Barth continued, have an original form in the accounts of Scripture. Scripture does not consider them an absurdity or a curiosity which we can replace with our own inventions. We may survive as a church, Barth said, without conscious resort to the angel dimension; but, he maintained, only "at a pinch . . . not without hurt and not without the underlying awareness that something is missing." [25] Barth did not hesitate to call the angels objective and authentic witnesses about God's action in Jesus Christ and he averred that without them God himself would not be revealed and perceptible. When God bypassed the angels and became man in Christ, said Barth, the angels entered the sphere of man with him. Because he felt that mysticism as a whole was not Christ-centered but man-centered, Barth, as we have seen, ruled it out as a part of the Christian revelation. With respect to the teachings about angels he was affirmative as long as angelology remains subordinated to Christology. Martin Luther was in Barth's thoughts as he wrote his dicta on the angelic. He regarded Luther as a good proponent of true angelology. Barth reminded his readers of "the unforgettable conclusion of the evening blessing in Luther's *Small Catechism:* 'May thy holy angel be with me, that the evil foe have no power over me. Amen. And then quickly and happily to sleep.' " Barth added: "This sentence contains the whole doctrine of angels *in nuce,* and decisively so on account of the address: 'Thy holy angel.' " [26] As we see, Hirsch's judgment on Luther's angel belief is almost at the other side of the spectrum, fired by confidence in rational power which practically excludes the mystical lore by transposing it to psychological needs or useful thought.

After this digression occasioned by Hirsch's reference to Luther's angelology, let us finally probe into Hirsch's appraisal of Luther's thought by selecting the discussion of Luther's place in the tension between *critical thought* in the forms alluded to above and the *primitive, simple mind.* In his exposition of primitive notions prevailing in early Christian times and persisting in Luther's day, Hirsch counterposed "a spiritually clear, thinking mind" and "the simple mind" in need of concrete guarantees including concrete manifestations of the divine. The standards of historical criticism, on the one hand, and the values of an unreflecting, primitive simple mind, on the other, were Hirsch's two categories whereby biblical material concerning metaphysical manifestations should be judged. The simple primitive mind needs unrefined beliefs and partly depends on crude ideas about the divine. Luther, notwithstanding his participation in a culture of much primitive belief in crude lore about the divine, was closer to the standards of historical criticism than to the values of the simple mind, Hirsch said. It was at this point that Hirsch cited Luther's lack of appreciation of angel lore, a healthy lack of interest springing from "an unadulterated strong faith." Such a faith had no need of supernatural lore which cannot be reconciled with modernity's demand for cognitive clarity.[27]

The effect of modern critical thought was, Hirsch found, that "the genuine, original faith" had been brought to the surface. Criticism in the modern scientific vein had expunged pre-Christian lore. It was a painful process, Hirsch conceded, but in the last analysis beneficial. The truly Christian had been crystallized in this way.[28]

As we noticed, Hirsch considered his method beneficial also for the clarification of Luther's thought. Whatever the trammels of primitive lore left either in Luther's own accounts or in the theologizing about him, the methods of historical criticism cleared them all away. Luther himself stood out as a man who long before the era of critical thought had adumbrated it by his theological style. But we have also seen that in order to arrive at this picture of Luther, Hirsch had to make strenuous use of an intellectualistic preconception with traits borrowed from the rationalistic philosophy of modern science. We are left with a Luther who subscribed to the common sense of rationalistic man but knew little or nothing about the world of experience from which mystical theology springs.

In his earlier writings on Luther *Heinrich Bornkamm* looked at mysticism as a spiritual attitude with which Luther, through his experience of personal salvation, was well acquainted and for which he felt kinship. Bornkamm considered Karl Holl the watershed in Luther research, not least through his emphasis on Luther's "rich notion of the Spirit" and on faith as a spiritual gift. Bornkamm was impressed with Dilthey's teaching about intuitive conceptualization and the latter's opinion that the Protestant mystic, Franck, was "the crown of the Reformation." He also noted the place accorded to mysticism in Troeltsch's sociological teaching.[29] He remarked that Luther actually embraced "Christ mysticism" and he observed that Luther employed the language of bridal mysticism.[30]

However, as was shown in the discussion of generalizations of mysticism, later Bornkamm works suggested an approach which reflected an altered frame of reference and a different yardstick. An ideological-theological stance became discernible in which the evangelicity of the immediate experience of God was questioned. Bornkamm spoke *for* "Protestant faith" but *against* mysticism's view of nature, terming the latter an "untruth." We said before that Bornkamm judged mysticism to be a homogeneous body of theological fallacy. In our current context we now add the tendency to contrapose two theological worlds from the angle of cognitive truth. Theoretical, dogmatic formulations about truth were invested with a measure of finality. This leads to the assumption that Bornkamm, in later thinking, came to opt for a more theoretical, didactic posture in systematics than was immediately evident in earlier interpretations. "Protestant faith" consequently appeared as a system of truths. As a result we find on historical-critical domain the same kind of confidence in cognitive formulation as among the orthodox Lutherans.

The operation of preconception in Bornkamm's interpretation of mysticism's place in Luther's thought can be observed first at the point just broached on which some elaboration will be offered: the question of conceptual truth; in the second place, the idea of the divine presence and, thirdly, the mystical in Luther.

Bornkamm's thinking about the mystical phenomenon became couched in the logical antinomy truth-untruth. He cited with approval Ritschl's verdict on the absolute distinction between the Catholic-mystical and the Lutheran-evangelical. The evangelical truth as propounded by Luther took comfort in the seemingly insignificant manger of the Christ child but the Catholic truth and more specifically the mystical truth, was an ascent to divine majesty. The evangelical truth Bornkamm described as one of sober, wakeful acceptance of a gift which did not require a corresponding movement of feeling and inner growth. The Catholic-mystical attitude was pictured as a selfish desire to possess the divine in psychic recesses of the soul.[31] Logical antinomy appeared to be the sustaining viewpoint on matters of faith. The antinomy was one between the Protestant truth and the Catholic-mystical truth. Having quoted the Luther dictum, "God is in each creature," Bornkamm explicated its theological meaning by asserting that Luther did not want to suggest that nature yielded "knowledge of God." The desire for antinomy doubtless actuated the absoluteness of the statement. For, as will be suggested further on in our study, the question of a general knowledge of God is not as unambiguous in Luther's thought as it appears in Bornkamm's judgment.[32]

The evangelical truth was set against the Catholic-mystical untruth so as to suggest that the contradiction is total. "The evangelical truth" was pitted against the claims of mysticism described as "untruth" or "fraud." [33] In this view the Protestant faith is a system of truths, a congeries of theoretical formulations. Truth as a logical-theological crystallization of what people say about their faith becomes the overriding concern. Trust as a living relationship to God which is not always amenable to logical strictures recedes into the background. The tension between truth and trust seems to have been resolved in Bornkamm's interpretation in such manner that logical-theological truth prevails and trust is relegated to the area of the subjective, the mark of mystical theology. The preconception governing the approach to Luther and his mystical vocabulary is intellectualistic, a receptacle made only for gathering of logical distinctions between truths. This bias, then, prevents an understanding of the language of trust which is the language of dynamic spiritual experience. The approach also affected Bornkamm's apprehension of terms for divine presence in Luther's language, as well as that of mysticism.

Secondly, in Bornkamm's generalized picture of mysticism the seeker is promised "immediate God-experience." Bornkamm's interpretative instruments reacted against this aspiration. Not even in the sacraments can immediate God-encounter be had, he objected. As noted, much depends on the meaning with which one invests the word "immediate." It may connote an alleged connection with the divine outside the media of holy word and sacrament. This immediacy was rightly ruled out by Luther. But the word may also bespeak the feeling-side of faith, experience "in the heart" that God is nigh. Numerous indications show that Luther knew this kind of immediacy and thought that it was a bona fide portion of true theology. However, Bornkamm can be understood to say that neither apprehension is in keeping with evangelical theology. Luther's sacramental theology did not contain suggestions about experience, said Bornkamm. The sacrament of holy communion is declarative. It declares that Jesus Christ is my God. The sacrament is "not a place for immediate mystical God-encounter in supernatural bliss." As Bornkamm saw it, Luther limited man's involvement in the sacrament to a confession of Christological fealty. The Reformer can in all probability be interpreted as saying more than this about the experience-side of eucharistic participation.[34] Our intent here was to see why Bornkamm, sometimes with some vehemence, consistently excluded the motif of "immediacy" from Luther's thought notwithstanding evidence that would open up for such a reading. The conclusion must be that Bornkamm's intellectualistic preconception, according to which the evangelical thrust represented the objective and declarative in the gospel and mysticism the subjective and desiring, eliminated the feeling-side of religion. Dogmatic logic and instituted order became the deposit of Luther's legacy.

Our third enquiry into the effect of Bornkamm's precon-

ceptions as he analyzes Martin Luther grows out of the foregoing. Did Luther evince any organic links with mystical
theology? The answer from Bornkamm springs directly out
of the previous discourse. The Catholic-mystical and the Lutheran-evangelical are dogmatically-logically contradictory.
The Reformer who provided the logical arguments to illumine
the contradiction cannot be supposed to abide in that which
he proved wrong. The subjective and experiential in the realm
of religion belongs to a manward quest manifestly opposed to
the objective, declarative address from God. The Reformer
must be on the side of the objective and cannot at the same
time be on the side of the manward and subjective. Mysticism
is part of a total system of untruth. The Reformer lifted out
the truth. This is a logical-dogmatic assessment of the question concerning mysticism in Luther's life. Seen from within
such a logical-dogmatic conception the following dictum by
Bornkamm becomes understandable: "Only dilettantes in the
field of spiritual history can call Luther a mystic." [35] But outside the frame of Bornkamm's particular perception this
dictum becomes presumptuous.

As in the case of other Luther interpreters, the nature of
*Gerhard Ebeling's* presuppositions can advantageously be observed in his treatment of Luther's relationship to Tauler.
In his work on Martin Luther's gospel explications Ebeling
asserted that Luther's acceptance of Tauler was bounded by
"an unconsciously objective limit." The acceptance was likewise conditioned by "a temporal limit." Attention was drawn
to these delineations in connection with Ebeling's tendency to
generalize about mysticism. Ebeling suggested that Luther
was not aware of the limits relative to Tauler but that later
scholarship in a sense has corrected Luther on the matter.
Let us assume for a moment that this vicarious correction has
been induced by a pervasive Protestant-Lutheran conviction
that Luther's thought could in no sense be termed "mystical."
The validity of this assumption can be partly tested through
some attention to an interesting Ebeling translation of a bio-
graphical notation by Luther.

In the foreword to his writings in Latin Luther told his
story of the inner change which made all the difference to
him. These were his words: *Miro certe ardore captus fueram
cognoscendi Pauli in Epistola ad Rom.* Ebeling's translation
reads: "A very unusual burning desire had gripped me."
"Mirus" is closely allied with "miraculum," miracle. It is certainly weightier than "unusual." It rather means "wonder-
ful," "mysteriously strange." It carries a numinous connotation. The German footnote translation by O. Clemen in the
Weimar edition has caught this spirit. It reads: 'I was gripped
by a wonderfully glowing desire." The mystery, the suggestion of a "beyond" is preserved in this translation. Presumably
in order to make the dynamic presence of something paranormal more apparent Clemen added these words: "And it still
had me in its command." This is to say, Luther's experience
was pervasive, not an isolated sensation. A past perfect tense
indicates that the initial experience was well behind him when
he began his second series of psalter interpretations, perhaps
in 1518. But the sense of the miraculous persisted.[36] Ebeling's
translation keeps the experience on a commonsensical level.
The connotation of "miracle" has been toned down. To say
"unusual" is to employ immanental language about an event
which obviously contained transcendental intimation and was
so expressed: *miro ardore.*

A certain reluctance to recognize that Luther may have alluded to metaphysical reality is in evidence in the translation
thus cited. Has not the translator revealed his own mindset
by his choice of words? The outlines of a specific preconception begin to emerge in the translated sentence. These outlines assume firmer contours in a subsequent passage where
the author announces the goal of his examination. The reader
should not, Ebeling warns, expect a biography, nor a picture
of Luther's personality, for instance Luther as "the eternal
German." (Ebeling definitely looks askance at the importance
which some German colleagues ascribe to Luther's Teutonic
virtues.) Moreover, one should not expect a systematic ar-
rangement inside the pale of traditional loci. Instead Ebeling

offered an introduction intended to bring the reader to an "encounter." Separate facts and individual thoughts are one thing, Ebeling suggested, the foundation of it all was another. Ebeling proposed to present precisely the foundation. He would delve into Luther's *thought*, not his *thoughts* and he felt that he was part of a movement toward complete understanding of the subject matter, Luther. He was not involved in copying, rather in a desire to assume responsibility.

His goal, Ebeling continued, required the employment of an antithetical method. He maintained that Luther cannot be understood unless a particular scheme for understanding him is accepted. Ebeling's scheme was a dialectical one. Luther's thought, he argued, developed in antithetical fashion. For example, Luther thought and lived in the tension between philosophy and religion, letter and spirit, law and gospel, faith and love. His thought was assertive and confessional. In the process of his inquiry, Ebeling declared, the inquirer would remain open for "an encounter with Luther as a language event." For what really fired Luther was a zeal to bring the Word into language in correct manner. Luther as a "language event" should, if I have understood Ebeling, be seen as an emergent of antithetical motifs and movements.[37]

By this type of analysis Ebeling hoped to transcend historically conditioned understandings of Luther. To take two examples: it would be necessary to demonstrate the erroneous image of Luther developed by Lutheran orthodoxy as well as by pietism. Ebeling's propositions with respect to the latter are of special interest in our context. Ebeling has found that pietists took a distinctive liking to Luther's earlier years. For it was during Luther's earlier years that "the so highly esteemed edification literature of German mysticism . . . seemed closely related to the gospel of penitence and grace." By Ebeling's account of pietism and its links with Luther, the pietists maintained a certain distance to the later Luther whom they deemed a "hardened" Christian reformer, a person who under the exigencies of the day moved into some "re-Catholizing" positions. To Ebeling this was an illustration of how easily the understanding of Martin Luther may come to "depend on general value judgments." Ebeling himself had a different ambition. His method was oriented toward in-depth ("eindringend") examination of the sources. Scrutiny of the traditions which were part of Luther's life, made it plain, said Ebeling, that two eras warred in him. Moreover, something dynamic and constructive had sprung from this tension. Luther found that his renewal was a rediscovery of "the antithesis between the old man and the new man." The question was not just historical. It was existential. For it bore upon the antithesis "time of law—time of grace." Luther raised a timely question, not just a historical one.[36]

However, the timelessness of Luther's renewal and its significance appear only to the "trained ear," Ebeling explained. Only those who have grasped Luther's deepest concern will escape the disappointment that sets in at the discovery of the Reformer's human weaknesses, at the realization that he was not a "holy man," Ebeling pointed out. This is the nexus where a "trained ear" discovers the essential, the tremendous force of Luther's struggles, "the great burden of historical responsibility." A "trained ear" learns about this Luther inside Luther not so much from psychological analysis, nor from doctrinal accounts or sheer biography. The spiritual contours of a person rather take shape for us as a "language event." Ebeling suggested that the language event was coterminus with Luther's pronouncement, *sola experientia facit theologum,* "only experience makes a theologian."

We must raise the question whether Ebeling and Luther mean the same thing by "experience." For our probe into the nature of Ebeling's preconceptions, that is an important query. Ebeling proposed to lay bare the "thought" of Luther by honing the analytical faculty. Only the trained analyst knows in the end what Luther's basic experience was. This affirmation limits the number of those who may understand Luther to a fairly select group. The analysts may come closer to an "encounter" with Luther through a study of "the language event," an event implicit in the traditions crowding in on Luther, and implicit in "the characteristics of his approach to these traditions." Mindful of this background, the analyst, by studying the language event, perceives how Luther through "mutations" in his thinking arrived at something we might call "his own." This, then, was the kind of experience Ebeling had in mind as he suggested that the Luther statement, "only experience makes a theologian," coincided with the analytical understanding of a "language event." [39] But the two notions hardly coincide. Luther referred to a spiritual-psychological state, Ebeling to an intellectual process. On Ebeling's view only the practiced intellectual ear that recognizes the different traditions surging in on Luther can understand Luther and come to a real "encounter" with him.[40] But Luther's understanding of "experience," and the way to understanding *his* experience, have little to do with a purely conceptual procedure, it would appear. The experience about which Luther spoke was a fiduciary experience, flowing out of a trust-relationship with God.

The above exposition may have seemed superfluous, yet it has been necessary in order to get a view of the mindset and the preconceptions from which Ebeling evaluates Martin Luther. Our attention to Ebeling's choice of words in the translation of *miro ardore* brought to light some reluctance to read anything metaphysical, miraculous or numinous into the experience to which Luther alluded. The picture of a preconception begins to assume shape at this point. It would seem that the *Vorverständnis* was not unaffected by empirical, commonsensical naturalism which is unable to recognize the non-rational as a proper source for conceptual work. We proceeded to examine the course charted by Ebeling for his study and observed an intellectualistic element which, in combination with the commonsensical approach, made it unlikely that Ebeling's notion of "experience" and Luther's would coinhere, as Ebeling suggested. The effect of a largely commonsensical and intellectualistic (or rationalistic) *Vorverständnis* can be observed in, among others, the following areas of Ebeling's discourse on Luther: the meaning of the cross of Christ; the

love which is directed toward God; the nature of man's co-
operation with God, and the structure of man's conscience.

One effect of the intellectualizing or rationalizing tendency
which we have noted, is that Ebeling accords no place at all to
the mystical in assessing Luther's theology of the cross. He is
persuaded that the dictum, "in the crucified Christ is true
theology and knowledge of God" must be adjudged the abiding fundamental orientation of Luther's theological thought.
Yet, living in the crucified Christ, albeit sounding like a theme
from passion mysticism, is only seemingly mystical, Ebeling
contends. *Theologia crucis* in Luther's thought betokened much
more than "a momentary concern or a peculiarity of the young
Luther." Thus stated the case becomes contiguous with a notion which, as already noted, is staunchly held by Ebeling,
namely, that mysticism was at most a stage in Luther's development and that it had nothing in common with the mature
Luther's evangelical theology. This persuasion now serves as
support for the idea of a non-mystical cross-theology. *Justificatio* had nothing in common with mysticism, according to
Ebeling. The theology of the cross was the essence of justification, ergo cross-theology in Luther's mind could not be
mystical.[41]

Although Ebeling's interpretation of Luther's cross-theology no doubt fits the master theory, can we say that it fits the
material? Luther rejected speculative mysticism and ego-
centered passion mysticism. But in his words about Christ's
suffering there was nevertheless a strong element of internalization. Luther did in fact speak of inner dying and resurrection as that which had to precede all external deeds. This
dying with the suffering Christ in faith opened the possibility
for Christ to live in man.[42] The similarity to much mystical
language is unmistakable, so much so that we must assume
that a common theme unites Luther and several medieval
mystics in this regard. It appeared plainly in the terminology
of bridal mysticism where Luther gave expression to a mystical understanding of justification, not just as imputed gift but
as a felt community of life and love.

Luther described the union under the cross as a heavenly embrace, when the bridegroom, Christ, enfolds the soul, the bride, and this heavenly embrace, he said, is an acceptance of the cross.[43] The passion of Christ was both sacrament and example, Luther held. The sacrament was a gift, the example exhorted to *imitatio* by suffering and death.[44] The cross-bearing Christ himself in mystical fashion becomes the "acting subject" and "the power in men." [45]

It is clear that Ebeling's *Vorverständnis* prevents a recognition of Christian cross-bearing as in any sense a psychological reality. His intellectualism impels him to assume a posture which in some respects resembles the orthodox forms of rationalism: justification solely as imputed truth existentially corroborated. Faith, Ebeling maintains in refutation of mystical passion theology, is an appropriation of the word, not an actual change of man.[46]

When, in a comment from 1515-16, Luther spoke of our "love for God" which is ultimately rooted in the inexpressible, in the unfathomable God, he called this experience a "transport right into the midst of the innermost darkness.[47] The statement sounds clearly mystical. The impact of Ebeling's intellectualistic preconception is visible in his comment upon this dictum. We have before us, he explicates, a manner of linguistically depicting a connection between faith and God which "still" lingers on and is a "loan" from the vocabulary of mysticism. The reference to religious feeling in Luther's comment, the love of God which includes love for God, cannot be handled except in the way suggested. Mysticism is considered a past stage with Luther, hence mystical terms must be registered as extraneous. On Ebeling's reading faith is one thing and a real actual change another. Luther embraced theological faith; Catholic mysticism subscribed to the religion of inner change. That is to say, in Ebeling's view it would presumably be theologically nonsensical to claim that the love of God should include a love for God in order to be meaningful. Evangelical theology on Ebeling's understanding does not calculate with human feeling and intuition as part of the theological concern. Thomas Aquinas' words that love unites with the beloved militate, we said, against Ebeling's schema of true theology. Such internalization, he holds, "points to the extraordinary depths of the confessional difference." [48]

Yet, can Luther's testimony about inner love, a love for God nurtured by experiences of feeling and psychic response, be relegated to the realm of obsolescent terminology which has no basis in "reality"? Ebeling's preconception demands an affirmative answer. But, as we have seen, much evidence would warrant a negative reply: with Luther justification includes a human love for God as well as overwhelming awe.

Ebeling introduced a seemingly orthodox note into his critical-intellectualistic score when, presuming to speak for Martin Luther, he said that man is not to be considered as acting in the face of God. This, Ebeling explained, does not mean that man is not challenged "as acting agent before God in the face of the world." But it does mean that man is not acting when he faces God. [49] The proposition is a paraphrase of a statement by Luther in *The Bondage of the Will*. It will be useful to go back to this statement. Luther wrote that God's mercy is the prime mover. It moves all and our own will moves nothing. [50] Ebeling's use of the word "act," acting in the face of God, obviates the thrust of the remark. The choice of words may be in keeping with the animus of his mindset and preconception. The prejudgment holds that subjective, psychic response and spiritual growth are to be repudiated, not of course as occasionally valuable human values, but as parts of an evangelical theology about the God-relationship. Yet, the Luther quote under discussion does not seem to undergird Ebeling's thesis. Luther, it should be remembered, wrote these words in excitement and irritation over Erasmus' book on the will. The sharpness of many a turn of phrase must be seen against this background. But even granted the qualification, the passage hardly lends itself to the non-mystical construction which Ebeling places on it.

Another Luther passage, this time from *On the Freedom of the Christian*, lends weight to the suggestion that the notion of complete passivity before God was not an organic part of Luther's thought. The book on Christian freedom was of course written in a situation quite different from the *Bondage* situation. Luther felt that the Pope might understand where the ecclesiastics did not. Here we meet Christ mysticism pure and simple. Luther testified that he was free in Christ. A liberated person has a right to be glad and jubilate. In trust the liberated person's faith grows as the will to be of service grows. There is a quality in the Christian life which distinguishes it from the world. The center of this quality is the new insight that the Christian is not doing Christian tasks in order to further himself or to please the priests or the world. He does them because he is in Christ.[51] There is no indication here that justified man is not acting vis-à-vis God. To say the contrary would be to make him an automaton. One does not preserve God's sovereignty by making man an automaton.

Luther's intention by the statement containing the word "agere" was not to withdraw acting responsibility in the face of God but rather to underline the sovereignty of God as the prime mover and activator. Man is still, to Luther's mind, an agent expected to act in the face of God, moved by God. A preconception assuming that the movements of religious feeling and the engendering deeds have no rightful place in a theology of justification by faith has in part eclipsed Luther's idea of the meaning of being an agent before God.

Our probe into the role of preconceptions governing Ebeling's Luther interpretation will be concluded with a glance at the connotation of the word *conscience*. Ebeling has become persuaded that Luther regarded the conscience simply as a symbol for the points "where God and the world wrestle with one another." [52] Ebeling concedes that Luther appeared to say more than that about conscience. He appeared to say that an interiorization process ensues after man's surrender to God, indeed a kind of spiritualization. It looked like the language of the mystics. But, Ebeling continues, this is only an optical illusion. Luther, he warrants, just resorted to nomenclature which intrinsically did not belong to his justification theology. His real intention was "to locate the God-talk." In other words, Luther was in large part involved in analyzing an existential situation.[53] In so doing he found that conscience provides suitable testing ground for phenomenological observations. His language is only on the surface a mystical language.

However, did Luther actually think of the conscience only as a symbol for the contact areas between world and God? After his liberation from a scholastic view of conscience Luther saw it as the place of encounter between God and man, a dynamic knowing-with-God for justified souls. He began to describe the life of the conscience as Christ's entry into the soul with all what that meant of moral and affectional change.[54] How could Luther avoid dealing with the conscience when he wrote that Christ is formed in us and we are formed according to his image? [55] When he described faith as creative of divine attributes "in us," what else did he characterize but the conscience? [56]

We have thus, on the one hand, various Luther dicta about the conscience as God's growth in man and, on the other, Ebeling's contention that such dicta were merely Luther's way of verbalizing man's ideas about God. It would seem that Ebeling's notion that Luther used words about mystical internalization, which in his case had no actual reference to mystical internalization, must be considered a result of an intellectualistic preconception. According to this preconception mystical experience can in no way be integrated with evangelical theology and in fact wars against it.

Ebeling's preconceptions governing his understanding of Luther have been formed by the concerns of common sense and reliance on conceptualism or intellectualism. These prejudgments are detectable in his concept of the task as a Luther interpreter and his description of Luther's task: the understanding for Luther rests, in the last analysis, with the linguistic analyst and Luther's own reformatory task was ultimately analytical. On Ebeling's view Luther had one great aim: "to think God and world into oneness." [57] This emphasis on Luther's thought as a primarily intellectual-reflective renewal, with an antipode in mysticism, creates a Luther image that is closer to the analyst than the inspirator, the scholar than the seer. On Ebeling's account the mystical and Luther have therefore nothing in common.

A recent American work exploring the theological relationship between Luther and two medieval mystics hypothesizes that Luther's and St. Paul's anthropology stands in diametrical opposition to "mystical anthropology." [58] *Steven Ozment* asserts that Luther presupposed no continuity between God and man, no uniting substance because an assumption of continuity would eradicate the borders between God and man. As a consequence, Ozment argues, Luther and mysticism have contrary views of salvation and think antithetically about the feeling-side of faith, "immediacy." Ozment's fundamental verdicts and sustaining suppositions are the following: Luther's anthropology assumes "a soteriologically de-substantial nature of human life." Conversely, mystical anthropology assumes a soteriologically substantial nature of human life. Ozment reinforces his basic a priori judgment concerning polarity between mysticism (especially its anthropology) and Luther's thought by declaring that his (Ozment's) study is both historical and systematic. The former method wards off attempts to make a-historical comparisons of ideas for polemical or ecumenical reasons. The latter method guarantees a holistic approach to a thinker's world and obviates the use of ideas in isolation, abstracted from systematic contexts.

The following conclusions form the context within which Ozment's assertions should be seen. Tauler's anthropology is regarded as basically non-Lutheran. According to Ozment, Tauler depicts "man's pre-creaturely status as 'one essential being' with God." Ozment considers this concept incapable of inclusion in Luther's thought. Moreover, in Ozment's accounting Tauler calculates with "human preparatory activity" in salvation. Luther did not. Lastly, Ozment avers that "the effort to interpret Tauler's understanding of the *unio mystica* as a *conformitas voluntatis* overlooks the fact that such con-

formity . . . is preparatory to a still higher union with God."
This would be far from Luther. Thus Ozment finds that Luther's thought, in contradistinction to Tauler's, discounts the
suggestion that there is something "soteriologically substantial" in the part played by man during the work of salvation.[59]

A study of Tauler, however, prompts the questions whether
it is possible to make such categorical distinctions and whether
a particular preconception may not be at work in this instance,
rendering the delineations sharper than the material warrants. The matter of a particular preconception will therefore
be broached with respect to the relationship between faith
and humility and the problem of evangelical preparation.
Then, in an effort to lift out aspects bespeaking Luther's essential ties with at least Taulerian mysticism the questions of
"substance" and "the cognitive and the spiritual in faith"
will be discussed.

The first topic to be considered is *faith and humility,* an
issue frequently chosen by theologians to illustrate the gulf
between Catholic manwardness and Protestant Godwardness.
Ozment draws attention to a study of 1918 by A. V. Mueller
who produced no less than thirteen points to prove that Johann
Tauler and Martin Luther "agreed about the powerlessness of
the natural powers within the order of salvation." However,
Ozment writes, Otto Scheel repudiated Mueller's thesis in
1920 by claiming that "the Catholic doctrine of grace under-
lies Tauler's mysticism, and this doctrine is the opposite of
the Reformation doctrine of justification." Ozment terms this
statement a "confessional dismissal" and declares that it is
"generally accepted today." [60] Ozment maintains that Luther
is the "demarcation line between medieval and modern" in
the sense that "a clear and firm line was drawn between divine and human *activity*" [61] (Ozment's italics). The delineation signified, in Ozment's judgment, a reversal in Christian
anthropological thought: "Pauline anthropology" superseded
"mystical anthropology." Ozment not only maintains that
confessional theology correctly—and with general approval—
dismissed the idea that mystic Tauler and Reformer Luther

were essentially akin. He also asserts that a certain verdict by Vogelsang is the final word "for generations past and present." This verdict regards the "mystical-psychological consideration of man" as "overcome and replaced by a theological understanding." [62] Ozment's conclusion concerning the theological complex of "faith and humility" is that mysticism has no place for it inasmuch as mystics, influenced by their total theological framework, assume substantial kinship with God. To Luther faith and humility belonged closely together for, as Ozment seems to think, before God man's only assumption could be that he is not of God's substance.[63]

Ozment's theory of dogmatic contradiction is also in evidence with respect to the concept of *preparatio evangelica,* the possibility of an inner preparation for the entry of divine grace. Ozment avers that Tauler makes "human preparatory activity an indispensible condition for divine presence." Man must "do his own, then the Holy Spirit enters." Quoting Tauler's sermon on John 3:11, Ozment imputes to Tauler a universal "natural creational claim to salvation." In this sermon Tauler said that God has eternally imprinted himself in the ground of the soul, from the point of view of substance, action and essence. That is to say, the soul is related to God in the sense that it can receive all by grace that God has by nature. Luther was not estranged from such discourses. He could say that he found "true theology" in Tauler.[64]

Therefore, what Ozment regards as the total *context* of Tauler's "natural covenant" views on the one hand, and Tauler's "isolated" utterances concerning radical sinfulness and distance between man and God, on the other, are not as irreconcilable as they have been made out. Luther's high regard for Tauler's thinking showed an intuitive understanding of the connection.

Tauler sometimes spoke of a preparation for God's advent. But he also spoke of the great distance between man and God and man's nothingness and sinfulness before God.[65] He told his listeners that "all our holiness and righteousness is nought . . . our renewal must take place in God's righteousness and

holiness." [66] "The natural people" do not understand "the will
and the pleadings of the Holy Spirit" for they are living in a
righteousness of their own making.[67] Notwithstanding the
Taulerian talk of God's eternal oneness with man in the
ground of the soul, the basic thrust of Tauler's soteriology
rather appears to be on the side of Pauline anthropology. At
the same time we should remember that Luther himself took
positions which reckon with man's eternal links with God.
We shall return to the soteriological meaning of such thoughts
when the discussion comes to "man's nature."

We have seen that Ozment is guided by a *Vorverständnis*
which views the problem of Luther's relationship to mysticism
from within an either-or mold of doctrinal conceptualism:
"medieval or modern," "Catholic or Protestant," "mystical or
theological." A counterthesis will pervade the following exposition of some essential topics in Ozment's study: the exclusively logical-conceptual approach to the question of Luther's
links with the mystical, results in a divisive absolutization by
which the non-logical and unitive elements in faith, equally
essential for the task of theology, are lost.

The questions to be discussed are the problem of *substance*
and the problem of separation between *cognitive and spiritual*
components in faith. If our elaboration on substance seems
detailed the defense would be that the central issue will not
emerge without attention to some details in Ozment's study.
Luther commented on the problem of substance in his marginal notes on a Tauler sermon. Ozment summarizes these comments in the following sentence: "God destroys man's substantial form." [68] The question is whether Luther was actually
carrying out a polemic against Tauler at this point, as Ozment suggests. My impression is that Luther is not debating
here, but elaborating on what his spiritual kinsman is saying.
Let us look at the texts. Tauler speaks of Jesus' exhortation
not to give up in supplication to God, to keep on knocking at
the door in prayer. In the beginning of the sermon Tauler
characterized man's predicament in the face of God as being

*in diesem inwendigem Armute* which Ozment correctly renders as "this inner poverty." [69]

Surprisingly Ozment draws the inference that Tauler at this point calculates with an inner substance or a "substantial form." True, Tauler had earlier encouraged his reader to *blibe allein bi dir selber* which, rather than Ozment's "hold yourself together," might mean "abide in yourself." But is this really a claim for divine status with respect to salvation if we see it in conjunction with the confession of inner poverty? As Tauler proceeds this question must be answered in the negative. Tauler writes about a *geburt die ist nach und sol in dir geborn werden.* Ozment renders this translation: "The birth of God is close at hand, and God will be born in you." "God" is here an addition made by Ozment. But does it clarify, or is it simply an indirect outcome of Ozment's prejudgment? The text speaks of a "birth that is near and will be born within you," that is to say, it will happen in you. This version changes the picture.

Luther, Ozment insists, provided a "response" in the margin to Tauler's pronouncement about the inner birth. A better word than "response" would be "comment" or "elaboration." For as I see it, Luther does not debate here, which is no doubt the impression with which Ozment leaves his reader. Luther simply remarked as he ruminated on Tauler's words about "the birth," that "we dictate the mode to God." This is to say, we tend to tell God how he should do it. Luther certainly did not contradict Tauler. Ozment's translation of the passage on the spiritual birth supports his contention that mysticism allows the *coram Deo*-relation, the relationship to God, to be determined by "a natural anthropological resource." To claim the possibility of a "natural creational 'covenant,' " he writes, to attribute "soteriologically significant resources to the soul of man" is Pelagianism.[70] Tauler's dictum does not support Ozment's contention that this kind of soteriology is Tauler's.

No doubt Ozment's discussion reflects sound dualistic theology. Luther indeed set himself against the idea that man in any sense saves himself. Our plans are inimical to God's counsel as long as they are based on the assumption that they substantially help bring about salvation. But when Ozment seeks an illustration of this fact in Tauler's sermon on Job 17:12 and Martin Luther's comments on it, he places more emphasis on a logical-dogmatic polarity than either the words or the intent of Tauler and Luther warrant. In an effort to support his polarity thesis Ozment "proves" two points which can hardly be proved with the aid of this particular material; first that Luther here disagreed with Tauler, secondly that Tauler preached from the Pelagian supposition that man's salvation depends on a "substantial form." On the first point one might ask why Luther could write as follows if he were actually debating with Tauler: "Thus, as he [Tauler] says here, the entire salvation is the will's resignation in all things." [71] On the second point, with reference to the foregoing analysis there seems to be little justification for believing that the otherwise forthright Luther would here be delivering a circuitus "explicitly critical non-explicit criticism" against Pelagian ideas.[72]

Has Luther, seeing Tauler's words "resignation of the will," become "totally uncritical?", Ozment asks. His answer is that Luther criticized Tauler "non-explicitly." But in the Tauler text we find only a mention of spiritual darkness and inner poverty without any indication that such conditions are to be induced by man as a method to gain salvation. To "abide in yourself" then becomes a statement about the fact that man in some way possesses a God-given ground for the divine encounter. Tauler and Luther are not at variance on that point. The "substantial form" of this ground or this material must be destroyed. The material, the ground, assumes a new shape through a new birth or naked faith. The clay in the hands of the potter (to use the biblical image in Luther's comments on Tauler's sermon) has changed form. But it is still clay belonging to the potter. Luther is not being uncritical. The question arises whether a preconception concerning mysticism has influenced Ozment's treatment of this Tauler text.

The effect of an a priori judgment, too categorically applied, can also be observed in the discussion of "pure disposition" which is an element of the discourse on "substance." In his attempt to show that Johann Tauler presupposed, as a theological cornerstone, a pure disposition in preparation for the receipt of God's grace, Ozment resorts to sermon 1. in the Vetter collection of Tauler sermons. The subject of this sermon centers around the "outflow" and the "inflow" as an interplay between the human and the divine. The author of the sermon speaks of "the origin" as a basic potential for development of the divine in man. This terminology does not occur in other sermons, something which should alert the reader. In an article entitled "On Tauler's sermons" Philipp Strauch has submitted results of his research on Tauler's printed legacy. Strauch writes that the Leipzig edition of 1498 contains five Eckhart sermons. One of them is precisely the sermon cited by Ozment as evidence of Tauler's theological incompatibility with Luther. Presumably Luther never read Eckhart and presumably he therefore never saw the sermon which Ozment uses as documentation for his tenet that Luther and Tauler on deeper ground did not see eye to eye theologically.[73] An absolutely held prejudgment, namely, that mystical theology is diametrically opposed to Luther's theology, has prevented the student of Tauler from noting that the theme on "outflow and inflow" as part of the divine "origin" is a singular occurrence in the sermon collection and that it is more Eckhartian in tone than Taulerian.

Tauler was quite conscious of that "substance" in man which is perverse. He would therefore not have derived much help from what at least superficially appears to be the total Eckhartian view of "entry" into "the ground," namely the encounter with that "substance" which is "God in man" and consists of man's powers as directed toward God.

Time and again do we hear in Tauler's sermons that the soul is "united to God in a supernatural way" but also that this will not be known "until the old man be driven out." God "preserves man's nature in a supernatural manner," Tauler would say. Yet, "if God is to enter into us . . . the creature will cease to exist" since "the poison of the first Fall has sunk into the very depths of our nature." There is in other words a sense in which God's entry into man means the same for Luther and for Tauler, namely the experience of becoming a sinner. And then comes the "going out," the grace-bound freedom.

We can only draw the conclusion that Ozment's use of a sermon which in all likelihood was Eckhart's, not Tauler's, reflects a methodological model according to which mysticism always represents the non-evangelical and "medieval" and Luther consistently the evangelical and "modern."

"Substance" means two things both to Tauler and to Luther. It is man's sinful estrangement from God but it is also God's indwelling in man, "potentially and substantially," a Luther dictum we quoted in the footnote to Ozment's statement that man before God proves to have no substance of God. The qualification, "soteriologically de-substantial," becomes somewhat redundant if one realizes that neither Tauler nor Luther thought that man's natural equipment could bring about salvation.[74]

Our last point of deliberation connected with the Ozment study concerns the relation between *the cognitive and the spiritual*. One of Ozment's leading pronouncements is that "Luther secularizes man, not man's justification before God."[75] The statement serves as a delimitation against the thinking of Karl Holl who placed positive emphasis on the latter salient, secularization of justification, thereby rendering Christianity a moral-ethical enterprise. By this delimitation, however, Ozment also appears to have closed the border to a theology which reckons with the immediacy of life in God and Christian man's potentiality in God. He would seem to rule out from Luther's world the aspect of spiritual growth and affinity with the divine. Martin Luther becomes, in Ozment's version of Luther's relationship to mysticism, a theologian who is "theological" to the exclusion of the "psychological-anthropological." It is assumed that the two areas, the cognitive-conceptual and the intuitive-experiential can and should be separated.[76]

As far as mysticism is concerned it becomes Ozment's aim to prove that there is, even in the case of Johann Tauler, an unbridgeable gulf at all essential points between the mystical and Luther's thought. Is this sharp distinction viable? To answer this critical question one must read what Ozment read.[77] Even though I cannot claim to have read all that Ozment read yet I would argue that pertinent critique of faulty structures does not necessarily demand coverage of the total waterfront. For one thing, even the material that author and reader "read together" may give rise to divergent interpretations. Also, the soundness of conclusions based on documented and submitted propositions may well be vitiated by documentation that the author has not read or chosen not to submit.

Ozment's exclusive logical-conceptual approach to the problem of Luther's relationship to mystics absolutizes the division between "theology" or "theological faith" (as a logical system based on doctrinal *loci)* and "mystical spirituality" (as the psychic and non-logical salient of the religious life). In order to maintain this intellectualistic, absolutized division Ozment disregards common ground on which some Christian mystics are "theological" and Martin Luther "mystical."

## C. Conclusion

The rationalism of Protestant orthodoxy was principally a pre-scientific rationalism whose reliance on theological concepts barred the inclusion of non-logical forms of spiritual experience reflected in mystical theology. Because mysticism seemed to arrogate importance to feeling, Protestant theology read past Luther's mystical utterances and transformed *unio mystica* into a concept inside a catechetical order of salvation.

Some Protestant theologies have been radically influenced by historical criticism and naturalistic empiricism with verifiability codes from Newtonian science. Although equally de-

pendent on *concept* and wary of feeling, the rationalism of
these theologies was, in part, much more apologetically oriented than that of orthodoxy toward a skeptical modern world.
On *this* ground the former ruled out the significance of Luther's references to inner, mystical experience and underplayed
Luther's professions of spiritual kinship with mystics. Liberal
theology answers to this description, whereas in neo-orthodoxy
the motivation for exclusive conceptualism has stemmed less
from apologetic concerns and more from a desire to recover
the centrality of Christ, lost in liberalism. From this aspect
mystical theology seemed too occupied with man's possibilities
and subjective moods and too little with credal faith. The possibility of a "mystical Luther" was discounted on that ground.

Yet, both of these strands of contemporary Protestant theology would place "theological faith" on one side and "mysti-
cal-anthropological theology," including "actual inner change,"
on the other. The former is conceptual and logical, the latter
is feeling- and intuition-oriented. Luther's mystical inclinations are likewise discounted through one method or the other
both by liberal and neo-orthodox theology. Depending on the
intensity of the individual theologian's confessional involvement, the absolutization assumes a more or less fervent character of confessional ideology, with two opposing camps in the
sphere of noumenal contention. Each camp purportedly represents theological-logical consistency either in what is termed
true or heretical direction.

The picture of Luther emerging from the special angle of
relationship to mysticism assumes varying shapes.

1. Luther is pictured by some in the liberal camp as a person of commonsense robustness and of a wholly non-mystical
bent. The codes of the empirical historian are applied to Luther's thought. They forbid the inclusion of mystical lore in
the statements of Christian faith.

2. Man's conscience stands at the center of Luther's theology, according to others. To them justification by faith has
become a new exciting *concept*, rather at war with emotional

mystical, spiritual *experience*. Luther is made to answer these criteria of faith.

3. There is the emphasis on Luther as a rediscoverer of the gospel sanctifying our existence in the flesh. This emphasis owes a great deal to historical criticism. The ethical implications of the imitation of Christ in such accounts eclipse Luther's words about a mystical formation into the likeness of Christ.

4. We have also met the suggestion from liberal-historical-critical quarters that Martin Luther's concern as a Christian and a reformer coincides with the intent and the results of critical research. When stripped of unessential supernatural embellishments faith becomes a process of inner actualization. This event is depicted as the truly Christian element in faith and Luther is pictured as a modern pioneer for that inner side of the creed.

5. Insistence on theological knowledge rather than trust or *fiducia* in a subjective sense has been noted. The knowledge of God's "for you" in Christ cancels out belief that the natural life offers knowledge of God. The evangelical becomes the antipode of the Catholic, the faith-borne the opposite of the mystical and Luther's Germanic presence the counterweight to passion mysticism.

6. At one salient of the historical-critical front one endeavors to systematize Luther's Reformation theology by analyzing it as a "language event." Luther's "thought mutations" may be best observed by applying antithetical word pairs like letter and spirit, law and gospel. Luther's religious experience is portrayed as an analytical venture rather than an inner drama of psychological significance. Luther's theology about the cross of Christ is described as "theological" in contrast to the "psychological." It does not involve a real, actual change of man. Moreover, this Luther interpretation considers the Reformer's mystical language only superficially mystical. In effect Luther's theological language deepens the confessional

gulf between evangelical faith and Catholic faith, the latter including mysticism.

7. The antipodean character of the encounter between Luther's thought and mysticism is underlined by yet another rendition which we have considered. With emphasis on Luther's gift of scholarly clarity it hears Luther say that human life is soteriologically de-substantial and reads mysticism as claiming substantial kinship with God for the purpose of salvation. Luther is "modern," mysticism "medieval," Luther a prototype of "the new man," the mystic the paragon of "tho old man."

The motif traversing these samplings of theological reflection on Luther and the mystics is intellectualism or rationalism as shaped by the so-called exact science of the 19th century. In my note on Ebeling's dictum to the effect that God and the world have to be "thought into unity," I suggested that Luther's kinship with some mysticism will remain an enigma as long as the *ratio* of naturalistic reflection must govern theological inquiries. Under those circumstances there can be little room in the thought structures for the numinous dimension, experiences of spiritual presence and feelings inspired by the Holy Spirit. In fact, it becomes an undeclared intention on the part of theology to remove all suggestions that manifestations of the metaphysical or the supernatural belong to faith. As we have seen under the rubric "mysticism generalized" one will go to quite some lengths in arranging the material so that it will affirm both the dogmatic delineation and the scientific ambition.

In the following chapters an attempt will be made to show that Martin Luther's theology may lose Martin Luther himself if shorn of its mystical elements. In the process the discussion will be continued with intellectualistic constructions of Luther's theological intent.

# CHAPTER 3

# The Pneumatic School

## A. The problem: intellectualistic abstraction

As we have seen, various presuppositions both in confessional-orthodox and liberal-critical theology have almost obscured the experience aspect of Luther's gospel apprehension. Experience is Luther's word for an immediate God-relationship through the mediation of Jesus Christ. We have observed forces which neglected this central fact and shaped a Luther image and a Lutheran kind of theologizing which lacks dynamics.

First, soon after Martin Luther's death there was a return to scholastic-rationalistic orthodoxy, where the Word became the focal point instead of the Roman Catholic tradition. That was and is the line of Lutheran orthodoxy.

Second, theology borrowed its apologetic frame of reference from modern Newtonian science which was making rapid advances. That which was explainable and scientifically verifiable, according to the codes of exact science, became theology's sole methodological norm. Luther was brought before the tribunal of modernity's sober causality-thinking and, like biblical events and personalities, found either wanting or profoundly modern. The mystical life in God was judged to be of no essential concern to him. Here we find a wide congeries of thinkers in what one might broadly term the critical-liberal tradition.

Third, theologians representing a wide range of theological opinion have, through their attempts to systematize Luther's thought, been governed by a desire to prove that every important dogmatic point of the Lutheran evangelical faith is in diametric opposition to its Roman Catholic counterpart. The result is that Luther's affinity with some mystics and his belief that the Christian life is in part an immediate experiential life in God have been disregarded. Both the orthodox and the critical-liberal interpretations of Luther's thought have succumbed to this confessional polarity thinking.

Ernst Benz writes:

The [intellectualizing] theology has since the 16th century accumulated a monopolistic power position behind which all other expressions of the Christian faith have receded and languished—the religious experience in mind and heart, religious poetry, meditation, the *charismata* which extend into the irrational, into the prerational, into the transrational and which played a decisive role in the old church. Let us not forget that one of the spiritual gifts that Jesus gave his disciples when he sent them into the world as missionaries was the one described in Luke 10:19: Behold I have given you authority to tread upon serpents and scorpions, and over all the power of the enemy; and nothing shall hurt you. . . . How often has not theology become a sort of abstract mathematics in which numbers and mathematical symbols have been represented by dogmatic codes and symbols. Surely, they enable well-honed heads to indulge in all manner of interesting intellectual combinations. But they reach only as far as the grasp and enjoyment of such intellectual games goes.

With this activity Benz compares the vision of the unreachable wholly other, the immediate experience of the reality of the world beyond to which the prophet and the seer can testify.[1]

Rudolf Otto described the attitude evidenced by those who have in some way experienced the charismatic, as "the religious conception of the world." The "religious conception of the world" has difficulty with "the naturalistic, 'mechanical' interpretation of life" and vice versa. It may seem strange that theology would find it hard to integrate essential aspects of "the religious view" with its purview, but this is so. In the field of theological discourse naturalistically molded reflection and the religious life-view frequently appear incompatible. The religious concept of the world, Otto held, never grows immediately out of the natural perception of things. Nor, he suggested, could the religious view of the world ever be exhaustively explained by natural perception; that is to say, the religious view of the world will not need to pronounce opinions as to the nature of the world and the meaning of existence. If it illumines our existence and lends purpose and meaning to personal being, that is sufficient.

It is enough, Otto thought, if in *this* regard reality conforms to the religious illumination by corroborating it. Reality does so in signs and moments pregnant with meaning. The religious view of the world can consequently act as apologetics for a non-naturalistic grasp on life but it is an apologetics aware of its limits. Moreover, the theological defense or explication must fetch its inspiration in a personal will to faith and joy in faith. Many enigmas will remain enigmas to the religious experience of life; the religious experience is less concerned with explanation than with decision and choice.

Genuine faith has never turned away from pain and insoluble riddles. In fact, it has always been much exercised by these questions. But the religious conception of the world does not try to solve them in an explanatory fashion. Otto quoted Luther to the effect that faith involves going against appearances. This means, Otto explained, that the religious conception of the world can never be congruent with a scientific or general study of things. Through suffering under appearance and contradiction the religious or sacral life almost floundered at times; yet frequently, and paradoxically, it found strength. Wherever faith has died under the pressure of appearances, the person with dead faith will assert that faith, as attitude of awe and reverence before God, was possible in earlier, naive eras but not possible for those who have developed greater insight. This, according to Rudolf Otto, is foolish talk. If faith dies in this fashion, he said, it dies from a childhood disease. Otto made the point which we wish to make here: reflection about faith from natural presuppositions and reflection on faith from charismatic or religious experience do not have to conflict, yet often do. Religion becomes irrational and natural reflection rationalistic. For the subject under review in this book it is important to observe that under the influence of naturalism "the spiritual sciences," including theology, have become patterned on natural science. The result is that spiritual inspiration and the movements of man's conscious life tend to be described as commensurate even in theological deliberation.[2]

The inspirational and the logical, however, are two parts of one theological whole. If the conceptual-logical takes the upper hand, the visionary who is also a scholar becomes a scholar without vision. Martin Luther was a visionary and a scholar. Much depends on where the accent fails. Two examples will be given for the purpose of showing the place of intellectualistic abstraction and its effect in the one case, and the place of the numinous apprehension in the other.

## Logic and numen

The mainstream of Protestant theology considers the essence of mysticism essentially foreign to Martin Luther's theological thought. Underlying such proposals is the general assumption that mysticism militates against Luther's thought or does not warrant mention when this thought is discussed. This has been plain in examples given from theology operating within the liberal and critical framework molded by ra-

tionalistic modernity. As an introduction to the problem
facing a pneumatic view of Luther's religion, attention will
now be drawn to two authors who have devoted intensive study
to Luther's *The Bondage of the Will.*

The first is Father Harry McSorley.[3] According to him Luther underwent a dogmatic evolution from *liberum arbitrium,*
the free will, to *servum arbitrium,* the unfree will.[4] McSorley
quotes from Luther's early writings, notably the first lectures
on the Psalms, marginal notes to Gabriel Biel's *Collectorium,*
the lectures on the epistle to the Romans, and the treatise on
the *Bondage.* The author claims that Luther in the years
1510-1524 (the latter marking the conclusion of *The Bondage
of the Will)* moved dogmatically from a nominalistic notion
of man's will to an Augustinian or even a so-called necessitarian concept of the human will as it relates to God. Mc-
Sorley points out that Luther began by affirming and extoll-
ing the natural powers of the will.[5] Then, in his marginal
notes on Biel Luther asserted that "they that really do good
works ... know that man cannot do anything from himself."
On Luther's view it would be an error to interpret the phrase
"to do what is in him" thus: "to do or to be able to do anything." [6] Although Luther already in 1515-1516 affirmed that
the will "is always naturally free," in his commentary to the
Romans he uttered words about necessity and contingency
which "indicate a departure from the Scholastic understanding
of these concepts." McSorley sees in this departure something
regrettable and inadequate leading Luther eventually to say
in his *Bondage of the Will:* "Free will is knocked flat and ut-
terly shattered." [7] In McSorley's opinion Luther "blurs the
distinction between natural freedom *(liberum arbitrium)* and
acquired freedom (Christian freedom)." McSorley argues
further that Luther, through his "lack of clarity" on this
point, lamentably departs from "the entire Catholic dogmatic
tradition" by not underwriting any longer his earlier—and
sounder—dictum that man is always free naturally.[8] In the
end Luther seems to make no distinction between a "necessitarian" view of God's omnipotence which renders the termi-

nology deterministic, and a "biblical" posture according to which God's grace precedes all.

Two methodological points should be mentioned in connection with McSorley's Luther study. The first one is explicitly announced. McSorley writes that he must necessarily limit himself "to a consideration of only one point of the 'dogmatic' side of these lectures (on the Psalms)," namely, the question of the *will*.[9] In fact, the entire work is so limited. The second point is implicit. Not only does McSorley not include "the 'existential' aspects," [10] he disregards entirely the mystical content of the dogmatic complex he treats.

Let us examine the first point. By limiting his impressive marshalling of Luther dicta on the bondage of the will to just that very important part of Luther's thought on salvation does not McSorley run the risk of actually employing the very mode for which he criticizes Luther's deterministic-sounding utterances: "Speculative theological reasoning"? [11] Does not the process of isolating the explicit documentation about the will lead us away from the central experience which constitutes the entire Reformation discourse on the will: the awesome and joy-filled encounter with the God who rights the wrong? When McSorley opines that neither Augustine, nor "authentic" Catholic doctrine, nor the Lutheran confessional writings calculate with determinism regarding God and the will, and then contrasts this fact with the unaccountably deterministic ring of Luther's *Bondage* dicta, does not his self-imposed delimitation assume the character of academic intellectualism? Is it possible to register "not only . . . what Luther said but also . . . what he meant" [12] when one limits the examination to the question of words on the will? Moreover, is the task just one of providing a sketch of Luther's evolution from one doctrine to another, as though the Reformation were primarily a succession of ideas, where sometimes *one* idea is expected to entirely supplant another? Roman Catholic McSorley shares puzzlement over Luther's "lack of clarity" about the difference between "necessitarianism" (or "theological determinism") and the "biblical" view of the will with several Protestant authors who have been endeavoring to render Luther acceptable despite his lack of cognitive clarity on this score.[13]

A clue to Luther's disregard for this lack of cognitive clarity is offered in McSorley's almost incredulous observation: "Luther, very uncharacteristically, makes no effort to give biblical support for this [the necessitarian] argument." [14] Here McSorley's implied persuasion is that any religious contradiction can be clarified by more theological cognition and biblical quotations. For once Luther is supposed to have slipped up on a dogmatic issue. Also implied is the suggestion that "biblical support" equals the number of supporting Bible passages available. The truth of the matter may rather be that Luther felt that he indeed based both his theological determinism and his notion of the powerlessness of free will without grace on the biblical message as he experienced it with increasing intensity in his own life.

The second consideration is suggested by the first. One could contend that neglect of the mystical experience in a study of Luther's life, as an implied method, leads precisely to the disappointment about Luther's lack of "clarity" and "poor terminology" [15] out of which grows the regretful judgment that "Luther's doctrine of responsibility leads him to an antirational concept of faith." [16] This could of course be just the point. Meeting God is to know increasingly that he knows and plans all and yet, irrationally, that he needs the will's assent and attunement of man's will to his. No intellectual attempts in this determinate existence can resolve this problem. When McSorley judges Luther's "rejection of the traditional argument for free will questionable" [17] he seems to speak too much in favor of something like a logical equation. Luther, on the other hand, communicated out of mystical *gemitus*-and-*raptus* experience, which simply says that the Pelagians do not know what they are talking about. Attempting to salvage "Luther's *intention*" from the shambles of his "misleading *terminology*" McSorley declares that Luther is not really questioning the fact of a free will within natural man, only its capability of contributing to man's salvation. McSorley goes on to state that this is Luther's fundamental intention, not a doctrine of determinism. According to Catholic teaching it is not heresy to say that prior to grace the free will can do nothing but sin, continues McSorley. After all, "it is a thesis of Augustine, the 'doctor of grace,' a thesis which has been accepted by the official teaching of the Roman Catholic Church." [18]

In response it could be argued that the attempt to attune Luther to the scholastic tradition probably does not promote the cause of ecumenical understanding as intended. There are deeper ecumenical affinities between Luther and the church he cherished and combated. The absence of the necessitarian element in much prior Catholic thought and in subsequent Protestant thinking tends to remove the mystical experience from the Christian dogma. It was precisely that experience which made Luther's unreasonableness on the necessity-issue "understandable." In one of his table conversations Luther referred to the difference between Erasmus and himself as one of non-experience of God and one of experience of the present power and the invisible worlds of God. From this kind of numinous, mystical experience issued the violent, "anti-rational" statement, the "exaggerations," to use McSorley's terms. But they are part of the spirituality which led to the Reformation and which is also of a mystical order.[19]

In his book *The Idea of the Holy* Rudolf Otto, expounding on the same work of Luther's, *The Bondage of the Will*, adds a dimension which is missing in McSorley. Otto, like McSorley, acknowledged that Martin Luther regarded his treatise on the captive will as very intimately his own, as belonging to the heart of his message. Otto, however, presented the doctrine of predestination with Luther as the meeting place between the rational and the mystical, the numinous, whereas McSorley treats predestination in the tradition of scholasticism. Predestination in Otto's Luther version became an analogical intellectual formula depicting the evangelical understanding of man's relation to God.[20] Otto maintained that for Luther a contrast prevailed between the *mirae speculationes,* the awe-laden reflection on the unspeakable in God and the *facies Dei revelata,* God's revealed face, i.e., between majesty and grace. Luther reminded his listeners that his teaching about the will as it approaches God, was not merely a subject for dispute or philosophical discussion, but a Christian's religious experience. In fact, he described the awe-inspiring, non-rational character of God and the lovely, human, gracious side of God as a force to be experienced, felt, as a mystical movement of mind and heart. Wrote Otto: "I grew to understand the numinous and its difference from the rational in Luther's *The Bondage of the Will* long before I identified it in the *qadosh* of the Old Testament." The unapproachable who becomes approachable—this can be grasped not by intellect alone but by "inwardness." This inwardness "finds only very dubious expression in the subsequent one-sided doctrine of the schools, where the mystical character of the 'wrath'—which is of the essence of 'holiness' infused with that of 'goodness'—is referred simply to the righteousness of God, and taken thus as righteous anger or indignation." [21]

Rational terms must be resorted to, Otto continued, when God's judgment and wrath are to be expressed. But "if we are to recapture the real Luther in these expressions, we must hear sounding in them the profoundly non-rational strain of 'religious awe.'" The mystical presence ringing through Luther's words about God's *tremendum* in *The Bondage of the Will* cannot be harnessed by

> the rational attributes of trustworthiness and love and the corresponding element in the mind of the worshipper viz. faith and trustfulness. No . . . the element of fascination is in Luther wholly interwoven with these rational elements and comes to utterance with them and in them. This can be felt forcefully in the boisterous, almost Dionysiac, blissfulness of his experience of God.

We have here "the mystical tone of Luther's actual creed." [22]

McSorley follows an important strain in the Protestant theological tradition in that he assumes that faith is a notion that can be rather exhaustively comprised in rational concepts. As noted, Luther's possible affinity with mystics remains unregistered in the McSorley account. This fact now becomes easier to understand. McSorley's logical approach to the problem of will as it relates to God allows no room for non-rational knowledge. To McSorley it is "unfortunate" that Luther denies that man has free will, not because he is a sinner but because he is a creature.[23] That is to say, in McSorley's view, if a theological suggestion breaks with the logic of *ordo salutis,* the rational should take precedence over the non-rational.

According to Otto, in Luther's religion faith "plays the same essential part, *mutatis mutandis,* as 'knowledge' and 'love' for the earlier mystics: it is the unique power of the soul, the *adhaesio Dei,* which *unites* man with God: and 'unity' is the very signature of the mystical." For Luther, Otto maintained, faith is the basis of the soul about which the mystics speak. Faith is also "an independent faculty of knowledge, a mystical *a priori* element in the spirit of man." Otto contended that

> there are definite features in faith, as the term is used
> by Luther, which justify us in classing it with the
> mystical ways of response to which it is in apparent
> contrast, and clearly distinguish it from the *fides*
> taught by the Lutheran school with its determinate,
> well-ordered, unmystical temper.[24]

McSorley is representative of those who attempt to find adequate formulations for predestination. In the case of Luther's necessitarian predestination McSorley does not find the logic, hence a rejection. Otto, on the other hand, pointed out that the necessitarian view of determinism is an analogy of predestination, not a formulation of theological logic. In contrast to McSorley, Otto found an "inner logic" for a necessitarian view of determinism in Luther's thought. It is not an isolated lapse of theological acumen but rooted in mystical intimation. The logical-conceptual and the numinous spheres complement each other but they do not coinhere.

But if the mystical presence influences Luther's thought so that the logical and the numinous interweave, how does Luther distinguish between biblically true mysticism and mysticism farther removed from the heart of the gospel?

## B. Mysticism differentiated

The hitherto surveyed theological opinions of mysticism's role in Luther's thought involve either a total disregard or a total generalization. At some junctures we have had occasion to suggest that a differentiation between varieties of mystical reflection may—all else being equal—lead both the school of total disregard and the school of total generalization to a reappraisal of the significance of Luther's mystical terminology.[25]

Martin Luther himself acknowledged his relationship to mysticism by particular approval and particular disapproval. He did not reject mysticism in general. For, as noted in the analysis of Protestant thought on the matter, there is no mysticism in general.

In 1515-1516 in the course of his lectures on Romans Luther pointed out that "Roman mysticism" pays too little attention to the incarnated word. Purity of heart comes only through the incarnated word. Only after the encounter with the incarnated word dawns the reality of the uncreated word.[26] In 1519 Luther warned against a different kind of mysticism, the one of Dionysius the Areopagite. Dionysius was not, said Luther, "a right mystic" for he spoke of "understanding" as a primary requirement. True theology must, however, go through "death and judgment." [27] It is clear that Luther felt little kinship for mysticism that dealt in speculation, in visions for their own sake, or as a method designed to find God. On the other hand, as Vogelsang pointed out, "all his life Martin Luther was grateful to Bernard (of Clairvaux) for the allu-

sion to the Crucified, the judgment and experience." What
made Luther repudiate one form of mysticism and give assent
to another? The yardstick for Luther in his relation to mysticism was the personal experience of justification by faith.
The differentiation of types of mysticism, especially Christian
mysticism, is a process which Luther himself initiated, and
it grew out of his deepest religious experience. But before en-
tering this area we have to consider a related matter which
by itself leads scholars to dismiss the discussion of differentiation since it often appears to render further attention superfluous. It is the debate about the "young Luther" and the
"mature Luther" with respect to mysticism. The question is:
Can one discern any basic difference in the attitude of the
"young Luther" and the "mature Luther" regarding the
mystical life?

## Young Luther and mature Luther on mysticism

Besides generalizing about mysticism and by this generalization trying to prove mysticism's inadequacy, much Protestant theology has employed another argument to support a
disclaimer for mysticism in Luther. It is the argument that
assigns Luther's mystical thought to his younger years, while
the mature Luther made a definitive distinction between the
mystical and the evangelical. The Reformer's youthful theological inexperience is thus contrasted with his later sagacious
theological realism and the issue becomes one of chronology.
Some examples from a few systematicians and historians will
serve as illustrations of the before-and-after school concerning
Luther's relationship to mystics.

Adolf Harnack maintained that Luther "during the first
period" used terms which showed that he "has learned" from
Augustine and the medieval mystics. We noted words to the
effect that Luther learned from the old mystics but "he found
what they sought." [28] Harnack described mysticism in general
as a complex of elevated feelings and a desire for psychological self-destruction. If any such proclivity was ever expressed

in Luther's vocabulary he later discarded this mood for active piety and steady, blissful certitude.[29] Harnack, who always pictured Luther as a soundly cheerful hero of the faith, held that Luther in his comments on Romans 8 discerned the historical Christ, attained certainty of his salvation, and "conquered mysticism."[30] We may consequently speak of a somewhat opaque Catholic stage followed by a lucid evangelical stage. The latter totally eclipsed the former. Luther totally abrogated Catholicism; Catholicism was tantamount to mysticism, hence Luther must have left mysticism behind him.[31]

The mystics who influenced Luther, Karl Holl averred, did their duty by bringing him to St. Paul and then fading out, for their erroneous notion was that man could satisfy God by meritorious deeds. St. Paul helped discard this fallacy; then there was nothing left of mysticism in Luther.[32]

In his earlier works Nathan Söderblom occasionally subscribed to the Harnack-Ritschl concept of a two-stage development in Luther vis-à-vis mysticism, the prior stage being completely erased by the latter. Söderblom's generalization of mysticism contained the notion that mysticism was a technique and a method for developing inner spiritual experience. From this viewpoint Söderblom spoke of "the mature Luther" rather than the young Luther. The mature Luther, he wrote, knew nothing of the methodical practice in passional inwardness. Because mysticism is method for attainment of God-union the Reformer could not in his mature theology have anything in common with it.[33]

Söderblom's compatriot Gustaf Ljunggren in his solid monograph on sin and guilt in Luther's theology subscribed to the same opinion. He spoke of "the completed Luther" in a way which suggested that the theological, somewhat mystical, past would be completely "conquered."[34]

"In his younger years," Heinrich Bornkamm asserted, Luther had gone the way of mysticism. He had endeavored "to climb into the Majesty before he had found his heart's comfort in the humble reality of the child in the manger." But soon his "German spirit," his "manly" inclinations drove him away from the less manly mysticism.[35] Luther went from the untruth of his younger years to the truth of the Protestant faith in his mature years.[36]

Gerhard Ebeling believes that continuity exists between the early Luther and the later Luther with respect to basic evangelical insight, but in the case of mysticism, a definite discontinuity prevails. Mystical elements in Luther's theological language are qualified by the words "still" and "seeming," indicating that, whereas some mystical vocabulary abides, its integral use belongs to the young, not to the mature Luther.[37] As noted in the previous section on historical-critical theology's way of dealing with the problem of Luther and mysticism, Ebeling uses his generalization of mysticism as an argument for his thesis that Luther constantly moved in dialectical fashion. Mysticism is not reconcilable with Martin Luther's *justificatio*. It represents a stage which later became wholly unimportant. In the evolution from the ideas of a young man seeking truth to the theology of a mature person, the mystical interest dissipated as it did not fit the mature Luther's theological discoveries. As noted, from this point of view Ebeling terms Luther's mysticism an *Augenblicksanliegen*, a passing interest.[38] The pietists, says Ebeling, have pressed to their bosom the Luther of earlier years when mystical edification literature seemed germane to the gospel of penitence and grace. But the later Luther was considered hardened and recatholicized. Ebeling had reached the conclusion that changes in the understanding of Luther depended on value judgments. Ebeling, however, offers a value-free "in-depth examination of the sources." It then transpires that Luther simply brought out "the antithesis of the old and the new man." Mysticism reflected the mode of the old man—Luther's mature Reformation teaching the new man, *simul peccator et justus*.[39]

We recall here our query into the possible reason for Ebeling's unwillingness or inability to assume a certain pervasiveness of and inter-relationship between spiritual motifs in medieval mysticism and Reformation theology. An illustration employed in this context was Ebeling's translation of Luther's words about the dynamic "wonder," the feeling of the numinous: *miro certe ardore captus fueram.* A point was made of the fact that Ebeling's translation obscures the mystical-numinous character of the sentence. An intellectualistic frame of reference renders the miraculous the "unusual," apparently without supersensible overtones. If the supposition is correct that Ebeling's scientific and personal apparatus does not record intimations incapable of adequate conceptual formulation, it becomes more understandable why the suggestion is offered that thoughts are formulated notions that supersede each other rather than, also, spiritual forces that interweave.[40] Attention is again drawn to Ebeling's words: "Later critical judgments show . . . a *zeitliche Grenze,* a temporal border line, in Luther's development." [41]

Wilfried Joest's viewpoint will conclude our sampling of what appears to be the majority opinion among Protestant theologians concerning "young Luther's" and "mature Luther's" attitude to mysticism. Joest takes for granted that all mysticism means "the immersion of consciousness in the ground of being." He contrasts the immersion theme with Luther's idea that the ineffable word is the crucified Christ. When Luther used mystical terms in *Operationes in Psalmos* of 1519-1521 "it should be clear that the Luther of 1519 cannot mean the immersion of consciousness in the ground of being. . . . For a long time already the *verbum innominabile* has a content: the crucified Christ." Here we see anew the notion that it is possible to delineate young Luther from mature Luther by drawing a certain temporal line.[42] It is assumed that mysticism cannot contain the crucified Christ and that the crucified Christ cannot be mystical.

There is a way of looking at the notion of a young Luther and a mature Luther which would make the distinction less categorical and less intellectualistic. Whereas traditional theology tends to see the issue in terms of dogmatic formulas analogous with abstract mathematics, a theology sensitive to the unpredictable dynamic of the Holy Spirit emphasizes the element of spiritual kinship between Luther and several mystics. For want of a better term we might call it "pneumatic theology." The feeling and experience of God and the immediate presence of Christ become links that unite Luther and similar spirits. It is not necessary to speak of influence. As indicated earlier, kinship is a better word for the affinity in question. If this perspective is applied it becomes difficult to draw a chronological border line between young Luther and mature Luther.

In his *The Idea of the Holy* Rudolf Otto said that many strands connect Luther with mysticism. Some of them are strong at the outset, decrease in strength later, but some never disappear. The explanation lies in the fact that Luther represented the numinous consciousness at first hand, not in a derived sense. Mystical doctrines, the miraculous thoughts of God's majesty, are intimately related to Luther's innermost religious life.[43]

Otto ventured the suggestion that non-rational elements in Duns Scotus' emphasis on God's *will* rather than on God's *being* were brought to fruition in Luther's theology. But this aspect has been expunged from later Lutheran theology as an unauthentic part of Luther's religion. It was treated as a residuum of nominalistic speculation. Yet we have ample reason to believe that the emphasis on God as *will* belongs to Luther's life-long view of faith as experimental and experiential. Numinous consciousness, said Otto, is at the root, rational dogmatizing is a derivative.[44]

Another voice addressed the young-mature problem as follows: "There is hardly an alleged 'mystical' statement with young Luther which could not be found with the allegedly 'unmystical' later Luther." This remark by Erich Vogelsang has immediate reference to Luther's comments on the penitential psalms. Both in young and mature Luther Christ is a mystical presence, not just a theological verity. He is dynamically present in the Word, for he lives in the words he spoke. By that token he is also in man's afflictions and joys.[45] Luther, Vogelsang asserted, never rejected mysticism in general since there was no mysticism in general to reject. He took umbrage at Dionysian mysticism but accepted the kind of mysticism that agreed with his own salvatory experience. The division between a theologically young Luther and a theologically old Luther who extirpated all that the young Luther said is not tenable. From Bernard, Luther had his definition of mysticism—mystical theology is experience, not doctrine. The young Luther spoke of Bernard, the mystic, as a spiritual friend who had experience. Bernard, as a mystic, knew that "the soul has rest only in Christ's wounds," wrote Luther. Not doctrine but experience brought him to this realization. The mature Luther said of Bernard—and, incidentally, about Bonaventura—that, as men of the mystical faith, they knew about "the incarnation of Christ." [46]

There was in Luther's theology a "continuous mystical approach" which harmonized with his deepest religious experience, writes Erwin Iserloh. This accord in feeling would rule out the method of fixing dogmatic stages allegedly holding mutually exclusive tenets at all major doctrinal points. Iserloh is particularly struck by the mystical tone of Luther's comments on Psalm 85:8. In meditation Luther discovered the illimitableness of the truth that God speaks in us. Only a still, contemplating soul can understand this. "A continuous mystical approach" would rule out the categorical two-stage approach.[47] The two-stage theory of drastic division seems to operate on the mechanistic presupposition that *one* thought can be irretraceably supplanted by another. Rather, *caritas Dei*, God's love and grace, has two inter-twined aspects, the objective one of justification and the subjective one of loving God, being affectionately tied to God. A solely cognitive scheme cannot accommodate that dual relation.[48]

In a penetrating essay on Luther and mysticism Heiko Oberman argues that Luther's attitude to mysticism did not change when he encountered Tauler's writings and the anonymous *Theologia Germanica*. Nor did it change fundamentally in the struggle against the *Schwärmer*. Not even the conscious turn toward the Reformation made a difference in that regard, irrespective of whether one places this event in 1514-1515 or in 1518. Luther remained positive towards mysticism as the experience-side of Christianity. Oberman confutes the frequent  allegation that "young Luther was a mystic until he discovered the dangers of mysticism in his encounter with the left wing of the Reformation." [49] In 1516 Luther wrote a marginal note to a Tauler sermon where he considered *theologia mystica,* insofar as it discusses the spiritual birth of the uncreated word, secondary to and derived from *theologia propria* which treats of the spiritual birth of the incarnated word. Luther did not deny the validity of high mysticism. Mary and Martha, he wrote, both belong to the total truth. God in his hiddenness and Christ in his revelation are interconnected. But there are some who would rather remain passively with God than actively with Christ.[50] In 1538 Luther commented on Genesis 19 saying that the true speculation about God is centered around God's power in man's orders, the incarnated and crucified son. True mysticism was not branded as questionable or impossible. Luther encouraged his readers to study the mystic Gerson and similar authors. Only he warned, in 1538 just as he had in 1516, against placing spiritual rapture before the access to Christ through faith.[51] Here we have young Luther and mature Luther both speaking positively of genuine mysticism. Striving to attain union with God outside the incarnated word is dangerous. But mystical theology was part of Luther's Christ concept. Luther often placed a *sic et non,* a yes and no, in the margin of mystical writing. But there was one author of the mystical school whom Luther accepted without that double comment: Johann Tauler. Oberman does not agree with thinkers who claim that Luther's enthusiasm for Tauler was a passing fancy. We recall that he makes use of a list of references to Tauler in Luther's writings according to which Luther, also in his mature years, often alluded to Tauler in positive ways.[52] Even if Tauler were the only mystic one could count as a spiritual kinsman of Luther, this alone would refute the allegation that Luther

in mature years placed "faith" against "psychological immediacy" and theologically denounced his "younger" days. This
is, however, not the only link with mystics that Luther maintained, as already indicated. He disassociated himself from
synergistic tendencies in mystical exercises. He also opposed
cognitive speculation as a road to the divine. But throughout
his life he reckoned with the mystical *affectus*.[53]

It seems clear, then, that Martin Luther did not fundamentally change his own stance concerning mysticism from his
"younger" period to the mature period of the Reformation.
The immediacy of God's presence was always part of his
*Erfahrung* (experience) and his *Erfahrung* came from will,
love and intuition rather than from thinking per se. Intellectualistic theology does not appreciate this distinction, hence it
makes more of the "young Luther-mature Luther" difference
than the facts warrant, especially if considered from within
a pneumatic-intuitive understanding. It is worth repeating
that Luther did not partake of mystical writings with a constant awareness that they were mystical, that is to say, the
trade mark meant little to him. He recognized a spiritual
temper in harmony with his own experience and acknowledged the kinship. Let us now return to Luther's differentiation of various species of mysticism.

## Threefold mysticism

From the above considerations it is clear that one has to
distinguish between different groupings of Christian mysticism. It is impossible to pass any verdict at all on Luther
as a mystic prior to such a sifting. Luther himself was selec-
tive on the subject, basing the evaluation on his fundamental
experience of a God that justifies by faith in grace. The theologies that, for a variety of reasons, treat mysticism as one
single block of identical motivation are too dependent on
specific prejudgments to make use of a diversification.

Erich Vogelsang made a valuable contribution to the understanding of Luther's links with mysticism, or kinship with

the mystics, when in 1937 he distinguished between the three following kinds of Christian mysticism: the neoplatonic form, emanating from Dionysius the Areopagite, the Romanic form with representatives like Bernard, Bonaventura and Gerson, and the Germanic form with the Frankfurter in *Theologia Germanica* and Johann Tauler.[54] It is not necessary for our purpose to study the details of these classifications. Should Gerson rather be classed with the Germanic school?[55] Is bridal mysticism part of Luther's faith?[56] Did Luther turn away from certain forms of mysticism at certain chronological junctures?[57]

The three groupings of Christian mystical thought as they crystallize from Luther's own acquaintance with Dionysius the Areopagite, Hugo and Richard of St. Victor, Bernard, Bonaventura, Gerson, Birgitta, Tauler, the Frankfurter *(Theologia Germanica* or deutsch Theologia) are: the Dionysian, the Romanic and the Germanic.[58]

1. DIONYSIAN MYSTICISM. Despite the fact that Martin Luther occasionally quotes Dionysius approvingly, the Reformer expunged dionysian theology. He found it insufficiently concerned with and rooted in the incarnated and crucified Christ. It was based on idle dreams, Luther judged. He warned that the person who rises with Lucifer to heaven runs the risk of falling.[59] The platonic concept of graded ascent to heaven, so prevalent with Dionysius, must be rejected as long as it leads man to think that he can climb to God on his own. Our ladder to God is he who descended to us, said Luther. We have to begin our ascent in his humanity and humiliation.[60] Sin cannot be extinguished with penitential works and efforts. Therefore, the Christian life does not begin with an emulation of Christ as the *exemplum*. It begins at the cross, in Christ as the *sacramentum*.[61]

2. ROMANIC MYSTICISM. Most of the mystics specified above belong to this category. Luther was in agreement with Romanic mysticism's discovery of Jesus Christ as a human being.

He felt at home with Romanic mysticism's emphasis on experience. But he objected to its ignorance of *Anfechtung* and he considered as dangerous its method of attaining mystical and ecstatic union with the divine without the medium of the external word, its claim to reach the "uncreated" word.

Romanic mysticism often spoke of man's life in God in metaphors lifted from the area of love between man and woman. It has long been a matter of some contention whether or not Luther's use of nuptial metaphor carries essential significance, i.e.the terms by which the God-union is depicted as a marriage-union. Vogelsang tended to believe that Luther preferred Tauler to Bernard precisely because the former used the love-union symbols more sparingly than the latter. Other scholars find an essential place for the bridal vocabulary in Luther's thought. According to this interpretation Luther would then be of one mind with Romanic mysticism. As suggested, Erwin Iserloh and F. Th. Ruhland belong to these interpreters.[62]

Martin Luther wanted his readers to be careful with the idea of participation in the godhead. This is evident from his antithetical treatment of much of Romanic mysticism, the *sic et non* treatment, the yes and no. In Luther's opinion man may on the one hand share in Christ's life but he can, on the other hand, never possess the whole Christ.[63]

3. GERMANIC MYSTICISM. We deal here primarily with two authors, Johann Tauler and the anonymous writer of *Theologia Germanica*, "the Frankfurter." But, as Oberman and others have underlined, the distinctions should not be made too hard and fast. Much of the wisdom termed Romanic may well fit the Germanic. Luther approved theologically of Germanic mysticism. A spiritual kinship existed between the man who found justification by faith in grace to be the heart of the matter and the writers who spoke of near desperation and resignation to hell as part of life before God.

In order to acknowledge and understand this bond with mysticism, not least the affinity with the variety called "Germanic," it is important, according to Luther, that we recognize the personal, subjective, experimental element in justification. The encounter with the incarnated Word is not mere pedagogical preparation for a closer walk with God, nor is it tantamount to observing a drama or engagement in moral discipleship. It involves community in the depth of the human person. It is subjective and experiential, an interpenetrating unity of external history and internal event. When we say that Luther was mystical in the sense that he recognized the presence of spiritual friends among mystics we are actually saying—and this bears repetition—not that he owed conceptual debts to mysticism but that he found some of its expressions of immediate divine presence congenial with his own deepest experience. This assertion is borne out by the fact that Luther often enough paid no attention to the theological species to which a spiritual friend among mystics belonged. The technical category of "mysticism" played only a small part in his thought. When he wrote his introduction to *Eyn deutsch Theologia* in 1518 he referred to its content as a "German theology," not as a "German mysticism." The theory of chronological stages in Luther's use of and appraisals of mysticism is hardly tenable. A pneumatic theological stance brings out Luther's differentiated view, rather than a universal rejection on his part. This differentiation is guided by *Wesensverwandtschaft* (Iserloh), an essential kinship, transcending abstract formulas. Intellectual penetration cannot adequately gather up this kinship, for here we deal with a style of religious life and personal spirituality, elements not interpretable by theological logic alone. In this bond of mutual spiritual recognition *faith,* according to Luther, and *love,* according to Tauler, become interchangeable terms. This fact carries an ecumenical overtone.

# CHAPTER 4

# Evangelical versus Roman Catholic: Critique of an antithetical approach

We have seen that a one-sided reliance on intellect and reason often leads interpreters of Luther's theology to underestimate the importance of the various forms of mysticism. Such a dependence on the intellect also issues in—or is perhaps encouraged by—confessional rampart-building: Luther dicta are marshalled as evidence of absolute polarity between the evangelical and the Catholic. Apologetic confessionalism both in traditional orthodoxy and historical-critical-liberal accounts, endeavors, as noted in the analyses of several Luther interpreters,[1] to systematize essential dogmatic *loci* in antithetical formulations. There are, however, strong indications of fundamental unity between the evangelical and the Catholic in Luther's descriptions of religious experience.

If, as we have suggested, the material does not permit a definition of mysticism as exclusively Catholic (hence heretical from a biblical perspective, according to Protestant thinkers such as Calovius, Harnack and their disciples), a proposal by Rudolf Otto takes on significance. Otto saw an "essential connection between Lutheranism and mystical religion" and suggested that this essential bond is more important than the historical relation between them. Otto came to the conclusion that the typical moments of mysticism—creature feeling and union with God—are more possible on the basis of Luther's faith experience (as *fiducia*, trust, and *adhaesio*, a

123

spiritual clinging to, a union with God) than on the basis of *amor mysticus,* the mystical love. The mystical temper of the following words by Luther is unmistakable and it brings him close to several medieval mystics: "He indeed who cleaves to God abides in light . . . from this emanates man's loftier perfection in this life so to be united with God that the whole soul with all its abilities and all its powers is collected into its Lord and God and becomes one spirit with him." [2]

The quality of Luther's faith was "ecumenical" in the sense that it bonded Luther to an essential element in Roman Catholic reflection which is trans-institutional in nature. The real Luther, Otto asserted, is to be found in the non-rational experience of religious awe. Vogelsang wrote that Luther recognized the mystical movements of his soul in his reading of mystics. All his life Martin Luther was grateful to Bernard, Vogelsang said, for pointing to the Crucified and to experience. Luther had even found a soul-mate in Tauler as far as spiritual *Anfechtung* was concerned. Yes, there had been an inner kinship with Tauler, not a dependence but a kinship. It was Tauler who had convinced Luther that eternal life begins on this earth and that eternal life should not be connected with reward. From Bernard Luther had his definition of mystical theology, as we have seen. Toward the end of his life Luther had the same feeling of closeness to Tauler and exclaimed once that he had found "sheer Jesus in Bernard." Luther and Tauler were one in the way in which they spoke of personal certainty of salvation in Christ and both of them knew that God was unfathomable majesty before whom man could only stammer.[3] There was potential ecumenicity in the way Luther and some mystics experienced God and Christ. Trust in and union with God as mystical experiences carry an ecumenical potentiality exceeding rationalized dogmatic statements.

Theological conceptualism tends to produce an absolutism of contradiction between Roman and Protestant theology which has devitalized the unitive theme of oneness in and with God. Protestant theology, Otto averred, has isolated certain conceptual themes in Luther and forgotten the central experience of the numinous. It has spoken of Luther's desperation, his religious catastrophes, his attacks of melancholy, his predestination theology and focused on his rational terminology: "judgment," "punishment," "God's wrath." [4] In this way oneness in God through Christ became bound in confessional concepts and therefore limited either to a Protestant or to a Catholic framework of thought.

Two works by Roman Catholic scholars may serve as illustrations of the ecumenical stirrings in Luther's style and also of the limitations placed on this style by an exclusively conceptualistic understanding of Luther's dogma. The latter seems to be the case in McSorley's Luther book already discussed here in a different context.[5] McSorley wishes to emphasize Luther's ecumenical importance. He proceeds as follows. Luther abandoned a good scholastic—and universally Christian—tradition when in *The Bondage of the Will* he denied the existence of a naturally free will. Luther introduced a necessitarian moment in his thinking about predestination, a deterministic theme, which is not biblical and not to be found in scholastic writing nor in the documents of the Lutheran school. McSorley would seem to speak for the ecumenical common ground—a universal tradition on free will—and against a non-ecumenical aberration on Luther's part. However, the case may be the obverse. Luther in his seemingly mechanistic and deterministic explication of free will *coram Deo* draws from a deep mystical source, a numinous feeling of God's majesty which prompts the theologically illogical statement that man has no free will whatever. Let us recall that Luther did not treat his theological determinism as part of a conceptual-logical scheme. McSorley appears to suggest that Luther's assertion is fallacious because it is not logical. Luther, on the contrary, gave expression to a religious experience which eludes ratiocination: man standing before a God who knows all about him and, in a sense beyond theological logic, also knows what man will do. The mystical, numinous dependence was at the center of Luther's deterministic idea of the will in *The Bondage of the Will*. Luther shared this awesome intuition with some mystics.

Perhaps one can say that McSorley's ecumenical proposal does not go far enough, remaining within the framework of dogmatic conceptualization. For the underlying assumption seems to be that if theological patterns can be brought to coincide on the question of a measure of natural free will the ecumenical potentiality would increase. McSorley appears to suggest that progressive rational discourse would be the only avenue of ecumenical rapprochement. Luther, however, pointed to a deeper mystical togetherness as he chose the language of theological determinism. His was the profoundly unitive experience of the God in whom we all live, move and have our being. Thus one can say that the ecumenical ground is mystical rather than conceptual.

The second illustration of ecumenical stirrings in Luther's theology is provided by another Roman Catholic scholar, Jared Wicks. Wicks has examined Luther's "early spiritual teaching" and suggests that the Reformer was *primarily* a man of spirituality rather than of dogmatic polemics. Wicks' work also suggests that the spiritual and mystical themes of Luther's earlier ministry should be considered more central and original than the categorical rational pronouncements of later years.[6] In Wicks' interpretation we find awareness of the significance of Luther's mystical contacts (Tauler and *Theologia Germanica.)* As we have seen, such an awareness is hardly detectable in McSorley's account. Both authors propose potential ground for Roman-Protestant encounter. McSorley submits that a partly revised and logically more consistent concept of free will than the one found in Luther's *The Bondage of the Will* could serve as a uniting force. Wicks thinks that the ecumenical significance of Luther's work lies in the mystical spirituality which the Reformer conveyed. McSorley places considerable emphasis on "concept," Wicks on "experimental spirituality." Wicks asserts that Luther's main concern in theology was not intellectual penetration of God's revelation but rather how a radical spiritual experience could be meaningfully translated. When a rationalizing theologian interprets Luther's thought on sanctification as the Reformer's attack against supernaturalism Wicks pronounces this a distortion of Luther's point. For Luther's thought included Christ's indwelling just as much as it insisted on a more objective imputation. It is good to hear Luther speak of a God at work within us, Wicks concludes. "Both Catholics and Lutherans can learn much here. As we learn together from Luther's earliest spirituality, this too could well be a work of God, actively drawing us toward unity and reconciliation." [7]

Here are two instructive attempts—interestingly enough by Roman Catholic scholars—to overcome the antithetical procedure which dominates much systematizing of Luther's thought. It appears that McSorley's endeavor is still moving inside the framework of traditional intellectualism whereas Wicks seems closer to the pneumatic interpretation which, from the perspective of our sustaining thesis, carries the deeper ecumenical promise.

Let it be clear, however, that no discussion of the antipodal character of many discourses on mystical components in Luther's religion should discount the real differences that exist between Roman Catholic and Luther's postures on grace, the church and man's nature. Our suggestion that conceptualizing about these differences may lead to theologically unrealistic absolutism should not be taken as an invitation to dismiss conceptualization. Yet, intellectualistic preconceptions often take no account of mystical components in Luther's thought for epistemological or confessional reasons. To be alert to this kind of omission is to realize that there are theological minds who function on the assumption that theological conceptualization is *not* permeated with the non-rational.

Antithesis as an all-pervasive method for depicting the relationship of Catholicism or mysticism to the Reformation can place an unrealistic construction on Luther's thought. The beginnings may lie with the Reformer himself holding forth in disputatious moods. Then his followers sharpened the distinctions in order to defend the fruits of liberation from an oppressive and still oppressing institution. Yet, whatever can be said for confessional distinctions between law and grace, tradition and word, papacy and evangelical freedom, institution and person, theology of glory and theology of the cross, they are conceptual whereas the links between those who knew that Christ was and is an ever present reality continue to transcend mere institutional and conceptual barriers. What Jared Wicks says about Luther's "spirituality" and Luther as a *homo religiosus* sheds light on one side of Luther which in a special way represents the ecumenical continuity of all Christendom, the numinous, intuitive, subjectively experienced, intimately private presence of Christ. This mystical element serves as a constant reminder of the limitations of antithetical polarizations.[8]

Luther's kinship with mystical modes of thinking is so much in evidence that absolute distinctions between two contrary theological worlds revolving around one leading tendency seems too simple to fit an ambiguous reality. We will now examine some bonds between mystics and Luther from three viewpoints: the picture of God, the image of man and the nature of salvation.

PART II

# Luther's Views
## on
# God, Man, and Salvation

# CHAPTER 5

# On God
# and God in Christ

Martin Luther did not speculate much about God's substance. The question of God's substance and presence in nature and history hardly constituted his primary concern. He rather asked how God is disposed toward man. Does God meet us in wrath or goodness, as death or life, through law or gospel? This became Luther's problem with the nature of God. This problem was resolved, insofar as it can be resolved in human existence, by the way in which Luther experienced God. "Since He [God] resides in my heart, courage remains. . . . I cannot get lost." [1]

God's life touches us in two ways, Luther said. He is first the hidden God emerging in creation's masks, that is to say, the phenomena of creation are the masked face of God. We have him in the smallest leaf, in our enemies, indeed in Satan himself.[2] But we also find God as the revealed one, in Jesus Christ. The only possible approach to the revealed God is to say, "Christ is my life." [3]

Behind the masks is God as the mysterious power, mysterious and non-rational. Behind the revealed God is the hidden one, the non-rational. Against that background we have to understand Luther's notion of reason as a "whore." No speculation can bring clarity about God's mysterious hiddenness. One can say that this is the paradox about God. But then one must add, that the paradox is essential. Luther said:

131

"In order, therefore that there may be a place for faith, all the things that are believed must be hidden." [4]

The paradoxical picture of God should be taken into account whenever Luther's concept of predestination is discussed. In *The Bondage of the Will* we find, says Otto, that "numinous temper" which is "religious awe" and which is nothing but the nonrational and mystical strain of the Christian faith.[5]

What Luther experienced on the personal side is evident in his theoretical thinking about God. God is the *tremendum*, that which makes man tremble. But he is also the *fascinosum*, the power that enthrals and fascinates. Faith and trust have a real, not an imagined source and Christians should be a blissful people; they have reason to "sing praises, stamp and dance and leap for joy," said Luther. Christians know that God is the great giver. "That should kindle a fire and a light in our heart. We should never cease dancing and leaping for joy." [6] In other words, God daunts the Christian but he also makes him glad.

Otto claimed that the *fascinosum*-element in the God picture probably gained the upper hand in western mysticism, at the cost of the *tremendum*-element. According to this proposition the feeling of mystery, fascination, and majesty would consequently abound in western mystics whereas the feeling of awe would be less strongly emphasized. Otto asserted that the nonrational dreadfulness of deity is an aspect especially prominent in Jacob Böhme's writings and that Böhme, like Luther, knew the dark night of the soul, the abyss, the agony, and barrenness. Luther's ideograms for that quality within the numinous which evokes a sense of awe, are "wrath," "fire" and "fury." An ideogram, however, must not be confounded with rational adequacy. The ideogram, the figure of speech, the analogy, are not rational concepts. The *Erfahrung* of the divine, an expression which we have seen Luther employ, includes the awesomeness of God, i.e., that which anthropomorphically is termed fury and wrath. *Erfahrung* also includes the aspect of God's goodness and love. Consciousness of the numinous lies behind the ideograms, and cannot be exhausted by the ideograms. Scholasticism, Lutheran orthodoxy in old and contemporary forms, and liberal rationalistic theologies—whether Lutheran or not in intention—often fail to make a distinction between the rational concept and the ultimate ground approachable in feeling and intuition. Luther, however, had a strong sense for the inadequacy of the ideogram. This can be seen from his use of the term "external word" as opposed to "internal word" or his persuasion that miracle has an "external" side which must be regarded as a mere analogue of something much more profound, God's love and power.[7]

It has become almost a theological cliché to say that Luther's view of God is counterposed to that of the mystic. Before adding some words about the concept of God-in-Christ as it emerges with Luther and with the mystics, let us pause for a moment to consider what a mystic close to Luther uttered on the matter of distance to God. It is important to note his words for much Protestant theology has claimed that the distance and the awe disappear in all mysticism and God becomes an entity so close to man as to render the two indistinguishable.[8] Johann Tauler wrote, in an enumeration of various captivities which keep men from God, that "the third captivity is the natural reason." People, he said, "vaunt of doctrine, of truth . . . they get puffed up in their reason." Human reason is unable to gather up God in its embrace. In fact, between man and God "a gigantic distance" exists. Tauler wrote: "In the gigantic distance between tiny man and the great awesome God it is evident that man must speak of God with fearful trembling." [9]

This dictum reflects a pervading religious sentiment in Tauler's writings albeit not repeated at each doctrinal juncture. It is therefore hardly correct when systematicians, adhering to the traditional Protestant interpretation of mysticism, assume the opposite. Ozment's reading of Tauler, for example, leads him to think that "the 'likeness' of created and uncreated spirit, of created and uncreated 'grounds' is an established presupposition in Tauler's thought." [10] It is obviously possible to read Tauler in different ways. It is *one* thing to say that man is related to, not only separated from essential reality, for if it were not so there would be no knowledge of separation. Tauler does indeed express this thought. It is a different thing to say that no distance divides tiny man and the awesome God. Tauler does not subscribe to this notion. Tauler's consistent rejection of the dogmatic scholastics should caution against adopting a counter-Lutheran theory about mysticism in general and Tauler's mysticism in particular with respect to their picture of God.[11] The subjective analogue of God's objective awesomeness, namely melancholy and an oppressive sense of guilt, is something Luther found and recognized in Tauler.[12]

One may thus obvert the common assertion about Luther's relation to mysticism's teaching of God and say that Luther endorsed some mystical knowledge of God as *tremendum* and *fascinosum* when he sensed that the mystic in question had experienced justification by faith through grace. This becomes all the more plain when we study Luther's view of God-in-Christ and collate it with that of his kinsmen among mystics.

In his work on Luther and mysticism Vogelsang implied that "the mystic" really never said: "When we hear the Gospel we hear Christ." [13] Here Vogelsang has for a moment abandoned his basic thesis that theology would do well in differentiating between various forms of mysticism in order better to perceive kinship with or alienation from evangelical faith. Tauler and the Frankfurter offer material which contradicts the above statement. Expounding a biblical text on a *pater familias* Tauler declared that the house father is, of course, "the Lord Jesus Christ." [14] In a meditation on the God-man relationship the Frankfurter explained: "It is indeed true that the creature is in itself worth nothing and can claim nothing." Only through spiritual poverty do we, through Christ, become debtors of all and debtors before God. "Were it not so . . . Christ would not have taught it in words and consummated it with his life." [15]

Luther conceived of God's work with us as objective and

subjective, objective in that it imputes a "for you," and subjective in that it abides at the same time "in you." The dual
experience can only be given through Christ. It occurs through
"the mystical Christ." [16] The process is so intimate that Luther
resorts to a language expressing tactile desire, words like *in-
haesio,* clinging to, and *conglutinatio,* cementing together. The
mystical Christ's presence engenders an inner transformation.[17] Whereas the mystics approvingly quoted by Luther had
not worked out a systematic, sustained Christology they nevertheless left no doubt as to the central place of Christ in their
thought and their understanding of the Bible.

As God is everywhere, Christ is everywhere. He is in all
creatures, in the stone, in the fire. But do not tempt God by
seeking him outside the word. This was Luther's exhortation,
not least when the battle with the Enthusiasts had begun.[18]
Through Christ God enters the soul. This entry has a moral
and affectional character. It is not just imputation; it is also
a matter of feeling and will.[19] Therefore, to have lost Christ
is to have lost God. Söderblom quoted Luther as saying in a
letter to Melanchthon: "I have almost lost Christ." Luther
also wrote in another letter: "Satan seeks to deprive me of
Christ." And in yet another letter he implored the recipient:
"Pray that the now weak Christ may grow strong in me." [20]
Luther expressed both the forensic and the subjective side of
Christian faith when he declared that faith justifies because
Christ is present.[21] The "God for me" is inherent in "faith
justifies" and the "Christ in me" finds its expression in the
words "Christ is present." The God who can be the object of
speculations comes into man's heart as Christ and "Christ lives
in us, works and speaks." It is not the life of the flesh, although
our life is lived in the flesh. "It is the life of Christ." [22]

God-in-Christ is both sacrament and example, Luther pointed out. Christ has carried our human nature through death to
victory. By becoming part of his death and by participating in
his victory, we are integrated with his divine life. The example became sacramental power. Christ is the original sacrament. His resurrection is not only a sign, a sacrament, of our

righteousness, of the fact that we have been righted with God;
in the example there is also dynamic power. Luther wrote in
his commentary to the Galatians: "St. Augustine teaches that
the suffering of Christ is both a sacrament and an example—a
sacrament because it signifies the death of sin in us and grants
it to those who believe, an example because it also behooves
us to imitate Him in bodily suffering and dying." [23]

There are mystics who experience the godhead as merely
unfathomable depths, as abysmal darkness—and remain by
that concept. This is the "negative theology" about God. Both
Luther and some mystics knew this side of the picture. When
this negative theological mysticism occasionally assumed an
intellectualistic ring, Luther disagreed. It endeavored to "understand" God. To Luther God's hiddenness is not the fact
that he cannot be discerned, perceived, understood, nor is it
mere darkness. It is rather hiddenness in history. A word came
to us in Christ, unbelievably much beyond our understanding,
yet lovingly near. However, the negative theology of kindred
spirits among the mystics basically corresponded to Martin
Luther's experience of the divine. One would rationalize Luther's thought beyond recognition by neglecting this fact. [24]
The numinous, the awe-inspiring, the sentiment inherent in
the experience by the burning bush is present in Luther's religion as in much mystical thought. When the conceptual and
the doctrinal begins to preponderate over the inexpressible,
the church communicates to the mind through the narrow
clefts of the cognitive understanding. Such a God and such a
God-in-Christ become too circumscribed. [25]

# CHAPTER 6

# Man's Nature

Is there an essential continuity between God and man? In our assessment most Protestant interpretations of Luther assume that it is evangelical to reckon with a radical break between man's being and God's being, a discontinuity, and that it is Catholic to calculate with an essential affinity, that is to say, continuity. Mysticism would then fall on the Catholic side. We will consider this problem by looking at the concepts of the soul, conscience and reason.

In his studies of Tauler Luther noted that God has made us into three parts, body, soul, and spirit. In the notes on the *Magnificat* he described the spirit of man as the noblest part. The spirit, he said, enables man to understand incomprehensible, invisible, eternal things. It is the house in which faith and God's word live. The soul vivifies the body. It is the place of rational knowledge and feelings. The spirit is potentially the power that makes man whole. Luther, in other words, does not regard the spirit as a separate faculty. As body and soul, man's sensory and rational faculties are ruled by the spirit and by the flesh. Spiritual man is according to Luther governed by God's spirit in faith. When God thinks of man he thinks of him as a totality—body, soul, and spirit. In order for man to become what he is in God, a whole being, he must be ruled by God's spirit in faith, working through man's spirit.[1]

Some mystics speak in similar fashion about wholeness in

God. The fact that some mystics so do renders the common generalization inadequate according to which the mystical notion of "the ground of the soul" inappropriately—and heretically—divides the material body as something lower, from the soul or spirit as something higher. On this basis, then, man is supposed to strive for "divinization." It is beyond the intent of the present examination to scrutinize all the mystics Luther knew in order to ascertain how close to or removed from each other they may be with respect to the idea of the soul. One will be mentioned here: Johann Tauler. His theology of the soul does not conform to the generalization just cited.

On Tauler's view the ground of the soul is the inner space where man meets God. Tauler employed the metaphor of the mirror and the sun to illustrate his point.[2] Luther spoke of the spirit as the house, the abode for God. Tauler's term for God's dwelling place in man was the ground of the soul. Both of them maintained the dualism man-God.[3]

Tauler also referred to the ground of the soul as God himself. The life of the kingdom eventually leads to a state in which "the spirit in this person . . . becomes so impregnated with the divine that it is lost . . . in God." [4] Man has to be reborn to experience his integrality in the union of God, according to Tauler. This can only take place through faith and justification. Luther spoke of the indwelling of the triune God in the faithful person. The nomenclature differs but the mystical, non-rational quality of the terms is in essence the same with Tauler and Luther.[5]

The human spirit has, in Luther's opinion, a side turned natureward. He calls this side "soul," as noted above. The soul contains a priori knowledge of God. In Luther's *Table Talks* we read: "The knowledge of God . . . is divinely imprinted upon all men's minds. Under the sole guidance of nature all men know that God is, without any acquaintance with the arts or sciences." [6]

Rudolf Otto, basing his conclusions on this and similar statements, asserted that Luther reckoned with "an a priori factor in religion" and that this notion on Luther's part is more basic to his thought than his occasional attacks against the idea. The latter occur in the context of repudiation of scholasticism's "whore reason." [7]

Jared Wicks submits a Luther saying to the effect that God batters the flesh so that the soul might rise more freely. There is some imprint of God in our soul despite contrary appearances. "Contact with Tauler thus served to strengthen Luther's conviction that God works in our lives beneath contrary experiences." [8] Even though Luther in his early writings turned "excessively dualistic" in his view of man as spirit and matter, thereby jeopardizing a holistic view, there is nonetheless in his theology the notion that we have "invisible realities . . . within the human spirit; they are reached when a person turns within to consider what manner of goods correspond to his own spirit. . . . when one turns within, one 'finds oneself' and then is open to the word of God, which itself speaks of invisible goods, of the true goods of the human spirit." [9]

Herbert Olsson has found the same content in Luther's notion of the soul. Olsson thought that Luther looked at natural religion as an area which shows that man simply cannot avoid God. Man has an autonomous existence with roots in God.

> The fact that man is created with his own *Wesen* (essence, being) and thereby exercises self-activity, must be taken for granted in any Christian view. For the opposite would mean that man's existence as creation, i.e., God's creation as such, would be sin.[10]

Luther made a distinction between body and soul. His pervading tendency was to regard the soul not as higher but more enduring than the body. In this sense, the soul as the invisible part of man is linked with God. The soul therefore survives after physical death, as a life-giving egress of God. This distinction between body ("this bag of worms") and soul seems to have been more antithetically conceived in his earlier years than later. However, the thought that man does belong to God was the overriding one. The soul contained this affinity in a special way. It was therefore in keeping with his general notion when he said that the soul at death, about to "depart from the body," undergoes "a transition from this life into yonder future life." [11] That is to say, Luther considered the soul's life something which continues in other, invisible realms after death but also as a part of man, partaking of this realm while in the body.

In his thinking about the soul Luther was thus persuaded that a certain continuity prevails between the human and the divine. This continuity is of course not qualified; the new birth must be experienced, yet it is there. In this regard Luther was close to Tauler who, as we have seen, calculated with a ground of the soul which is of God, as part of natural religion. The same Tauler, however, spoke of the self's "nothingness." There are people, he asserted, who treat of their own nothingness "as though they were in possession of this noble virtue and in their self-appraisal they therefore appear to themselves taller than the city's cathedral." But alas, they deceive themselves. Few, "maybe three of all who are sitting here" know the Nought. When you perceive that your desire is to draw people's attention, then you should lower yourself "to your deepest ground." [12]

As indicated in the discussion of Ozment's analysis of a purported all-pervading contrast between Luther and Tauler it seems inappropriate to speak of Luther's thought as "fideistic" in the sense that the psychological and the naturally anthropological are ruled out from it, and of Tauler's theology as "a mystical anthropology" which knows nothing about the kind of faith which inspired Luther. Asking the reader's indulgence I permit myself to recall some of the discussion on Ozment's analysis.[13] When in a comment on a Tauler dictum Martin Luther wrote, "We dictate the mode to God," he did not argue with Tauler but rather elucidated his words by saying: to all intents and purposes, that is the way man acts. Ozment presumes that Luther was engaged in polemics. He believes that Luther was correcting a false idea, namely that *synteresis* is valid only before men but invalid from the point-

of-view of salvation. He also believes that Luther here taught
Tauler that "faith and not a natural anthropological resource
determines the relation to God." Ozment goes on to suggest
that Tauler is guilty of Pelagianism claiming the possibility of
"a natural creational 'covenant,' " attributing "soteriologically
significant resources to the soul of man" (the "Seelengrund"
or the *synteresis*). Arrogating such resources to the soul of
man may well be Pelagianism. But one cannot use Tauler's
41st sermon and Luther's marginal notes on it as evidence of
polarity between Tauler and Luther concerning the nature of
the soul. As demonstrated by previous quotations, Tauler knew
not only about affinity and continuity between God and man,
he also knew about the dualistic relation. If Luther had not
sensed this he would hardly have written: "Thus as he [Tau-
ler] says here, salvation is through resignation of one's will
in all things." [14]

A theology that must presuppose confessional contrariness
at each dogmatic locus has difficulty eliciting a certain measure of continuity between the human and the divine in Luther's teaching. Luther was admittedly ambiguous on this
score. It depends a great deal on the context of an utterance
whether a dictum from him comes out on the continuity or the
discontinuity side. On the subject of salvation he was anxious
to disclaim any synergism on man's part, thus discontinuity.
When he dealt with the question of divine omnipotence he
accorded divine substance to man and the created world, hence
continuity.

The second topic for our consideration of the continuity-
discontinuity issue will be the meaning of conscience. According to much medieval thought *synteresis* is the top quality in
man's equipment, i.e., conscience, that which "knows with
God." Is this synteresis something of a divine substance in
man or was it destroyed both formally and materially at the
fall of Adam? Luther apparently ceased to employ the term
after his earlier years, replacing it with *fides* as a symbol for
trust and mystical union with God. But he always recognized
that God reawakens his own substance when he awakens man

in the rebirth. Man's conscience, taken in the wider meaning of synteresis, dormantly relates him to God and points to the goal, which is to be righted with God. But on Luther's accounting synteresis does not show man the road to the goal.[15] The sometimes anguished longing for God, *gemitus,* suggested to Luther that man is born with a synteresis, or conscience in its religious function. His opinion in this regard was no different in later years when he preferred the terms *fides* as *adhaesio* to the term *synteresis.* The essential fact remains: the synteresis is a substantial part of man. Bonaventura was particularly explicit in this regard and Luther interpreted his own rebirth the same way. The synteresis belongs to man's *esse* in the sense that it enables us "to understand and love the invisible things." It is helpless love without the righteousness of the Christ, but it is there.[16] Synteresis is the anthropological locus of the words about the Spirit in Romans 8:26 where Paul says: "Likewise the Spirit helps us in our weakness; for we do not know how to pray as we ought, but the Spirit himself intercedes for us with sighs too deep for words." [17]

In natural man there is material for formation by God. The old man is material for the new man. Luther, on the one hand, and Tauler and *Theologia Germanica,* on the other, agree on this.[18]

The question about divine "substance" in the human soul was taken up once around Luther's dinner table. Luther said: "God is not bound to a locality. He is not excluded from any place nor the captive of any place. . . . He is even in the lowliest creature, in a leaf or a blade of grass, yet He is nowhere." Someone queried him as to whether God was everywhere *potentialiter* or *substantialiter.* Luther: "I answer: in both ways in each creature. The creature acts by virtue of *qualitas* but God acts . . . *essentialiter.*" The recorder of the table talk continued:

> When someone said: "That I don't understand," he answered: "Don't you believe that God is at the same time on the cross and in the virgin Mary's womb?

In either case it is impossible for our reason to believe. As God can be housed in the virgin's womb, He can also be housed in the creature." Another person said: "Would God consequently be in the devil?"—"Yes, certainly in substance even in hell . . . as Psalm 139 says: 'If I make my bed in sheol, thou art there.' " [19]

Tauler spoke in a similar vein about the innermost ground which is always there as a link with God.

Man must go into his own ground, into the innermost, and there seek the Lord, as He himself has demonstrated when he spoke, "God's kingdom is in you" . . . seek in the innermost ground where God is closer to the soul and more intimate, closer than the soul is to itself."

But just as Luther experienced this "natural" link with God as unqualified from the point-of-view of the gospel, Tauler taught about the unsettling encounter with the divine which makes nought of possible human claims. "When man enters this house and has sought God in this innermost ground, God comes and seeks him and turns the house totally topsy-turvy." [20]

We come to the third topic selected for the discussion of man's nature in mysticism and Luther's thought. In accepting Luther's verdict that reason is no bridge to the birth of God in the soul many theologians have over-rationalized it. The issue of continuity and discontinuity, the nature of the soul and the conscience, brings this home to the student of Luther's kinship with mystics. Luther's repudiation of reason has been taken to mean that Luther's faith has no part whatever of the psychological and the anthropological in man's quest for God. True faith recognizes that there is a non-rational element in man's bond with the divine and that this element must be joined to the rational in order for us to retain the dynamics of spiritual life. The a priori factor in reli-

gion, the unity and goodness of the divine nature, is according
to Otto based on "an a priori knowledge of the essential interdependence of the rational and the non-rational elements in
the idea of God." To know that there are such factors, such
imprinted divine signs "latent in the human spirit" is to
utilize a faculty which is present with man albeit in em-
bryonic form, namely the faculty of "divination." [21]

Perhaps one could say that reason comprises a non-rational
factor, a faculty with roots in the para-human. This renders
it necessary for Luther to make a distinction between human
reason which to scholasticism simply becomes the voice of
God and reason which is an imbedded sign from God and
points to him. On the one hand Luther criticized reason. On
the other hand he evaluated reason positively. On the one hand
he could say: "If you wish to live for God, you have to die
entirely to the law. Reason and human wisdom do not understand that doctrine." [22] On the other hand he would assert
about the first article in the Creed: "Intended is that I shall
believe that I am God's creature, that he has given me body,
soul, normal eyes, reason. . . . " [23] And another example: "No
one is so morally perverted that he does not feel reason's call
and his synteresis (the sense of the divine) . . . in accordance
with Revelation 3: 'I stand at the door and knock.' " [24] Luther
wrote in yet another context:

> The natural reason itself is forced even here where
> there is no holy scripture to grant it [namely the
> truth that the general human reason possesses many
> true cognitions of what 'God is in himself or in his
> inmost essence'], convinced by its own judgment.
> For all men, as they hear it treated of, find this belief
> written in their hearts, and acknowledge it as
> proved, even unwillingly: first that God is omnipo-
> tent and can neither err nor be deceived. . . . These
> two things are admitted by heart and feeling. [25]

From the above survey of Luther's and some mystics'
thoughts on the soul, conscience and reason we draw the fol-

lowing conclusions. First, Luther presupposed a knowledge of God preternaturally impressed upon man's mind. Second, Luther assumed that under the mere guidance of nature—without any acquaintance with the arts and sciences—all men know that God is. Luther essentially shared these two persuasions with his friends among the mystics. Together with some mystics he looked at the preternatural knowledge imprinted on all men's minds as emanating from extraterrestrial dimensions. Like some mystics he took for granted that man's very denial of God is a concession that God is. For one cannot, said Luther, deny that of which one has no knowledge. Man's conscience testifies to and affirms his potential, integral relationship to God.[26]

The mystical experience, the experience of God's presence now and here, is in some sense dependent on the possibility of a certain continuity between man and God, a "substance" in man which is of God, a faculty of recognition as the things of God and his patterns emerge. It seems clear that Martin Luther shared precisely that recognition with his friends among the mystics. The danger with much theological treatment of Luther's dicta about man is, we reiterate, that Luther's antirationalism becomes too rationalized. Luther's "dualism" is not as unambiguous as it appears when theology claims that the Reformer defends the *theological* line in contrast to mystics and others who are understood to follow only *psychological* and *anthropological* leads.[27] This bisection would suggest that faith in the evangelical and Reformation sense has once and for all parted with the psychological and the anthropological from the point of view of theological explication of God's activity among men. The question for Luther was quite a different one. Luther asked where the theological point of gravity lies in a true religious existence. He found that it could not be lodged in the soul, in the conscience, in reason. The initiative was God's. The natural powers cannot save. On this crucial point Luther and mystic Johann Tauler entirely agree. Tauler said: "In us man must always die." [28]

On the other hand, to withdraw from the theological concern the fact of the *psyche*—the emotional, intuitional and numinous as vehicles for growth in God—and the likelihood of divine patterns in human existence is to misunderstand both Luther and his mystical kin. Christ can become our substance, wrote Luther.[29] But did he thereby say that we are void of that substance which enables us to invite him? The psyche is certainly involved. How else could Luther claim that in communion with Christ he entered paradise itself? Was not his psyche stirred in that experience? And did this not mean that the hidden depths in his being responded to a call from an invisible spiritual home? [30]

# CHAPTER 7

# Salvation

We have observed that outer similarities between Luther and mysticism may decrease in number but that some deeper concerns unite them. Our analyses of the picture of God and the view of man provide illustrations of such essential consanguinity. In turning to descriptions of the meaning of salvation we will also find basic unity. The saints do not contradict each other, runs an adage. It proves to be sound wisdom in this context.[1]

For a consideration of our theme, Luther and the mystics, in its bearing upon salvation, the following procedure will be applied. First we will consider the question of unity with God; second, the question of faith as a mystery; third, the mystical meaning of *gemitus* and *raptus;* fourth, the bride-bridegroom analogues; fifth, salvation as *Erfahrung* and personal change; sixth, participation in God, and finally, seventh, the supernatural moments in salvation: salvation as confirmation of and testing ground for the supernatural dimension.

## A. Unity with God

What unites us with God is just as important to Luther and his mystical friends as that which divides. The second article of the Apostles' Creed makes this clear to the Reformer. Christ is our salvation and therefore the basis for unity with

God. But, as we have said, the first article of the same creed also gave Luther occasion to declare that knowledge of God is imprinted on the minds of men. Man's mind knows this *proprio suo iudicio convicta,* persuaded by its own autonomous judgment. When the truth about "God in himself" is expounded man grasps it by dint of reason.[2] Luther could say about this potential unity with God or recognition of the God-fact that *homo conditus est ad imaginem Dei,* man is constructed as an image of God.[3] Man is a potential temple of God and as such harbors a predilection for God (but not necessarily a predilection for the good).[4] Just as there is an unrighteous humanity within us so there is a righteous humanity, an image of God according to which we are made. Tauler asserts likewise: just as there is an unrighteous "ground of soul" so there is a genuine, longing ground.[5] One can paraphrase Luther and say that "the natural life is the beginning of the eternal life." There is a dormant unity between man and the divine.[6] In both instances, with Luther as well as with the mystics, the soul recognizes God, albeit latently.

However, this recognition of God is not the same as salvation, nor is it a matter of conditioning the soul for receipt of the Holy Spirit, as Tauler's theology has been described (by Ozment). It is rather a matter of a perhaps long forgotten affinity with the power that has created us. When God saves he saves that which is part of him in fundamental structure. Yet, this is important common ground with respect to salvation. Against this background we can speak of mystical unity between the savior and the saved, once the rebirth has taken place. Man is then worthy of becoming "part of the divine nature."[7] God's "being becomes our being."[8]

## B. The mystery of faith

Luther's "faith" was *fiducia,* trust, as well as *adhaesio* or *conglutinatio,* a cleaving to God. Faith is a gift which generates *Gelassenheit,* a spiritual ease anchored in the confidence that God provides the everlasting arms. To Luther "righteous-

ness" meant that man has been "righted" by God-in-Christ.
It was not grounded in moral probity, neither in love produced
by man, nor in humility by spiritual techniques of diverse
kinds. Experienced righteousness connoted God's birth in the
soul. Luther maintained that rebirth was a mystery. God instilled faith in him when he was at a loss: the struggling monk
felt that he had contributed nothing but his own despair, like
the tax-collector in Jesus' parable. Faith was devoted trust in
God's mercy and, as such, a mystery. Luther wrote: "He who
puts his all on God . . . gets from God everything he wants." [9]
But the gift was unaccountable. God came even if the recipient did not understand. Faith existed in an "independent divine spiritual life." It meant much more than an intellectual
acceptance of Christ's deed, imputed to man. Because faith
was more than mere appropriation by the mind Luther could
speak of a *spiritual* use of the sacraments and of the institutional church as housing the hiddenness of the Christian life.[10]
This is to say, everything in faith was not exhausted by the
outward sign. In Psalter glosses of 1513 Luther dealt with
the mysterious aspects of faith by employing the following
revealing terms: the secret of faith, the mystery of faith, the
invisible grasped in faith, the calling to the invisible, the secret spiritual force, God as all in all, the conjuncture of soul
and God.[11] To have all and yet to have nothing, to mourn yet
not to mourn—such antinomies emerged from corresponding
experiences, and warrant the suggestion that faith in Luther's
vocabulary bespoke relationship to the invisible and a presence
of the Spirit; both are enveloped in mystery.[12]

We already referred briefly to the important fact that Luther made a distinction between "the historical faith" and
"the true faith." [13] They are interlocked and the one should
never be separated from the other. The historical faith is
readily prepared to make the concession that the credal confession "Christ has suffered and certainly also for me" is
proper and true. But, said Luther, the historical faith, if left
to its own ways, does not add this feeling-laden, experiential
knowledge which the marital union image conveys. The true

faith is the necessary inner, non-rational affect which prompts the faithful to exclaim: My beloved is mine and I reach out for him with gladness. This feeling-side of faith is not grounded in our natural capacity for feeling but rather in our discovery of sinfulness. The important point to make in the present context is that spiritual knowledge, the knowledge imparted by faith, is more than the apprehension of Jesus Christ as a cipher aiding our self-understanding or as an assurance of eternal life; faith is also "an experiential knowledge," according to Luther. By experience does the justified know.

Faith, then, in Luther's thought encompassed more than a conviction that certain eternal verities were true; it contained a strong mystical strain. On Luther's view faith was the kind of trust which gives rise to feelings of immediate presence. We have seen what these intuitions or sentiments might be: perhaps the feeling of the *tremendum,* perhaps the experience of the *fascinosum.* In the very event of faith there was a non-rational element.[14] The mystery of faith which Luther experienced was akin to the mystical faith of Tauler. As noted, Tauler held no brief for the scholastic rationalists. He characterized the birth of faith as moments when a person has reached "his radical nothing" and could "throw himself in the abyss of the divine will . . . sink down on your smallness, your incapacity, your ignorance." Tauler exhorted his listener to say what Peter said to Jesus: "Lord, depart from me for I am a sinner." Then the mystery of faith will enfold the supplicant.[15]

Faith in its mystical dimension—and this goes for Luther as well for the mystics he cherished—was not only an acceptance of a public, external creed. Faith was also a private, personal surrender and—however odious the concept may appear to many theological systemizers—private experience. Christ invites his followers to precisely an inner event, Luther maintained as he preached on Mark 3:35 and Luke 8:21. He asked: "Who is Christ's spiritual father and mother?" The answer was: "All faithful persons are Christ's spiritual mother." The private, intimate, mystical nature of the Christian faith and mission is betokened by a passage belonging to the same sermon. "As often as a person comes into faith anew, so often Christ is born in him." [16]

## C. Gemitus-raptus

The terms *gemitus* and *raptus* are used by Luther and some mystics about salvation. Professor Oberman has devoted some instructive inquiries into the meaning of these two poles of a mystical life with God. He qualifies his conclusions by terming the problem thorny, yet insists that we are now able to discern patterns in Luther's thought with sufficient balance and clarity to venture the claim that the *gemitus-raptus* complex belongs at the center, not to the periphery of Luther's theology. Hence another unmistakable mystical theme moves into our purview.

*Gemitus* signifies the religious affect engendered by God's awesomeness. The term refers primarily to the reality posited in Romans 8:26, ". . . the Spirit himself intercedes for us with sighs too deep for words." (We alluded to this passage in Chapter 6.) In medieval scholasticism and mysticism the *gemitus* had its anthropological place in *synteresis,* the root of conscience. In Luther's thought about salvation anthropological theory played an unimportant role. Luther soon supplanted the term *synteresis* with trust-filled faith. *Synteresis* provided the goal but did not offer the way. It is a justified sinner's faith that offers the way in Luther's view. God-given faith brings man into *gemitus,* the sighing which is too deep for words and which is actually done by the Spirit for man, in face of divine majesty. *Gemitus* is inextricably interwoven with man's life in faith. Yes, *gemitus,* like prayer, presupposes faith. This was of course not the case in every mystical accounting. Some mystics would regard *gemitus* as preparatory practice for the development of proper humility or as an attribute of a sinless part of man. But for Luther—and some mystics—God-given faith simply issues in *gemitus* as a sign of the righted relationship with God.[17]

What man knows in the awesomeness of the *gemitus* experience before God is that boasting and self-congratulation do not belong to any genuine man-God relation. Such constant reduction to true proportions serves as a counterweight against the other element in a salvatory experience, *raptus,* with which Luther also dealt. A cross theology thus kept the mystical *raptus* from painting the Christian gospel as a theology of glory.

The counterpoint in what can be termed a coincidence of opposites is then *raptus.* One becomes a right theologian (read "a true Christian") *in raptu et extasi,* said Luther. *Raptus* is a refuge into "the righteousness extra nos," from outside us. The *raptus* experience is a spectrum with many rays.

First, in *raptus* man sees Christ with his mystical eyes and is overwhelmed. This vision combines a transportation beyond visible limits and the cross experience. For, whereas the experience engenders life in the soul, it is simultaneously a partaking of Christ's sacrifice, a sense of dying and being judged, as Luther noted.[18]

Second, a silence beyond the babel of many voices reigns in the depth of religious enrapture, according to Luther. The right theology or the right Christianity is engendered in complete silence, "in the highest reaches of the mind." [19]

Third, this spiritual transportation changes man's affects and his trust. Man's psyche is moved. (To Luther this did not seem to mean an ontological change.) The salvation that comes to man from outside himself coinheres with *raptus* as an empirical psychological event. Luther's notion of *raptus* consequently rules out a merely forensic interpretation of salvation, the idea that man's liberation is analogous with a juridical acquittal, a declaration of guiltlessness devoid of corresponding movements in man's psyche.[20]

Fourth, *raptus* in Luther's accounting connoted passivity with respect to the soul. But, if we read Luther correctly, the mystical state of stillness before God was not an elitist achievement by a few who knew their exercises well, nor did it imply complete non-action on the part of man. Regarding the former observation it is clear that Luther did not agree with the kind of mysticism whose exercises for the attainment of an ultimate state of passivity could only be carried out by a few experts. Luther democratized the mystical attitude of passivity. God invites everyone, he said, to be "transported" or "led," or God desires men to "let" him lead them into his grace. Such a democratized mystical theology rather prevents than promotes a quietistic interpretation of faith and salvation. The latter observation, concerning inaction, distinguishes the mystical passivity of total inertness from the mystical passivity of participation. The Christian who surrenders in a *raptus* experience is not a dead tool, nor is his justification an incentive to quietism.[21]

Fifth, *raptus* is an experience of the created word, not of the uncreated word, of the incarnated God, not of the "naked God." Hence Luther often made it a point to place the *accessus* before the *raptus*, the justification in faith before the ravishment in spirit. He brought the question to the fore, for instance, when expounding Romans 5:2, "Through him [our Lord Jesus Christ] we have obtained access to this grace in which we stand." God's grace in Christ was the *umbraculum*, a shaded, protected place, the Reformer pointed out in another context. The mystical *raptus* was mediated through Christ.[22]

Sixth, yet behind the experience of God's salvation focused in Christ as the incarnated word was a kind of *raptus* which Luther called a "hidden circumstance." [23] The testimony about God in Christ in some fashion depends on such encounters. When St. Paul mentions in 2 Corinthians 12:2 that he had been caught up to the third heaven Luther did not dismiss the dictum as not belonging to the center of the gospel.

From his comments about *raptus* as a taste of ineffable reality we can draw three conclusions: Luther himself had had the same experience as Paul; Luther warned that it was rare and could be dangerous; and finally, without such frontline glimpses of the supernatural, the transmission of the gospel would lose its dynamic force. Luther said that he "was

once caught up into the third heaven." [24] He thought that such
events were rare and that they should not be sought for their
own sake; they are the fruit and reward of love rather than
love itself.[25] Yet Christian witness and life are permeated with
the numinous experience which is beyond words. St. Paul is an
illustration, Peter, James and John are others, said Luther.
Luther himself was obviously in the same category, we might
add. But, like the others, he did not let his direct teaching
revolve around such mystical experiences. Just as the convey-
ors of the gospel in Scripture, his words were often in indirect ways satiated with the mystical knowledge.[26]

Mystical theology or personal faith experience thus depicts
the Christian life as *simul gemitus et raptus*, the unspeakable
sighing and the enrapture. The common root for this coincidence of opposites is the mystical presence of Christ. Although
the accent falls differently in several regards if we compare
Luther with mystics, on this point there is doubtless agreement
between the Reformer and the mystic about whom Luther
said that in him he had found "more solid and pure theology
than among all the scholastics," Johann Tauler.[27] Tauler spoke
of the nothingness of the person who faces God.[28] This is the
*gemitus* aspect. Tauler also wrote that thinking of oneself as
nothing and all that one does, or can do, as nil constitutes the
beginning of the road to true bliss.[29] Here we find the *raptus*
notion. Whatever the verdict on similarities between Luther
and some mystics in the area of *gemitus-raptus* reflection, we
can conclude that mystical experience pervaded Luther's use
of the terms. In fact, reflection upon *gemitus-raptus* experience served eminently as a counterbalance to exclusive intellection in Luther's thought. Intimations of the supernatural
aspects of salvation found expression in the two mystical
terms discussed here (besides others, like *excessus* and *ecstasis*). The supernatural character of the *gemitus-raptus* experiences served as a corollary to the natural and historical
components of God's saving activity. Luther once put the
interdependence between mystical awe and rapture, on the
one hand, and natural existence on the other, in the following

words: "The eternal majesty lets himself deep down into my poor flesh and blood and unites fully with me." [30]

## D. The bride-bridegroom analogues

Another important aspect of the picture of salvation offered by Luther is the bride-bridegroom image. We recall some reflections on this topic in connection with mystical motifs as potential ecumenical links. In our discussion of the mystery of man's faith in God the point was made that Luther spoke of "the historical faith" as something inadequate when left by itself. Basing his verdict on a life-long occupation with experiential spirituality he drew attention to the empirical-psychological side of salvation-through-Christ which "the historical faith" did not register. "Historical faith" rightly stated that Christ has suffered and also that he has suffered for the individual person. But "even the devil believes [the historical statement that Christ suffered] and praises God, as well as some heretics also." The imputed justification must contain experiential insight, empirical spiritual *Erfahrung*. We have found that Luther, in order to depict this experience, frequently adopts nuptial metaphors which abound in mystical literature. He did so also toward the end of his life, something which is worth remembering in the face of assertions that he abandoned bridal mysticism in his mature years. Luther never ceased insisting that there is a way to "know" religiously-theologically which "historical faith" hardly discerns. The love-union on the earthly plane is an analogue of *agnitio,* the insight or knowledge deriving from the spiritual experience that is a necessary part of salvation by justification. The following statement by Luther brings out his emphasis on experience as well as his persuasion that mysticism's nuptial imagery fittingly describes the reality he wished to convey.

> Knowledge is, however, of an empirical nature, and faith has reference to this word: "Adam knew his

wife." That is to say, experience-wise through his
senses did he know his wife, not in a speculative or
historical way, but experientially *(experimentaliter)*
. . . the historical faith admittedly says, "I believe
that Christ has suffered, and suffered for me." But it
does not add this sensitive and empirical knowledge.
However, true faith states this, "My beloved is mine
and I embrace him with gladness." [31]

According to Luther the "experience" which belongs to
faith and constitutes an inextricable part of God's address to
man in justification, exceeds all other kinds of experience.
Precisely bridal metaphors proved useful to bring this theological insight home.

Life with Christ is like "a secret wedding." [32] The soul is
like a bride who "with cordial trust relies on her bridegroom." [33] Faith "unites the soul with Christ as a bride is
united with her bridegroom." [34] "This Bridegroom, Christ,
must be alone with His bride in His private chamber, and all
the family and household must be shunted away." [35] "For he
who relies on Christ through faith is carried on the shoulders
of Christ, and He will cross over successfully with the bride,
of whom it is written that 'she comes up through the desert
leaning on her beloved.' "[36]

On Luther's view, grace is not just concept, nor just a
static property. Grace is always active. For the Spirit is a
living, not a dead thing. "Just as life is never idle, but as
long as it is present, it is doing something . . . so the Holy
Spirit is never idle in the pious, but is always doing something
that pertains to the Kingdom of God." [37] Luther had movement and sensitivity in mind when using the language of
bridal mysticism.[38]

The terminology of bridal mysticism should not be construed as exclusively individual and immanental only in an
individual sense. There was also a corporate element in the
bridal images Luther set before his readers and listeners.

Luther spoke, as we have seen, about "the mystical Christ,"
present as spiritual power, and plainly suggested that Christ
lets himself be experienced as "a spiritual essence, present in
the hearts of the faithful." Christ is not only living in the
individual's discipleship. The organism of the church can
only be understood from the perspective of Christ's presence.
Were it not so, one would not be entitled to speak of the
church's transcendence. The church is the body of Christ.
She is the bride for whom he, the bridegroom, has suffered.
The suffering and the victory which occurred when Christ
was incarnated in a body become the example, sacrament and
salvation of his mystical body, the church.[39] Christ guarantees
the continuity of the church. There is a continuing bridal
relationship between Christ and his body, the church. Luther
employed the thought of Augustine about the church when
he said that a joyful exchange takes place between the head
and the members.[40] In one of the basic passages for the teaching on Christ as the bridegroom of the church Luther spoke
of Christ as the initiator of "spiritual generation" in baptized
people and as the initiator of the church as "the new manifestation of the gospel." [41] Christ's marriage relationship to
Christendom is also depicted in Luther's writings on the Magnificat.[42] The presence of Christ guarantees the survival of the
church even when everything else crumbles in the world. As
Christ's bride she has always been protected and sustained.[43]

Luther said about this mystically-sustained and miraculous-
ly-surviving church that "Christ has not abandoned nor ever
given up his church." [44] What church did he then have in
mind—the *ecclesiolae* being formed under the impact of Reformation teachings or the papal church? During the latter part
of his life Luther seemed to have come to the conclusion that
one had to reckon with Christ's presence in both. There are no
firm borders between the churches. For even the true church
receives visits by the devil unbeknown to herself. She, too, is
"a mixed body." The fact that the church survives when everything else crumbles is a sign of Christ's presence. Even if

debased the bride is in the bridegroom's thoughts and care. As the validity of the institution as such receded in Luther's estimation he always kept on repeating that ecclesiastical continuity was safeguarded by the proclamation of the word and resting on the foundation of baptism. But to speak of "God's word" and its proclamation, on the one hand, and "Christ's presence," on the other, is not necessarily the same thing. For is Christ "automatically" present where the order of regular proclamation and baptism is preserved? This question is not always clearly posed in interpretive reflection on the Reformation teaching about the church. To be able to defend "order" and answer accusations of independentist views in Luther's world of thought it is either assumed that proclamation and Christ-presence are interchangeable or that Luther's ultimate concept of the church's continuity did not contain "spirituality" or "independentism." [45]

Yet it should no doubt be taken seriously in the ecclesiological framework as well when we so frequently hear Luther say that there is a personal, "experiential" side to the Christian life. The sacrament ought to be administered by "a Christian who has the spirit of Christ." [46] In the determinate, external church there is "the true church." [47] You do not see it but it is there, for Christ is there and without this faithfulness in the midst of the widespread unseemliness of the external church and the world there would be no church. Luther thought of the invisible *ecclesia spiritualis* when alluding to the promise of Christ's presence wherever two or three are gathered in his name.[48] The danger in many interpretations of Luther's Reformation thought is that the inner dimension, the possibility of "presence," recedes under the impact of attempts to render the entire evangelical faith a cognitive undertaking, a mere ordering of concepts. Like the mystics Luther could speak of Christians as people who "live by faith and in spirit, that is, by the recognition and love of what is invisible." Resting in God, "man is called inward and hidden in that he does not live in a worldly and carnal fashion. . . . "

Therefore every believer is part of a "tabernacle" (Ps. 27:5) which "in a mystical sense is also the church." [49] On account of the living Christ "the Lord and the church are one body, head and body one mystical Christ, and so one beloved." [50]

No doubt "the word" and its proclamation is at the center of the church's task. But it is a word which radiates the presence of Christ and thus exceeds "the orders." The Christ-radiating word lends "inner" meaning to the individual as well as the corporate components in the idioms of nuptial symbolism which Luther had in common with many mystics. The magnetism of the biblical word seizes the *individual* in the first place. The nuptial imagery leaves no doubt about this. But the Christian's corporate setting, the church, transmits the word to the individual and is transformed in the process. When we become right with God, when we receive the grace of righteousness, when we cease to struggle as our own saviors, the Savior enters, and then "we always adopt a passive attitude as a woman does toward conception. . . . Yet when grace does come and the soul is to be impregnated with the Spirit, it ought neither pray nor act, but only be still." [51] With a keen sense for Martin Luther's mystical-soteriological personalism Roman Catholic theologian Erwin Iserloh illustrates his assertion that "after the justification there is a thing like a (mystical) experience of salvation," by citing the Reformer: "After I have already been justified and acknowledged that the sins are forgiven without my merits through grace *(gratia)*, then it is essential that I begin to feel so that I may in some measure understand." [52]

The concern Luther expressed in these words about feeling-induced understanding was precisely the same as his concern when he employed metaphors from the field of human love. History and institution were essential as vehicles of salvation but, in the last analysis, the question comes to the individual. It is a personal question like Jesus' question to Peter: Do you love me? And the affirmative response is like a trusting nuptial relationship.

## E. Experience and personal change

In one of the most sensitive analyses in the 19th century of Luther and his kinship with mysticism, Hermann Hering pointed to what he called "Luther's cross vision." He added that it was this experience of the cross of Christ which made Luther slowly see the needs for reform in the church. The church did not see the cross. She was steeped in power, honor, possessions, worldly glory, competitive ventures with dukes and kings. The cross vision had faded. But without it man's proper relation to God becomes distorted. "The more inwardly perceptive Luther grows" the more does he sense this distortion, so common among Christians. Hering suggested that Luther radically experienced the mutually exclusive relationship between worldly glory and cross vision in the period 1513-1515.[53] The new insight coincided with a more discriminating approach to mysticism, said Hering, in that Luther consciously selected what he termed "German mystics," partially excluding "general mystics." Tauler and the Frankfurter moved into focus in Luther's meditations on matters of salvation. Mystics like Bernard, Gerson, Augustine and Dionysius the Areopagite became the objects of occasional critique, at least on isolated issues. Why was Luther drawn in a special way to *Theologia Germanica,* Johann Tauler and Staupitz?, Hering asked. His answer: they confirmed and supported Luther's own discovery of the biblical message. They spoke of trust in Christ and not in one's own work. Their "German mysticism" was crystallized in doctrines of piety, not theoretical speculation. It was anchored in life with God, in experiences of life as forgiven and justified sinner. When they said "come to God" they meant it as personal invitation from a personal savior.[54]

Scholastic doctrines offered the world both speculation and thought structures. Having declared that God is unfathomable it proceeded to explain what God is. Luther was critical of this approach. In mystical writings he found people who longed for life in often conscious rebellion against speculation.[55] Luther was attracted by the spontaneous directness of mystics like the Frankfurter. The adjectives for their approach to the divine were "longing, heartfelt, edifying, simple." *Theologia Germanica's* language is simple, Luther said in the introduction to the 1518 edition of that devotional book. He liked the "simplicity." The Bible and spoken German were also simple. Verbose and artificial language could not be a medium for encounter with God. There was a profound significance in Luther's observation that the mystical tract in question was "simple." From the incidental observation concerning language Luther proceeded to the essence of simple, direct mystical experience: God is always ready to meet with us in the stillness of our hearts, his own chapel within us, unused because of our sin, available despite our sin.[56]

In his comments to the Ten Commandments Martin Luther applied terms expressing "interiorization" and *Gelassenheit,* a trustful surrender to God. A Christian should throw everything on God; he must plead with and flee to God; he must meditate on Christ's sufferings; he ought to "go to Holy Communion in a spiritual way," become spiritually poor so that all his works be God's works, not his own. Humility is the fruit of this posture. Humility is also the basis for human fellowship. If man knew about himself only a fraction of what God knows about him, he would become "a sweet kindly heart" in his relations to others. From poverty of soul emanates sharing with others. In this spiritual destitution lies the meaning of being harmless like doves. The final commandments speak of salvation from temporal lust and this is a partly attainable goal for a justified person. But a Christian should remember that the consummation is beyond the temporal.[57]

We find similar notions about the element of experience in salvation as we move to Luther's explications of the Apostles' Creed. Hering pointed to terms that express devotion, terms Luther had in common with mystical marriage imagery. The trust that emerges from salvation is characterized as "devoted ('hingebend') trust." "He who puts everything on God . . . gets from God everything he desires." This means that man has reached a point where it becomes truly genuine to say: I trust no creature "whether in heaven or earth"; I trust "only the mere invisible inconceivable God who is *one* . . . the sole ruler of creation." I believe this, Luther commented, "not less if abandoned and persecuted by all men. I believe it not less if poor, misunderstood, unlearned, despised or lacking everything. I believe it no less if a sinner." For "my faith (devoted trust, *nota bene)* must soar ('schweben') above all . . . sin, virtue, above it all, so that he [the Christian] keeps to God singlemindedly and purely in accordance with the first commandment." Luther wrote about the second article of the Creed that Christ "is risen to give me and all his faithful a new life." He "has awakened us with himself in grace and spirit so that we shall not sin from now on, but serve him alone in all kinds of graces and virtues." [58]

In these Luther statements from 1520, *Erfahrung*, experience clearly stands out as part of the picture of salvation. We also have here a "for you"-theology which engages the whole self, not just the intellect. Ten years later, in his Small Catechism, Luther did not repeat the mystical terms. "But in the exposition of the commandments the high demands of the mystical life have remained," Hering asserted. *Innerlichkeit*, the warm inwardness, and simplicity were signs of Luther's kinship with the mystics. Hering suggested that Luther's struggles with "distorted mysticism" in the wake of the Reformation necessitated a tighter "objective" doctrinal language about the goods of the kingdom and the two sacraments. Yet, the personal *Erfahrung* aspect was still present as part of the salvation event. To undergird his suggestion Hering drew attention to a letter Luther wrote about the Zwickau prophets, post-Reformation mystics: "Have they experienced *Anfechtung*, divine birth, death and hell?" God in his mercy does not normally speak directly with men. Mary was frightened when the angel came. Luther grew suspicious of Dionysius the Areopagite due to the latter's words about direct communication with the ultimate Majesty. Who can converse with ultimate Majesty? In Zwickau they did not use Scripture, he fancied. They simply read from their own heart.[59] But the experience that God is close comes through the word which is Christ.

*Sola fide,* faith alone, can consequently not be understood as a repudiation of mysticism in Luther's theology. The word *raptus,* examined above, illustrates how "feeling" becomes an integral part of the mystery of salvation. "Faith with Luther clearly carries mystical traits and in Luther's theology it is delineated by one of mysticism's central concepts, *raptus,"* Iserloh contends. Luther knew religious ecstasy and called it *sensus fidei,* the knowledge of faith which includes "heart," feeling, not just intellect. Luther also termed this ecstasy "the spirit's *Hineingerissensein,* the state of being enraptured into the knowledge which emerges from faith." [60] Particularly in the lecture on the letter to the Hebrews we find allusions to the mystical dimension of salvation which can be experientially sensed and which Luther doubtless felt. Sometimes Luther described the participation in God as an experience even surpassing psychological or sensate categories. Thus faith as rapture received the following description in one of the comments on Hebrews: "The Christ faith is a being-taken-away *(raptus)* and a being-carried-off *(translatio)* from all that is experiential *(fühlbar)* inwardly or outwardly to that which is experiential neither inwardly nor outwardly, toward God, the invisible, the totally exalted, inconceivable." [61] But, whether reducible to psychological experience or not the participation in God leaves an indelible mark in "the heart," the symbolical sanctum for feeling. Salvation experience brings awareness of God's true relation to the heart and the heart's true relation to God. "Faith," Luther wrote, "causes the heart to cling fast to celestial things and to be carried away to dwell in things that are invisible. . . . For this is how it happens that the believer hangs between heaven and earth, . . . that is, that in Christ he is suspended in the air and crucified." [62]

Luther's language of feeling made him sound in certain contexts like one of those theologians whom he would fiercely attack, the ones that seemed to suggest that man could spin

God out of himself and that, therefore, constant positive change and transformation are possible by man's effort. He did indeed sound like them occasionally, and it is important for us to be aware of the soteriological context of such apparently unevangelical utterances. Luther wrote: "It [faith] is the creator of divinity, not in the substance of God but in us." [63] Within which framework was this enunciated? Obviously within a framework of salvatory experience where man in his godlessness was a perverse creature and a *homo mendax*, a mendacious being, but where once the power of God's righteousness in Christ had set in, " . . . through faith Christ is called our 'substance', that is, riches, and through the same faith we simultaneously become His 'substance,' that is, a new creature." [64]

Having opened himself to the power field of Christ, man changes into the likeness of our Lord. Luther and some medieval mystics were in agreement on this point. A formation takes place as a result of salvation. It is a mystery how conformation with Christ can occur since *homo mendax* continues to incline toward the devil even after a spiritual rebirth. But conformation with Christ does occur. Mystics knew that something happened to the totality of their existence when they had come to the cross. The Frankfurter, one of the closest to Luther among his mystical confreres, called the process of change "divinization" (or "deification"), a word which sits less well with a Protestant.[65] But did he not mean the same as Luther, that is to say, not a self-propulsion through ever higher spiritual spheres but a walk with the crucified and risen Lord? This walk changes Christ's companion, according to Luther and some mystics. With this in mind one should listen carefully to the following words by Luther. For here he said, on the one hand, that man cannot become divinized, and, on the other hand, that he can become divine. It all depends on the spiritual context.

Much has been written about how man shall become divinized. One has made ladders on which to climb

to heaven. But this is empty nonsense. Here [in the
gospel of justification by faith in grace] you are
shown the right way . . . so that your life . . . becomes wholly divine.[66]

The process of change, a result of salvation, is intimately
connected with Christ power. But is that power not mediated
only through the two sacraments? Luther's idea of personal
experience of Christ certainly transcended mere institutional
sacramentalism. A change, a transformation takes place in a
justified person, not just theological but psychological as well,
a tuning-in to the Savior. The attunement alters man's spiritual-psychological form. The formation comes about in human
relationships, through musings on the word, by prayer and in
holy communion. His experience of personal salvation widened
Luther's concept of the sacramental, although he was responsible for a numerical reduction of sacraments as liturgical
acts. He wrote: "All words, all stories in the gospel are sacraments, as it were, i.e., holy signs through which God generates in the believer what these stories signify. . . . "[67]

That Christ is generated in his followers—this must be
understood as the driving force behind "change" as an outcome of salvation, according to Luther. Therefore, the transforming power of God in Christ was not confined to the two
sacraments as administered by new evangelical parishes. Luther contended that God works with us and builds us up
everywhere, in conjunction with the power of the word which
is Christ.[68] No special place, no special order emerging from
institutional traditions are conditions sine qua non for the
work of God in a soul. Places and institutional sacraments are
useful—in the case of baptism even essential—but they are not
the only channels of grace. In this manner Luther's thought
on the relation between sacramental orders and personal regeneration can be summarized.[69]

Yet, Luther's relatively strong emphasis on personal experience does not mean that he regarded the isolated interior
meeting with the divine as something more glorious than the

exterior medium. His pamphlet against the "heavenly prophets" made this clear. He did not want the new enthusiasts to
render as a pious necessity the disregard of orders and customs. For knowing the human heart, Luther thought that precisely the disregard of orders and customs would become a
new law, a new yoke. God sends us external signs to bring us
into faith. He comes in the external, historical Christ who encounters us through the externality of words in the Bible,
through sermons and through baptism and holy communion
as emergents of the biblical word.

However, having made the case for the visible signs in
refutation of attempts to interiorize and spiritualize the salvation process, Luther turned the matter around: we have our
human external orders, however, in the area of faith, the interior precedes the exterior. The heart names the work, the
work does not give the name to the heart.[70] The externality
of word and sacraments is essential in drawing the soul away
from its involution, but the outward ordering as such brings
man no closer to the gist of the matter: love as life in faith.
Witness the *Schwärmer*, who advocated freedom from order
and landed in new legalism. God's very call to interiorization
and love had become a legalistic subordination of the outer
to the inner.[71] The man of faith obviously walked precariously
between two temptations of legalism in Luther's view: the
temptation of external order and the temptation to make of
interiorization a new law. But the Reformer always returned
to the interior, personal cross experience as basic to his view
on the meaning of revelation.[72]

In his thoughts about the bondage of the will Luther included the following words which give an indication of his
attitude to the "institutional" and the "subjective-interior"
components of salvation.

> Since Scripture testifies that God is present every-
> where and fills everything, the pious mind asserts,
> no, not only that, it experiences and knows it also,
> that he is present everywhere. Were it not so I

would not pray to God if a tyrant should take me captive and throw me in a dungeon or a cesspool and not believe that He is close to me until I come back into a stately church.[73]

To fall into God's arms and begin to change in that embrace—that is the inner salvation story. But the orders of dispensation of word and sacraments are entry gates and outer signs without which there would be no proper growth.[74]

The mystics emphasized the experiential element in faith as well as inner transformation. To Luther the mystical side of the Christian life was precisely this experiential side and this conformation to Christ. Obviously Luther's search had brought him to the same kind of insight as some mystics, hence his joy to discover that he was not alone. But did the mystical writers he regarded as co-pilgrims have the same kind of respect for the external and historical in God's work of salvation? They certainly did not have his keen sense for concreteness and history. Yet they were by no means unaware of the determinate media through which God works.

*Theologia Germanica* which spoke of transformation as "divinization" at some junctures, took pains to point to "the Writ" as primary source. The tract used the expression "God speaks" immediately followed by the Bible passage to be expounded. Enumerating the components of a Christian life it placed "the word" first: "the word, works and the way to live."

Johann Tauler who described the road of salvation as a total reduction of the ego, an acquaintance with the nought as antecedent to a tender calm, a loving trust, a friendly confidence, a holy hope, was also certain that God communicates through external signs. He wrote:

In many lands one cannot teach and preach any more, nor warn. This I will tell you in advance, as long as you still have the word. . . . The noble divine word is little understood. That depends on its getting locked up by the senses so that it does not reach the interior.

It is being destroyed by other images . . . the roads
will have to be cleared . . . much of God's word gets
lost and remains unapprehended by those who are
not yet free.

Furthermore, Tauler placed great emphasis on the outer sign
and its observance. In order "to cleave firmly to God" it was
necessary, said this mystic, to attend with regularity "the
Sacrament of the Body of the Lord." This should be done not
primarily in order "to attain to a state of great perfection"
or on the basis of "great deeds." [75] It rather had to be done in
accordance with Jesus' insight into the nature of salvation:
those who know that they are ill need a physician, not those
who think they are well.[76]

As we see, the two mystics alluded to here were not un-
acquainted with the importance of maintaining the right balance between the word and the inner light. Martin Luther's
spiritual intuition concerning the theological soundness of
some mystical insight proved accurate.

Experience and change were parts of Luther's picture of
salvation. When God moves into man's life, man feels it and
begins to grow in conformity with Christ. Utterances of this
sort in Luther's theology may, as we noted, be misinterpreted
as expressions of enthusiastic mysticism which seemed to
disregard the outer incarnate forms of the gospel or accorded
undue weight to man's own powers. In order to understand
Luther's language about experience in the life of faith we
have to relate it consistently to his basic emphasis on justification. According to Luther's basic view the other extreme,
as one faces the experience side of Luther's faith, is to discount entirely any suggestion that knowing, feeling and
growing are parts of an empirical psychic process within
faith. In this instance the tendency is to fasten upon words
by Luther which, for fear of minimizing the power of grace,
in fact postpone its effects until the life to come. Here again
we have to focus on Luther's central teaching which issued
from a joyful experience of liberation. A theological-logical

dilemma is no doubt present in the obvious dichotomy in Luther's thought between, on the one hand, the idea that a Christian's faith can increase his knowledge of being in and cooperating with God, and, on the other hand, the assertion that, since grace is all or nothing, no correspondence exists in the human realm which would issue in actual change. We will have to keep this dilemma in mind as we consider the nature of man's participation in God.

## F. Participation in God

Martin Luther spoke of man's participation in God not only as an appropriation of a "for you" but also as an immanental "in you." Luther's terms for this participation were "conformation" and "union." Conformation and union implied both a process of human integration and an awareness of oneness with the mystical Christ, the spiritual sun behind the visible sun. We will first consider the question against the background of forensic and liberal-humanistic interpretations of a Christian's participation in God; then we will examine the problem from the aspect of Luther's use of the term *communicatio idiomatum;* thirdly, participation in God will be seen as a reflection of union with invisible realms; fourthly, participation in God will be looked at as a source of human integration.

First, we ask how Orthodox Protestantism and liberal-humanistic theologies conceived of man's participation in God. From our account thus far it is clear that the exclusively conceptual and historical methods applied by orthodoxy and liberal theology tend to disregard psychological and supernatural implications of man's participation in God. In order to see the limitations of such methods let us recall the twofold sharing in things divine which characterized Luther's thought. In one way, more distant and impersonal, human existence encounters God in creation's *larvae,* i.e., masks of God. This is to say, God meets us masked.[77] In another, more personal fashion God reveals himself to man in Christ.[78] Man shares in God in this dual manner. In our discussion of the picture of God we saw that Luther took for granted that man is endowed with a general knowledge of God. To Luther it was theologically proper to state that man naturally concedes that he lives, moves and has his being in God. But this concession commits man to nothing. Before Christ, the Lord, who is both judgment and grace, man is called to a new kind of participation in God. This new participation emerges from crucifixion of the desire to be one's own savior and it leads to a sharing in Christ's life. It implies a growth from glory to glory, as St. Paul said.[79]

Orthodox Protestantism accords no soteriological significance to natural religion and ascribes no theological validity to the claim that man is "religious" and that life in God is "mystical" or experiential. Its approach to the question of participation in God becomes correspondingly rationalistic. We have observed that *unio mystica* in the accounts of Lutheran orthodoxy assumed the character of conceptual assertion, an intellectual appropriation of a deed done by Christ for man. Orthodox Protestantism regards justification as *unio mystica* but the union envisaged is a rational event by which man recognizes that justifying grace has been imputed or engrafted from the outside without any other involvement on man's part but the recognition of a concept. On this view justification becomes a basically juridical occurrence, a forensic element in man's grasp of the divine. Man is acquitted before God's judgment seat by virtue of Christ's redeeming deed. This means that grace, according to this interpretation of Luther, does not induce a process of transformation in man's psyche. The forensic is wedded to the eschatological so that God's gracious activity on behalf of man is pictured as carrying an eschatological promise which has no relation to an ongoing life in God.

The liberal or humanistic approach to the question of participation in God discounts the possibility of a mystical sharing in the divine as "only an auxiliary concept" (Ritschl). Participation in things divine is considered coextensive with an ethical existence. The ethical existence is based on rational decision-making rather than on experience of non-rational numinosity.

The orthodox as well as the liberal approach omits the strains of mystical spirituality which we have noted in Luther's theology. In his work on Luther's view of *unio mystica* Erich Vogelsang took exception to these avenues of Luther interpretation as being too rationalistic. Luther, Vogelsang wrote, regarded participation in God as a gift of grace but also as a felt response and a contact with a quickening invisible power. Vogelsang cited a dictum by Luther to the effect that "Christ is God's grace . . . given us without any merit on our part." But in delivering the gift Christ does not remain outside the soul. This would be "dead justice," Luther wrote. Rather, "Christ himself is there," in the same manner as "the brightness of the sun and the heat of the fire are not where sun and fire are not." [80] Vogelsang commented that possession of Christ's gifts is impossible according to Luther without "the real presence of Christ himself." Luther's idea of *fröhlicher Wechsel,* joyful exchange, between Christ as bridegroom and man as bride, has a constant premise, namely that Christ is mystically present, and that knowledge comes through faith by way of Christ's incarnation.[81]

With partial reference to Vogelsang, Iserloh underscores the same notion. He points out that Luther in this regard was in tune with "patristic teaching on redemption" but in disagreement with the scholastic teaching on satisfaction which "remains tied to the moral-juridical level." The church fathers, and especially Augustine, described man's relationship to God as follows: Man has alienated himself from life; he lives in disobedience to God. In fact, he has surrendered to the forces of death. But Christ took upon himself the flesh that was under the dominion of death. Death could not hold the prey which seemed to be lost on the cross. Christ's abundant life was too powerful for death. Christ's humanity was the bait "on the fishing hook of Christ's divinity" and this led to the undoing of death. Having emptied himself in obedience through his death on the cross Christ redeemed human self-glory, rendered death powerless and brought sanctifying divine life to man's nature. Iserloh underlines that Luther had in mind redemption of the kind just described, rather than forensic satisfaction, as he employed "the mystical notion of faith as marital act between the soul and Christ." This idea emerges most prominently in *The Freedom of the Christian* (of 1520).[82] Luther wrote:

> Not only does faith give so much that the soul becomes like the divine word—full of all grace, free, blissful—but it also conjoins the soul with Christ like a bride with her bridegroom. Out of this marriage follows, as St. Paul says, that Christ and the soul become one. Thus the possessions, the good, the bad, yes all belonging to the two become common property so that what Christ has belongs to the faithful soul and what the soul has belongs to Christ. Christ has all goods and bliss: they are the soul's own. The soul has all unvirtuous and sinful things resting on it: they become Christ's. Here emerges now the joyful exchange and struggle. Since Christ is both God and man, who never sinned and whose piety is invincible, eternal and omnipotent, making the faithful soul's sin his own through the wedding ring, that is the faith, and acting not otherwise as though he himself would have committed the sin, the sins must be swallowed up and drowned in him. For his invincible righteousness is too strong for any sin. Only through its dowry, that is to say because of its faith, the soul becomes free and endowed with the eternal righteousness of its bridegroom Christ. Is that not a joyful deal when the rich, noble, pious bridegroom Christ takes the poor, despised, wicked little whore into marriage and liberates her from all evil, adorns her with all good things? Then it is not possible that the sins condemn her for now they rest on Christ and are swallowed up

in him. Thus she has such a rich righteousness in
her bridegroom that she can remain upright against
all sins even if they are already besetting her. On this
Paul says in I Corinthians 15:57, "But thanks be to
God who gives us the victory through our Lord Jesus
Christ, in whom death with the sin are swallowed
up." [83]

From Luther's remarks on participation in God we draw
the conclusion that one does not do justice to his view of sharing in divine life by concentration on the "for you" of redemption or by a reduction of redemption to the ethical. On
Luther's view the freedom engendered by the gospel was not
simply a declaration of grace, but an experience of joy and
inner change.

We come to the second notion chosen to illustrate Christian
man's participation in God. The exchange of properties, the
*communicatio idiomatum,* between the divine and the human
in Christ's nature, was according to Luther applicable to this
divine-human encounter, often depicted as a joyful marital
union. Luther suggested that there are qualities in Christ's
humanity which belong to the divine. In like manner, Luther
said, man harbors aspects of Christ. Incarnate man is in part
spiritual. The dialectic of this situation was brought out in
Luther's notes on Paul's letter to the Romans:

> For in this way there comes about a communication
> of attributes, for one and the same man is spiritual
> and carnal, righteous and a sinner, good and evil.
> Just as the one and the same Person of Christ is
> both dead and alive, at the same time suffering and
> in a state of bliss, both working and at rest, etc.,
> because of the communication of His attributes, al-
> though neither of the natures possesses the properties
> of the other, but are absolutely different, as we all
> know.[84]

Like the church fathers Luther made use of Philippians 2:5 when he wished to describe the exchange between the divine and the human which takes place in the spiritual life: "Have this mind among yourselves, which you have in Christ Jesus." Christ divested himself of God's form and robed himself in a servant's form. The former is wisdom, power, freedom, the latter is our sins. Taking onto himself our sins is an expression of God's essential justice. The fruit of this divine righteousness is our righteousness. We have cooperated in bringing it about. Again Luther resorted to man-woman imagery when he wished to describe what occurs. We cooperate, we are co-workers and this is like the love exchange between bride and bridegroom.[85] Iserloh elaborates on the mystical aspects of this exchange: "The new righteousness is understood as a mystical union with Christ in the depth of the person, yes in faith the Christian receives in Christ a new person-ground," writes Iserloh, citing Luther:

> But faith must be taught correctly, namely, that by it you are so cemented to Christ that He and you are as one person, which cannot be separated but remains attached to Him forever, and declares: "I am as Christ." And Christ, in turn, says: "I am as that sinner who is attached to Me, and I to him. For by faith we are joined together into one flesh and one bone." [86]

The person who has entered such a mystical relationship —as we have seen, Luther does not regard redemption as just an address to man which man only *cognitively* appropriates— radiates works in keeping with Christ's nature. Luther asserted that such works are "incarnated faith." In the midst of these deeds is Christ's divinity, a hidden power. Luther said about this hidden interplay between divine power and human aspiration that "humanitas" alone achieves nothing, but the divine conjoined with the human achieves it.[87]

Thus we are on safe ground in assuming that *communicatio idiomatum* in Luther's thought partly connoted an experience of Christ's presence transforming the ego-centered sinner into a Christ for others.

Third, man's participation in God was seen by Luther as a reflection of union with invisible realms. To participate in God was tantamount to partaking of invisible power, a dimension of life which Luther described with the aid of analogies from both the celestial and the corporeal.[88] Behind the visible sun is the real sun, Christ. His constant radiation of the warmth of love renders participation in God possible. Communication across the boundary between the visible world and the invisible one is consequently a precondition for participation in God. The mystical, cosmic, spiritual Christ continues his incarnational work after his redeeming death and resurrection.[89] In other words, as there is no life on the earth without the visible, natural sun, so there is no life in a deeper sense without Christ and the natural sun is only the manifestation to our senses of the Christ power in and beyond the natural sun. Luther's mystical intuition led him to this profound suggestion, perhaps too esoteric for most of our explanations of the gospel. Man's calling to participate consciously in God is also, according to Luther, underlined by the symbolism of the human body. God's invisible world is a para-world with corporeal correspondences in the natural world. The body represents visibly what both heaven and earth are invisibly, the eyes are visible manifestations of sun and stars and the forehead is the symbol of heaven.[90]

Participation in God thus conceived, this is our fourth consideration, would then be the source of the integral unity between body, soul and spirit which, as noted, Luther experienced as an outcome of God's activity in our lives. Even the carnal, bodily life becomes an integral part of the mystical Christ. Faith is a spiritual pilgrimage where human wholeness is at least a promise and a potentiality. Martin Luther's thought on mystical participation in Christ seems to have included the possibility of a transmutation of bodily vitalities and ego-centered desires into harmony with the indwelling Christ. The person of faith is being formed according to the

Christ image. To be a Christian is to experience God's being become our being. Christ's daily advent changes us so that body, soul and spirit vibrate to one theme, the love of Christ.[91]

With respect to the subject of oneness within the human person as a result of participation in God it is instructive to read Luther's comments on a mystic's view of the matter. On a sermon by Tauler treating of man as three yet one, Luther approvingly remarked that there are indeed three parts of man, sensual man based on sense organs, rational man relying on reason and spiritual man resting in faith. Luther agreed with Tauler that "this all is one man." [92] Peace between the warring parts of man is the outcome of participation in God. Luther wrote:

> These three commandments prepare man for God as pure material so that he reposes in heart, speech and work, id est relative to the interior and the exterior and the central part of man, which has reference to the senses, reason and to the spirit. And thus pure peace reigns.[93]

In another remark of similar intent Luther affirmed that

> he who cleaves to God abides in light . . . from which follows that it is man's loftier perfection in this life to be united with God in such a way that the entire soul with all its abilities and powers is collected (gathered, held together) into its Lord God and becomes one spirit in him.[94]

The element of inner participation in God—experiential more than theological in a purely cognitive sense—was a trait which Luther had in common not only with some medieval mystics but also with, for instance, Lutheran mystic Johann Arndt. Rudolf Otto wrote about Arndt:

> Johann Arndt says at the commencement of his *Four Books of True Christianity* (ch. 5) : 'By this heartfelt confidence and heartfelt trust man gives his heart to God utterly, reposes only in God, surrenders him-

self and attaches himself to Him, unites himself
with God, becomes a sharer in all that is of God and
of Christ, becomes one spirit with God. This is simply Luther's doctrine (his *fides* as *fiducia* and *adhaesio)*, clarified and raised to a higher power. These
expressions might well be found in Luther's *Of the
Liberty of a Christian*—indeed the meaning is to be
found there. Paul says the same in Gal. 2:20 and
I Cor. 6:17.[95]

The typical moments of mysticism are not necessarily pictured by "transcendent quasi-nuptial rapture," Otto asserted.
That may well be. But judging from the frequency with which
Luther resorted to nuptial metaphor it must have said something essential to him about participation in the divine. Do not
the "really typical 'moments' of mysticism—'creature-feeling'
and 'union' "—in large part find expression in the bridal
imagery of mystics?[96] The participation, the "sharing in all
that is of God and of Christ," became a transforming venture
also in Otto's Luther interpretation. He heard Luther say
that "faith transforms us inwardly and brings us forth anew."
Faith to Luther, Otto reminded us, was "the Holy Spirit in
the heart, the mighty creative thing." Participation in God
transforms, conforms and unifies for it implies a sharing in
something which is more than, and beyond, man. This was, it
would seem, Luther's thought on participation in God.

## G. Salvation, Confirming and Testing
   the Supernatural

Salvation in grace by faith implies a new sense of being
part of a paranormal world. Not that supersensible experience
and conviction about parahuman realms of being would not be
possible without the kind of faith-experience about which
Martin Luther spoke. They admittedly are, in all sorts of religions and investigative psychic societies. But salvation often
intensifies the awareness of sharing in the life of non-physi-

cal worlds. Moreover, the new communion with Christ provides a testing place, a spiritual sifting ground for the assessment of diverse manifestations of the supernatural.

In the process of studying Luther's approach to mystical themes references have been made to his consciousness of being part of an invisible world impinging on man's physical existence. This awareness belonged intrinsically to Luther's story of salvation. As we saw in the analysis of liberal-historical theology's way of discussing mysticism, it is hardly possible to "demythologize" either the biblical or Luther's world of thought without doing violence to the nature of the Christ-revelation itself. Luther doubtless shared what "modern thought" would term naive or primitive biblical views of the supernatural. The question we must raise is whether supernatural assumptions may not be inextricable parts of the life of faith. That is to say, accounts of supernatural intimations should be considered germane to the theological quest.

Luther regarded the determinate world as a part of a much larger invisible one. On his view it was essential to take "the invisible" into account in theological expositions of faith and salvation in Christ. In his evaluation of Luther's theology Rudolf Otto suggested—justifiably, in my opinion—that Luther shared Duns Scotus' emphasis on God as "willing" in contrast to the God of "being," for the simple reason that Luther's own experience responded to a God who is will, not just cognition. The non-rational elements in Luther's religion thus found a theological home. But, Otto added, "this aspect of Luther's religion was later tacitly expunged and is today readily dismissed as 'the not authentic Luther' or as 'a residuum of the scholastic speculations of the nominalists. . . .'" In point of fact, Otto continued, this is not a "residuum" at all, but beyond question the mysterious background of Luther's total religious life, obscure and "uncanny," and to estimate it in all its power and profundity we need to abstract the lucid bliss and joyfulness of Luther's faith in divine grace, and to see this faith in relation to the background of that mysterious experience on which it rested.[97]

The tacit expurgation to which Otto alluded with respect to the volitional-mysterious and the numinous experience is also a fitting locution for what has happened to Luther's accounts of more specific manifestations of the paranormal as parts of salvation. In keeping with the prevailing cultural climate of the western world most theological writing has assigned these accounts to the area of timebound notions which have not survived the exacting tests of ever more intense cultural illumination. That which is not experiential in accordance with the codes of exact natural science cannot, so one argues, be the object of scientific research. The assumption that there exists a supernatural world is regarded as "metaphysics," unscientific in the sense that it cannot be demonstrated to the satisfaction of science or theology-as-science.[98] The supernatural dimension lives on embryonically in the word "transcendent." But spiritual phenomena which do not fit the thought-mold of causality, dominating much western thought, are often relegated to the category of psychologized angelology or demonology. According to psychologized reports of the other-worldly that which cannot be or occur by the rules of science or is not normally experienced by people in general, are attributable to the mechanism of psychological symbolizing.

Martin Luther's salvation experience included the experience of a "Beyond" whose powers interweave with human existence. He spoke, we recall, of the "daily advent of Christ." To demythologize his supernatural intimations would be to truncate his theology. It has begun to dawn upon our age that our yardsticks for acquisition of knowledge may be too limited, technical-rationalistic in a doctrinaire fashion. Experiences of the "Beyond" may simply be a natural part of faith. In any event, Luther's life with God should be taken as a whole. To him the invisible was not just a lovely thought along the dotted line from our sensate life. It was real, and without it he would not have had the courage to continue.

But a "theology of experience," expressions of experiential piety, should not, it may be argued, go further than to acknowledge feelings and intuitions involved in faith. Angelology, demonology, healing and parapsychological experience, although present in Luther's world of faith, were not typical for his thought, one might object. They were characteristic for Luther's times, but not for Luther.

As we now proceed to precisely such areas of invisible reality in Martin Luther's life, we do so in the persuasion that belief in living beings, invisible but real, and a sense of contact with invisible hierarchies and a present "mystical Christ" were integral parts of Luther's thinking. This means that Luther did not allude to supernatural dimensions and their various manifestations in the determinate world only because such accounts abound in the Bible. He made the allusions because his experience had corroborated the biblical reports on celestial realities and their paranormal appearance in the realm of Christian faith. Luther did not at this point simply share in time-conditioned beliefs but dealt with elements in faith pervading Christian experience from biblical times to our days.

One can therefore say that the mystical as a feeling of spiritual presence often became concretized for Luther in experiences of and belief in the proximity of angels and demons and in what we today would term parapsychological events. Luther integrated such manifestations with the Christ drama as it unfolds in persons, in the church and in the world. Evidence of the invisible was part of Luther's faith, just as it is part of biblical accounts. It was not centrally important. Christ as living Presence was. But manifestations of the invisible were integral elements in the life of faith. In this way Luther reminded us that the life of the Spirit is more than a general undifferentiated "invisibility." It is living, invisible reality and some of its forms are as differentiated as our earthly existence.

# PART III

# Luther
# on the Reality
# of the Invisible

# CHAPTER 8

# Beings Beyond

## A. Angelic and Demonic Powers

Perhaps because he found what he termed mere "historical faith" so inadequate, Luther makes it a point to underline the mystery of faith by employing the word "invisible" as a characteristic of God's influence in our lives. Otherwise one would have thought that religious things should not need that particular designation. But with Luther, and in much biblical writing, this extra specification appears rather frequently. God sees in the invisible, Luther said, *à propos* Psalm 1 ("Blessed is the man who walks not in the counsel of the wicked.") You think you can avoid his gaze but you cannot. It is the same with faith. Faith also sees in the invisible. The world may be dark around the soul, yet faith sees.[1] Psalm 18:11-12 speaks of the darkness which God sometimes causes to cover his glory, but the coals of fire he sends through his clouds emanate from his brightness. Not to be seen, yet seeing all—that is God's way, Luther commented. Applying the verses to faith, Luther wrote that faith sees nothing, yet sees everything. God rules through the written word and the spoken word, but those who believe merely in the external word have only part of the gospel. The righteous possess faith deep in the heart. To live in the invisible is to have trust despite appearances that do not seem to favor faith's vision.[2]

As "the word" in Luther's conception was not just a document in history but also God's eternal spiritual self-revelation, so faith is not just a stating of facts about the redemption but actually invisible influence of spirit. When Luther elaborated on Hebrews 11:1 ("Now faith is the assurance of things hoped for, the conviction of things not seen"), he again underlined that, when involved with God, man is involved in belief in the invisible.[3]

Luther's awareness of being watched, guided and used by invisible forces was strong. Subsequent to his departure from Augsburg, after negotiations with Cajetanus, he lived in "both fear and hope." The pope threatened him with exile by way of the provincial lords. "Many big men" viewed his tribulation as overwhelming, but "I am filled with joy and peace." [4] In Luther's Table Talks we find a comment on Erasmus which bears on the same quality of awe and expectation before the invisible, indeed a childlike spirit of anticipation. Erasmus was for some unknown reason certain that God is not and that there is no ongoing life after death. Luther was unable to understand this. Erasmus was as certain in his theological agnosticism "as I am that I see." Luther trusted the invisible intuitively through the faith that God had given him.[5]

In letters written from Wartburg during his "Patmos year" (his own description) he spoke of the living Christ who hides himself, as it were, yet surely has something in store for his servant. "I am a strange prisoner, since I sit here both willingly and unwillingly: willingly, since the Lord wants it this way; . . ." [6] In a letter addressed to Melanchthon during this period Luther wrote: "But who knows whether Christ does not wish to accomplish more by this plan, not only in my case but also in all others? We spoke so many times of faith and hope for the things not seen! Come on, let's test at least once a small part of [Christ's] teaching, since things have come to pass this way at the call of God and not through our doing." [7]

Those who knew Martin Luther in the flesh definitely had

the impression that they had met someone who lived by the invisible and had charismatic power. Erasmus Alberus in his book against Carlstadt thought that Luther was indeed a right prophet. "He could turn away God's wrath. No one could more tenaciously and more seriously pray and appeal to God, no one could comfort better." [8]

Luther's concept of the invisible was spelled out in more concrete detail. When he thought of the cosmos in the hands of good and evil he did so in terms of personal invisible entities. The devil ruled over the evil powers, bad angels, lesser devils and demons. On the strength of Christ's deed they lacked ultimate power but they could cause a great deal of harm.[9] Hierarchies of spirits, saints and helpful angels were Christ's messengers to the world. The closer a Christian comes to Christ the more energetic and subtle do the devils become. They are, one might say, like the obsessed in the land of the Gadarenes; they smell catastrophe for their cause at the approach of Christ. From his Wartburg time, when in all likelihood he was more sensitive as a psychic than at any other time, Luther wrote to Duke Fredrick:

> You know that I have the gospel not from men but only from heaven through our Lord Jesus Christ. The devil read my heart very well when I came to Worms. He knew that even if there had been as many devils as there are tiles on the roofs, I would cheerfully jump right into their midst.

But as there is a personalized world of entities that work against God and feed on all kinds of human lust, there is a spiritual counterpoint in good angelic forces. The angels see us when we die, he said in the framework of man's need of confession of sins.[10] But we are the objects of loving attention and care not only at the time of our death. Luther believed that there can be constant awareness of union between this world and the other one. Spirits of departed ones could be conscious of those left behind in the physical world. To a clergyman in Bremen he wrote in January 1546:

I shall pray for you, I ask that you pray for me. As little as I doubt that your prayer is effective for me you should not doubt that my prayer will be effective for you. If I depart this life ahead of you—something I desire—then I must pull you after me. If you depart before me, then you shall pull me after you. For we confess *one* God and with all saints we abide in our Savior.[11]

Concerning Luther's angelology there was reason to discuss it in connection with Emanuel Hirsch's views.[12] Suffice it to say here that Luther believed that angels rule invisible realms under God, that there are dark and light angels, that we might become "apostates from God to angels" and that the holy angels are used by God.[13] Are such ideas in Luther's legacy only theoretical, dogmatic supernaturalism or should they be regarded as biblical information reinforced by personal psychic sensitivity?

## B. Luther's Personal Psychic Experiences

We emphasize anew that Martin Luther was careful not to use his own "revelations" for the purpose of buttressing the persuasive power of his preaching. Even in this regard he showed his spiritual genius. For one thing, a personal story about psychic-spiritual experiences will soon lose its freshness and its impact both with the speaker-writer and with the hearers and readers. But it is undeniable that Luther's faith was permeated with intuitions of numinous Presence and experiences of the power of supernatural forces.

We begin our inquiry into Luther's psychic-spiritual impressions by looking at his concept of prayer. The little treatise, *How to Pray,* mentioned in the discussion of E. Seeberg's generalized picture of mysticism, offers good insight. Few favorable things can be said for "the jabber prayer" ("Plappergebet") practiced by many rosary devotees. Instead Luther recommends the interior, concentrated prayer as "true heart-talk." Coupled with this inner musing should be the demand for "methodically conducted contemplation." [14] The themes which the praying person puts before himself should not be sentimental passion-contemplation, nor should there be exercises around visions of hell or paradise. Solid media should be utilized: Our Father, the Commandments, a psalm or "several of Christ's or Paul's sayings." To these media should be applied a method of contemplation. Luther wrote: "Warm the heart and render praying enjoyable, filled with desire, that is the purpose of Our Father." But the thoughts of Our Father can be expressed

> in many other words, in more or fewer words. I myself do not attach myself to words and wonts, rather today this way, tomorrow in another way, all in accordance with how warm and desiring I feel.

But can prayer be said to belong in the category of Luther's psychic experience, the topic under consideration here? Prayer is normally not considered experiential in the same sense as psychic or parapsychic impressions. Yet, we may have to reshape our thoughts on this matter after listening to the continuation of the proposals in the little pamphlet on prayer.

> Frequently when I come to a certain part of Our Father or to a petition, I land in such rich thoughts that I leave behind all set prayers. When such rich, good thoughts arrive, then one should leave the other commandments aside and offer room to those thoughts and listen in stillness and for all the world not put up obstructions. For then the Holy Spirit himself is preaching and *one* word of his sermon is better than a thousand of our prayers. I have also often learned more from one such prayer than I would have received from much reading and writing.

In connection with preparatory meditation around the commandments Luther offered additional glimpses from his experience of the invisible through "inner prayer." In his inimitable fashion he proposed that

> if the Holy Spirit would come in the course of such thoughts [methodical preparation for worshipful prayer] and begins to preach in your heart with rich, illumined thoughts, do him the honor, let these rationally formulated ("gefasste") thoughts, reflections and meditations fade away. Be still and listen for he [the Holy Spirit] knows better than you. And what he preaches note that and write it down. In this way you will experience miracles.[15]

It is of course well known—and often a cause of some incredulous mirth—that Luther claimed to have had encounters with devils or the devil. Psychological theories have been advanced in attempts to find immanental behavior roots of what one is inclined to term "hallucinations." Yet the question should also be raised whether psychic phenomena such as clairaudience and clairvoyance do not enter our sensate world from beyond it. Or we may interpret such phenomena as combinations of paranormal ingression and reflections of psychological conditions. This is to say, the voices and the visions could well symbolize concrete human situations and at the same time be the impingement of parahuman reality. We may thus interpret the following words uttered by Luther concerning experiences during his time in the castle of Wartburg:

> Two good lads, who brought me food and drink twice a day . . . had bought me a bag of hazelnuts which I ate on occasion, and I had placed the bag in a closed box. . . . I turned out the light at night . . . and went to bed. Then the hazelnuts came down upon me . . . one after the other smashes against the rafters mighty hard. I am rattled in my bed. . . . I fell asleep briefly, then it begins to make such a noise in the staircase as though someone were throwing a bunch of vats down the steps. But I knew that the

staircase was well protected with chains and irons, so that no one could get up. Yet so many vats were falling. I get up, go to the stairs to see what is up. But the staircase was locked. And I said: If it is you, so be it. And surrendered myself to the Lord Christ.

The devil would sometimes take the shape of an animal to Luther's vision. "I looked out of my cell window," he recalled, "and saw a big black sow running around in the yard. Yet no swine could come into that place. It was the devil." At Wartburg "I saw a dog once in my bed. I grabbed him and threw him out of the window. He did not bark. The following morning I asked if there were dogs in the castle and the warden answered No! Then it was the devil, said I."

The envisioned animals no doubt have psychological feeding grounds. But the encounters which Luther described also issued from parapsychic dimensions. It is biblical to assume that he who goes far in obedience also becomes a special target for attacks from the forces who strive to prevent victories for God's righteousness. Some of these forces are parasensible.

Luther understood the letters to the Ephesians and the Colossians in a metaphysical fashion respecting their references to "spiritual hosts of wickedness in the heavenly places" against whom the faithful contend. "The principalities of darkness" were more than psychological metaphors to St. Paul and to Luther; they were part of the invisible realms. Most of us are perchance not sufficiently advanced in obedience to become targets of assaults by "the principalities." One has to be a threat to dark powers in order to draw their attention. This possibility should make us less condescending in our treatment of Luther's reports of experiences with dark invisible forces.[16]

But there were brighter revelations of the unseen in Luther's life. In the discussion of Hirsch's angelology we noted that angels, according to Luther, must be integrated with God's "economy" in Christ and in prayer and meditation treated as real, though invisible.[17] Luther must have had a vision when at the age of 22 he decided to become a monk, Söderblom suggested. His promise "was caused by a vision. Perhaps God had spoken . . . through one of his holy ones." [18] Luther's claim that he was once caught up into the third heaven has been alluded to in the present account.[19] It is reported from a conversation between Luther and Cochleus in Worms 1521, that Luther was asked if he had had a special revelation. Luther then called to mind 1 Corinthians 14:30: "If a revelation is made to another sitting by, let the first be silent." Cochleus said: "Have you had a revelation?" Martin Luther looked at him, was silent for a moment and said: "Est mihi revelatum," yes, he had had revelations.[20]

Luther thus had experiences of a clairaudial and clairvoyant nature. A third form of psychic endowment in the Reformer's spiritual life was precognition. In the early part of 1532 Luther became extremely ill, after having had forebodings. The physician spoke of apoplexy and declared that Luther would not recover. At four o'clock one morning Luther felt a most painful roaring in his ears and a powerful depression gripped his heart. He sent for Melanchthon and Rörer. When they remarked that the papists would certainly triumph were their friend and leader to die now, Luther suddenly spoke with vigor in his voice and said,

> I shall not die this time, I am certain; God will not strengthen the hateful cause of the papists by my death now . . . Satan would be glad to see me dead; he is constantly treading on my heels, but he will not be gratified, and God's will alone must be done. He controls all things.[21]

Luther seems to have had a precognition concerning himself when he said prior to beginning his last lecture series: "I shall linger over the exposition of this book and shall die in the process of doing so." He started his work on Genesis in 1535 and concluded it three months before his death. His last lecture proved to be his last academic presentation.[22]

The year of 1538, Luther presaged, would be an evil and perilous year; it would bring much sickness. Luther could read this prediction into the future for two reasons, one a natural reason and the other a spiritual reason. The natural reason was, said Luther, a conjunction of Saturn and Mars, and the spiritual reason was the godless and sinful life of the people. As far as Luther's own circumstances were concerned in the year that followed his prediction, the prophecy came true. He developed a severe stomach disorder, had to walk with a cane on account of foot trouble, had pain in an arm and was confined to bed for a while with fever.

No doubt Luther had paranormal experiences. Some of them were of Pauline magnitude, both experiences of a hostile invisible world and experiences of a benign invisible world. A few of the latter sustained his faith in the same manner as St. Paul was sustained by his clairvoyant and clairaudial Damascus experience.[23] Without them faith would be just rational play. But Luther used these paranormal intuitions sparingly in his gospel propagation. The reason is obvious. *Homo mendax*, man's mendacious, ego-involuted self, tends to turn the extraordinary experiences into self-glory. Besides, both Scripture and Christian experience teach us that some forms of occultism can be deleterious.

# CHAPTER 9

# Occultism, Healing, Deliverance

## A. Rejection of Some Forms of Occultism

Although Luther knew from his own experience that man is linked to invisible forces, his rebirth by grace in Christ made him doubly suspicious of any endeavor to attain salvation or achieve power by occult manipulations. Such suspicions appear early with reference to the kind of mysticism which does not relate to the word and to Christ and thus indulges in an impossibility, self-salvation. If you wish to rise to heaven, you may have a fall.[1] Dionysius, one of the suspects among mystics, does not seem to have discovered Christ. "Have faith in Christ . . . Dionysius' mystical theology is qualified nonsense."[2] Magic by which invisible power is supposed to be bent man's way, and according to man's wishes, is rejected outright.[3]

Luther recognized that God works miracles, but he always made a distinction between the outer miracle and the inner one. The outer miracle could easily be a magic trick. The question was what God wanted to do with the miracle. This was always a matter of inner attitude, penitence, salvation. Miracles in the outer sense were nothing but "apples and nuts for children," led nowhere as far as salvation was concerned.

The devil deludes people into believing that they are experiencing real miracles, Luther asserted, when in fact these miracles were performed by this potentate himself. Man should be aware of this deception. Luther was saying this, he added, to keep the faithful from believing in any and all signs of power. We should remember, he continued, that already the Old Testament warns of false prophets and the New Testament mentions anti-Christian miracles. Man must judge and consider all wonders and miracles in the light of God's word. Luther advised his listener and reader that if one is guided toward

> any help other than the doctrine and the works of the Lord Christ, you can conclude freely that this is the devil's work and his false miracles, by which he deceives and misguides you, just as he had done so far under the name of Mary and the saints where Christ was never known and taught aright. . . . Christ alone performs true, divine signs and wonders.[4]

All attempts to forecast the future were unbiblical, Luther averred, for only God knows the times, not even the Son knows them. Hence astrology could not be a *bona fide* part of the gospel.[5] (Yet Luther could sometimes allude to astrological knowledge as a reflection of "natural" cosmic interrelationships; we have just cited an example of this concept.)[6]

Behind rejections of the kinds illustrated above lies a profound concern for and knowledge of what God's righteousness means. It means a turning over to God everything that is in man, holding nothing back. For no divinatory techniques can attain salvation. It is opening up to God that does. So Luther warned all those who try by other means. He was persuaded that the devil has his hand in all such attempts. The devil knows extremely well our spiritual position and our intentions. And he has indeed nothing at all against watching us break our neck. "If outside of Christ you wish by your own thoughts to know your relation to God, you will break your neck. Thunder strikes him who tries." [7]

However, Luther's rejections of contact with the invisible that was not rooted in Christ must not be construed as rejection of the invisible. To be saved by justification was to have become a conscious part of a supernatural power-field. With Luther the "public" creed had a "private" experiential counterpart. The manner in which he claimed power from beyond was indicative of this.

## B. Healing and Exorcism

We have pointed to Luther's view of wholeness as an effect of salvation. Distortions of many sorts can be corrected by the power of Christ, he who straightens that which has become crooked. The healing and unifying process includes total man—body, soul and spirit.

Did Martin Luther in fact know and practice healing, the making-whole about which St. Paul writes in 1 Corinthians 12, and which many Christians have experienced throughout history as part of a charismatic revival? The answer can only be in the affirmative. It would indeed have been surprising had Luther omitted charismatic healing as part of the work of salvation. His total grasp was after all based on a keen awareness of the dynamic interrelationship between body and spirit, incarnate existence and invisible grace. With his keen experience of the power of the gospel the Reformer could not and did not hear Jesus merely command men to proclaim and teach. He heard the equally important admonition to heal.[8]

Under the impact of rationalism the church has often relegated spiritual healing to a bygone age. Healing miracles occurred when Jesus lived in history, it has been said, but no longer. Some theologians have been known to claim that miracles (occurrences out of the ordinary, beyond the range of normal causality) perhaps never actually were historical facts but rather faith's understandable adornment of the beloved memory of the Teacher. Martin Luther did not think that way, and it is futile to reconcile him with modernity in this regard, as some of his interpreters did and do. With respect to the psychic force of faith in Christ his belief was not bound by his era. The healing impact of the gospel issuing in the paranormal healing miracles is part and parcel of God's offer to mankind. Man has access to the integrating center of the cosmos, the power center that makes cosmos one, the sun which is Christ.[9] By that token man can be healed, inasmuch as the force of the sun may be claimed in the name of Christ.[10]

To Gerhard Wilskamp, Luther wrote about an illness from which he was suffering: "Christ has so far triumphed. I commend myself to the prayers of yourself and the brethren. I have healed others, I cannot heal myself." In other words, Luther had placed himself at God's disposal for spiritual healing of people sick in mind and body. At this particular juncture he despaired a little about the possibility of being healed himself.[11] When Philip Melanchthon lay gravely ill Luther turned to the window in the sickroom and poured out his soul in the boldest and most glowing prayer for his friend's recovery. About this occasion Luther wrote:

> This time I besought the Almighty with great vigor. I attacked him with his own weapons, quoting from Scripture all the promises I could remember, that prayers should be granted, and said that he must grant my prayer, if I was henceforth to put faith in his promises.

Luther then took the hand of the sick man saying:

> Be of good courage, Philip, you will not die; although the Lord might see cause to kill, yet he does not will the death of the sinner, but rather that he should turn to him and live. God has called the greatest sinners unto mercy; how much less, then, will he cast you off, my Philip, or destroy you in sin and sadness. Therefore do not give way to grief, do not become your own murderer, but trust in the Lord, who can kill and bring to life, who can strike and heal again.

It is clear that Luther knew Melanchthon's inner struggle at the time, namely that Melanchthon was blaming himself for too little stoutness in the defense of the evangelical cause. Melanchthon would rather have passed away in peace than have to return to earthly strife. But the power channeled by Luther's prayer recalled the sick man. Melanchthon recovered from what appeared to be the brink of death. He wrote later: "I was recalled from death to life by divine power." [12]

Luther was often aware of having been the object of intercessory prayer in times of illness. After an attack of "the stone" in 1537 he wrote to his wife:

> I was all but dead, I had already recommended you and our children to God and our Savior, in the full conviction that I should never see you again. I was greatly affected when I thought of you, thus on the brink of the tomb, as I thought myself. However, the prayers and tears of pious men who love me have found favor before God. This last night has killed my malady; I feel quite as though newborn. [13]

After his recovery from the stone about a month later a good friend asked Luther what remedy he had used. Luther replied: "Prayer, for in all Christian congregations they fervently prayed for me according to the direction of the Apostle James 5:14-15." [14] Although Luther had apparently undergone a kind of operation to relieve his pain and enjoyed the best physical care, he was still persuaded that intercessory prayer lay at the root of his recovery. As we have noted, such a posture was quite in line with Luther's mystical conviction that life in faith draws upon invisible, extra-human resources.

Myconius, pastor in Gotha, testified that Martin Luther healed him by prayer. It happened in 1541. In a letter to Myconius Luther had written: "I will pray with you that God may keep you here long." Myconius had apparently been rather seriously ill with a lung ailment. Martin Luther's prayer for spiritual healing, wrote the pastor, "showed such a power" that he recovered. Six years later Myconius, moved by the death of his leader and friend in Christ, wrote the little tract from which we have this piece of information on the matter of healing.

Let us digress at this point and say that Luther hardly made the matter of healing a subject of doctrinal discourse. The subject belonged to the realm of interior, mystical experience and was, as such, so personal that one could not use it in theological argumentation or in preaching. But to Luther healing belonged to the possibilities in Christ. In fact, it was part of that inner side of subjective, private legitimate experimentation with God's promises, without which the public side of revelation would be lifeless.

So, says Myconius, our Doctor Luther wanted me to stay on in this life as he felt I was sorely needed. Luther wrote: "I would be left alone among these devilish folk . . . would that I, after so many crosses and so much suffering, be permitted to precede you." God brought me back to this life through Martin Luther's healing prayer, Myconius told his readers.

> Now I crawl into my sick-bed to await the moment
> when the Lord bids me to put down my physical bur-
> den—I am now only skin and bone—and permits me
> to follow Luther to the Lord Christ. I would long
> ago have followed my dear Father Luther, had not
> the prayers of my brethren in several churches kept
> me here.[15]

Let no one who still considers the healing service of the church a dubious undertaking from the vantage point of Lutheran reformation believe that Luther's allusions to and recommendations of spiritual healing were incidental and thus not built into his concept of Christ's power. There is among Luther's letters a document which shows us beyond any doubt that he viewed spiritual healing as an integral part of the pastoral task of the church. He did not forget that medically trained people should be consulted. But especially when their counsels seemed at an end the constant necessity for intercessory prayer stood out plainly. The petitions should be regular and ritually ordered. Thus reads the letter from Martin Luther to pastor Severin Schulze.

To Pastor Severin Schulze, Venerable Sir and pastor, The tax collector in Torgau and the councilor in Belgren have written me to ask that I offer some good advice and help for the afflicted husband of Mrs. John Korner. I know of no worldly help to give. If the physicians are at a loss to find a remedy, you may be sure that it is not a case of ordinary melancholy. . . . This must be counteracted by the power of Christ and with the prayer of faith. This is what we do—and we have been accustomed to it for a cabinetmaker here was similarly afflicted with madness and we cured him by prayer in Christ's name.

You should consequently proceed as follows. Go to him with the deacon and two or three good men. Confident that you, as pastor of the place, are invested with the authority of the ministerial office, lay your hands upon him and say: "Peace be with you, dear brother, from God our Father, and from our Lord Jesus Christ." Thereupon read the Creed and the Lord's Prayer over him in a clear voice, and close with these words: "O God, Almighty Father, who has told us through your son, Verily, verily, I say unto you, whatsoever you shall ask the Father in my name, he will give it to you"; who has commanded and encouraged us to pray in His name "Ask and you shall receive"; and who in like manner has said, "Call upon me in the day of trouble, I will deliver you and you shalt glorify me"; we unworthy sinners, relying on these your words and commands, pray for your mercy with such faith as we can muster. Graciously deign to free this man from all evil, and put to nought the work that Satan has done in him, to the honor of your name and the strengthening of the faith of believers. Through the same Jesus Christ, your son our Lord, who lives and reigns with you, world without end. Amen.

Then, when you depart, lay your hands on the man again and say: "These signs shall follow them that believe: they shall lay hands on the sick and they shall recover."

Do this three times, once on each of three successive days. Meanwhile let prayers be said from the chancel of the church, publicly until God hears them.

To the extent to which we are able, we shall at the same time unite our faithful prayers and petitions to the Lord with yours.[16]

It will be noted that the kind of healing Luther described here was in part exorcism. If we recognize the likelihood or accept the certainty of a "peopled" dimension beyond the natural sphere determined by our senses, we have to reckon with the reality of obsession. Luther's sermon on the angels plainly does.[17] It may seem an impossible idea in a modern scientific world. But then both western experiences on the mission fields and a new sense for the occult overtones of human existence in our day and age have altered some presuppositions. Not a few ordained clergy in the western world are "part-time exorcists," in the name of Christ. More of them are building into the curriculum of the parish services intercessory prayer for the sick. An equally growing number are laying hands on the sick in private pastoral encounters.

The world that opens up through the salvation in Christ contains discoveries of the order just described. Luther's views on life after death seem to support our contention that the Reformer's concept of "spirituality" included the notion that man's existence in the flesh is enveloped in an existence of a subtler, invisible order. The remarks that follow are based on findings gleaned "in passing" while investigating Luther's relationship to the mystics. Doctor Martin was persuaded, through his faith, that God is not a God for the dead but for the living, for to him all live.[18]

# CHAPTER 10

# Luther
# on Life after Death

Luther was once asked directly what he thought of the soul's destiny beyond death. In his written reply he began by saying that his answer certainly did not satisfy him. Was it not true, the questioner had asked, that the souls of the righteous "sleep" after death, also that they are "unaware until judgment day as to where they are"? Luther was "inclined" to believe this, he wrote. A word in 2 Samuel 7:12 influenced his opinion. He translated the passage as follows:

"They sleep with their fathers."[1]

> And the dead who were raised again through Christ and the apostles testified to the same when they were awakened from sleep, as it were, namely that they were unaware of where they had been. To this come the ecstasies of many saints. So that I know of nothing by which I might annul this opinion.

But then Luther had second thoughts on the subject. He continued:

> However, whether this is universally valid for all souls I do not dare assert, on account of Paul's, Elijah's and Moses' *raptus;* the latter certainly did not appear as fictions on Mount Tabor. For who has

known in what way God may act with respect to departed souls? Could He not intermittently bring them to sleep, or rather as long as He pleased? After all, He puts them to sleep while they are in the body. Moreover, that passage from Luke 16 about Abraham and Lazarus does attribute consciousness to Abraham and Lazarus. Although it does not insist on universality, it is unacceptable to twist it to mean the [final] day of judgment.[2]

From the statement above it would seem that in his thinking about life after death Luther moved between a Hebrew concept of *sheol,* the shadowy realm of the dead, and a Christian view of life after the bodily death as a life in gladness based on conscious spiritual perception.

Luther said in one context that when the final day of resurrection arrives Adam will think that he fell asleep just a little while ago. About himself in that situation Luther maintained that he will sleep until Christ knocks at the door of the sepulcher saying: "Doctor Martinus, rise now!" Then he, Luther, will immediately rise to be with the Lord in eternal bliss.

One might ask whether Luther painted the continued life in this fashion to give a popular picture of resurrection in general. He certainly did not always hold to the idea that the main occupation of the soul in the other dimension is sleep. As noted, that would be the Hebrew notion of sheol to be found, of course, primarily in the Old Testament but visible also in the New Testament.

In other contexts Luther followed New Testament suggestions to the effect that those who die in Christ will enjoy gladness, that is to say, a conscious experience. It is moreover hard to think that St. Paul desired to be with Christ in order to sleep. If we can speak of an intermediate state between the death of the body and the ultimate consummation and resurrection, that state is within the dominant New Testament view of life where impressions are received, conscious decisions taken and development and spiritual changes occur. The question is even if after death man might not discover that the after-life is really to be living and the earthly existence is actually to be dead. Luther put it this way in another dictum on life after death. "When we are dead we have different eyes. Then we perceive that the whole world is dead. That is why the Lord said to a learned scribe who wanted to go and bury his father: 'Follow you me and let the dead bury their dead.' " [3]

We find in Luther's writings a good deal of evidence that his faith included the conviction that life continues after death, not as a sleep but as wakeful existence. Luther frequently thought of life after death in connection with the martyrdom of a true Christian. Part of the triumph of faith was to him the fact that life continues after death. The martyr may face the verdict that

> he is to be hanged, beheaded, burned or drowned. Then, too, a road stretches out before him that he must walk . . . a way which he cannot see, on which feet cannot tread, on which he cannot travel by wagon. Yet, one commonly says: 'He is departing, he is gone." But this is not to be taken in a physical or literal sense. . . . Our reasoning ceases to function and neither knows nor understands how the transition from this life to that one takes place, much less how and by what means it is to be attained.[4]

The transition from this natural life to "that other life" is no doubt a transition from one form of consciousness to another.

> For faith does not err and stray; but wherever the Christ is to whom it adheres, there it also must be and remain. And the stronger the faith is, the more surely this Way is traveled. For this walking is nothing but a constant growth in faith and in an ever-stronger assurance of eternal life in Christ.

If I persist in this faith and death attacks me and
throws me down, if it chokes me in my prime or takes
me by sword or fire and takes away all my five senses,
then the journey is over, and I am already at my des-
tination as I leap into yonder life.[5]

We see this persuasion about ongoing awareness which continues in a totally different dimension, as we read Luther's
account of his daughter Magdalen's death. The fourteen-year-
old girl died in 1542. Catherine, Luther's wife, wept bitterly
and Luther who had prayed with great intensity for her recovery said to his wife:

Dear Catherine, console yourself; think where our
daughter is gone, for sure she has passed happily
into peace. The flesh bleeds doubtless, for such is its
nature. But *the spirit lives and goes to the place of
its wishes.* (Italics mine.)

When they placed Magdalen's body in the coffin Luther said:

Poor, dear little Magdalen, there you are, peace be
with you. Dear child, you will rise again, you will
shine like a star, yes, like the sun. . . . I am joyful
in spirit, but oh, how sad in the flesh. It is marvel-
ous that I should know that she is certainly at rest,
that she is well, and yet that I should be so sad.

The tenor of these words is the belief that man enters a rest-
ful existence after death but certainly not a continually som-
nolent one. As the people came to carry out the coffin and expressed their sympathy for Martin and Catherine in their
grief, Luther said: "Friends, be not grieved, I have sent a
saint to heaven." Perhaps Luther was strengthened in his belief in an afterlife of a conscious order after a dream which
Catherine had had in the night preceding Magdalen's death.
Catherine had seen two beautiful, exquisitely dressed young
men come to her, asking her daughter in marriage. Philip

Melanchthon had interpreted the dream as follows. The young men, he said, were a vision of holy angels preparing themselves to carry away the dear girl to the true nuptials in the heavenly kingdom.[6]

We are now in a position to see that Luther's presumably predominant view of the after-life was a concept of conscious existence. But the after-life is not necessarily an unqualified blessing. It is important to distinguish between immortal life and eternal life.

There is, I believe, sound theological coverage for the suggestion that the New Testament makes a distinction between immortal life and eternal life. Immortal life is considered a natural fact. To speak in spatial terms, it belongs to the realm of "quantity." Eternal life is centered in the life of Christ and belongs to the order of "quality." The soul continues beyond death as a "natural" fact. But this has nothing directly to do with salvation. Rebirth through and faith in Jesus Christ does. And that is eternal life, encountering us in our earthly existence, leading us on in the other existence. Martin Luther did not make exactly this distinction—but almost. In his comments on the epistle to the Hebrews he explained:

> "Christ's believers are most properly called heavenly because if 'the soul is present more where it loves than where it lives,' and if it is the nature of love to change one who loves into what is loved, it is true that those who love heaven and God are and are called heavenly and divine, though not because they are heavenly by nature or in a metaphysical sense."

From this spiritual heavenliness Luther distinguished a natural-metaphysical heavenliness. In that sense "immortality" is a fact. "Even the demons and absolutely all the souls of men would be heavenly, since they are of a certain heavenly, that is, incorporeal, nature." [7] What else does this distinction mean but the notion that immortality is a "natural" fact of a quantitative kind if that term be permitted about a dimension invisible to physical eyes? Does not the distinction made here by Luther also mean, on the other hand, that "eternal life" involves the salvation of the soul and is of a qualitative kind? It is not the same as limitless time, as sometimes suggested, a condition beginning with the death of the body. Eternal life interpenetrates the sphere of material existence and the "invisible" sphere.

Later on in the same lecture series on Hebrews, Luther, dealing with the words about Abel, suggested that God "points out somewhat obscurely that the soul is immortal and that there is eternal life, yet He does so with power." In this remark by Luther the same thought found expression: there is an undeniable immortal life awaiting the soul. However, this is not the same as eternal life which is a life bent upon God and his Christ. Abel, who in his lifetime on this earth could not even teach his only brother by faith and example, though dead "lives far more vigorously, and teaches the whole world." [8] That is to say, Luther thought that man lives consciously after death and he thought that this kind of life should not be equated with eternal life which God imparts.

Luther wrote on Matthew 22:31-32:

> Moses himself testifies (Exodus 3:6) with a strong argument that there is another life after this one, for God was Abraham's God. This they had to concede, but they did not understand. So he asks: Do you wish to make God a God of the dead or any other thing, which is nil or has no being? . . . Since Moses says that God is Abraham's God, Abraham must be something and be alive. But reason speaks: Oh, Abraham has been disintegrated a long time; how can God then be his God? If I now were to say that God is Abraham's God according to the manner of the soul, this is not enough . . . Abraham has body and soul . . . there is a resurrection of the dead,

especially of the just . . . Christ says: he [Abraham] shall remain, rise . . . Abraham and all saints live even though they die. . . . How this occurs reason cannot see, nor conceive . . . the soul does not know . . . yet it shall not be dead. For the rising of the dead will surely take place . . . Moses . . . says . . . that we shall rise again for life shall prove stronger than death . . . Abraham . . . has body, and soul, which the order of death shall touch only a moment. . . . Twenty years ago I heard Cardinal Cajetanus who spoke of the Christian faith so that I shuddered . . . in this manner each burger and peasant will become a despairer of the resurrection of the dead, yes blind." [9]

Augustine tells us about a physician who doubted the immortality of the soul, Luther reminded his readers of the Genesis lectures. A certain physician regarded the doctrine of the resurrection and immortality as uncertain. However while he is dreaming, a young man appears to him and says: "How is it that you see me when your eyes are closed in sleep? How is it that you hear me when your ears are not open, but you are asleep? [Luther comments:] Therefore learn and believe that there are other spiritual eyes with which those who believe in Christ see when the eyes of the body have been closed by death." [10]

In his observations on the epistle to the Galatians Luther again indicated that life after the death of the body is conscious existence.

It is as though he [Paul] were saying: "It would indeed be fine if someone kept the Law. But since no one does so, we must take refuge in Christ, who was put under the Law to redeem those who were under the Law (Gal. 4:4). Believing in Him, we receive the Holy Spirit and begin to keep the Law. Because of our faith in Christ what we do not keep is not imputed to us. But in the life to come believing will cease, and there will be a correct and perfect keeping and loving. For when faith ceases, it will be replaced by glory, by means of which we shall see God as He is (I John 3:2). There will be a true and perfect knowledge of God, a right reason, and a good will, neither moral nor theological but heavenly, divine, and eternal.[11]

The aspect of "sleep" is notably absent in this eschatological picture, especially if "that future life" is to be interpreted as "the intermediate stage" before the final consummation in the last judgment. And a different connotation seems out of the question.

In a table conversation of the year 1540 Martin Luther referred to his book on John 14-16 as "the best book I have ever written." Theologians will dispute the adequacy of Luther's grading and suggest that he would probably have thought differently about it had he been "modern." Yet, perhaps he knew what he was saying. The book stands out even in a setting of modernity. With respect to Jesus' words about being the way, the truth and the life Luther found occasion to speak of "life beyond," among other things. When the time comes to say farewell to human activity one should not trust good bygone deeds. One must hold on to the words of Christ that he is the way. One shall also feel Christ mystically.

Make sure that then these words are firmly imbedded in your consciousness, so deeply that you can feel Christ's presence and He can say to you as He does to Thomas here: "Why are you seeking and looking for other ways? Look to Me, and reject all other thoughts regarding ways to heaven. You must expunge these completely from your heart and think of nothing but these words of Mine: 'I am the way.' See to it that you tread on Me, that is, cling to Me with strong faith and with all confidence of the heart. I will be the Bridge to carry you across. In one mo-

ment you will come out of death and the fear of hell
into yonder life.[12]

Although there is a continuing life, only the certainty that
God accords through faith—faith which, in Luther's comments on Hebrews 11, is tantamount to life in God—permits
man to traverse into the other dimension. ". . . God be
praised, as a Christian I do know where I will go and abide;
for I was assured of this in Baptism, in absolution, and likewise in the Sacrament. . . . Christ calls Himself the only Way
. . . He wants our heart and our reliance to rest completely
on Him when we are to depart this life; and He promises to
transport us across safely and take us to the Father. . . . " [13]

It seems clear that Luther's thought about the after-life
tended toward the notion of a life in wakefulness, despite
occasional difficulties to reconcile the traditional Hebrew sheol
concept with the view emanating from Jesus. Jesus indicated
that life after death is characterized not by a sleep-filled existence but by consciousness, either simply as unredeemed immortality or as the eternal life in Christ which man is invited
to enter already in his determinate earthly life.[14]

Luther's reference to Christ's story about Abraham, the
rich man and the poor beggar Lazarus contains, it would
seem in the light of other Luther statements on life after
death, the view which was more germane to his total theology.
Luther's persuasion about the angelic world, already touched
upon here, suggested the main direction of his thought on
immortality and eternal life. In a sermon on preparation for
death we read that the Christian should know that when he
dies he has invisible company.

> He can rest assured, as the sacraments indicate, that
> a great many eyes are directed toward him: first
> God's eyes and the eyes of Christ himself . . . then
> also the eyes of the dear angels, of the saints, and of
> all Christians . . . the sacrament of the altar shows
> us that all of these together hasten to him as one of
> their own, help him overcome sin, death and hell, and

bear all things with him. In that hour the work of
love and the fellowship of the saints are intently and
powerfully at work. In the venerable sacrament of
the body of Christ . . . are . . . pledged the fellowship, love, comfort and succor of all the saints in all
times of need.

Elisha is one among the many who knew this to be true. He
said to his servant: "Fear not for those who are with us are
more than those who are with them." Obviously, Luther
points out, this was not true as far as the testimony of most
*external* eyes was concerned. All one could see all over the
place was enemies. But "the Lord opened the eyes of the servant" and then he saw the invisible facts: they were surrounded by friendly forces, "horses and chariots of fire." [15]
To Luther such knowledge was not symbolical immanental for-
tification of faith conjured up by the mind as it meets life's
challenges. To him it was a statement of a comforting parasensible fact to which faith opened the door.

In the above dictum about man's invisible allies it should
be noted that Luther, like many mystics, reckoned with three
kinds of entities who uphold man from the invisible: spirits
of men, saints and angels. Moreover, it is clear that these
beings are not asleep but very much awake and at work as
man's helpful associates. Whatever the "intermediate stage"
might be between death and final resurrection, in Luther's
prevailing view it is an existence of largely conscious participation.

Luther encouraged the reader to look up Psalms 34, 91 and
125 for assurance concerning the living world of angels around
a human being. He reminded the reader of the psalmist's assurance that God directs his angels to protect the faithful in
all trials. "I will fill him with eternity." That is to say, the
soul is immortal but what counts is the eternal. The eternal,
we reiterate, is not illimitable time. It is not the kind of
time that takes over when earthly time is no more. In his
theological sensitivity Luther saw that eternity is a qualita-

tive notion. Eternity begins in time, not just after the physical death. It meets us in Christ and "through such insignificant signs as the sacraments." [16] A human being is called to prepare himself for the after-life by surrendering his involuted self to the eternal and mystical Christ here and now.

On Luther's accounting the two sacraments, baptism and eucharist, stood out as bridges for intimations of a life beyond. They show man that he should "call upon the holy angels, particularly his own angel, upon the mother of God, and all the apostles and saints." [17] In the sacraments man meets God's "angels, all saints, all creatures" and they "join God in watching over you, to be concerned about your soul and to receive it."[18]

To watch and to be concerned—the verbs do suggest that the world to which the soul goes is evidently not considered in the main as a place for sleep until the latter day.

The feeling this constant connection with the world beyond induces in the person of faith is beautifully described in Martin Luther's last sermon which he preached in Eisleben in February 1546. The text is Jesus' thankful prayer to his Father that the things revealed through his ministry could be appropriated by simple and childlike minds, not by those who thought a great deal of their wisdom. As a presage of the world that receives the passing soul at death the person who lives in God may experience God's love in the midst of tribulation. The world leers at those who are steeped in God; it views them with disdain and hatred. The great dukes, the emperor, the pope, cardinals and bishops are all hostile because of what he, Luther, had uttered. That must be endured. Our cause is beyond the grasp of the world. Christ, the Lord of invisible hosts, said that those should come to him who are heavy-laden. Luther paraphrased it as follows:

> Just cleave to me, hold on to my word and let go whatever thereby goes. Should you be burned or beheaded for it, have patience. I will render it so sweet for you that you shall sustain it well. As it has

been written about the virgin St. Agnes, when she was led to prison to be killed, she had the feeling that she was on her way to a dance. From where did this come to her? Ah, from this Christ, from believing this word: 'Come to me all who labor and are heavy-laden, and I will give you rest.' If evil befalls you I, the Christ, will give you the courage so that you will even laugh about it all, and the pain shall not be so great for you, and the devil not so bad. Even if you walked on live coals, you will have the feeling that you walk on roses. I will give you the heart to laugh. . . . Only come to me. . . . If you face oppression . . . do not be afraid, it will not be heavy for you, but light and easy to bear. For I give you the Spirit, so that the burden, unbearable for the world, becomes a light burden for you. For when you suffer for my sake it is my yoke and my burden laid upon you in grace so that you shall know that your suffering is pleasing to God and to me and that I myself am aiding you to carry it, giving you power and strength. . . . Waiting upon the Lord in faith you have already conquered, and escaped death . . . and by a large margin left behind you the devil and the world.[19]

# PART IV

# Conclusion

# CHAPTER 11

# Luther
# and the Mystics

The study which is herewith drawn to a close points to a deficiency in discourses on God's self-disclosure in Christ: inability to deal with the *Third* Article of the Creed. Theology has always found it hard to annotate in integral fashion the stirrings of the Holy Spirit in a Christian way and view of life. It registers admirably the historical and phenomenological data of revelation, whether the revelation is considered a once-for-all event or regarded as an ongoing process. But what can a linear and logical mind do with a wind which bloweth whither it listeth or a Lord who pledges that he will be present after his death wherever two or three are gathered in his name or that his Spirit will, through his followers, do greater things than he did?

Claims of this nature contradict the testimonies of our commonsense existence. They have therefore been treated with measured skepticism in Christian history ever since Doubting Thomas insisted on tangible proof. This is to say, man tends to restrict the range of God's possibilities to the determinate, palpable and ordinary.

Moreover, assertions about the power of the Holy Spirit have been tempered by the claims of exact science and their philosophical echoes. To keep in touch with the times many theological systematizers have adopted verifiability codes from scientific materialism. They fail to bring the gospel's mystical and supernatural components into their theological purview. The church continues to repeat a credal paragraph about the Spirit as an account of past occurrences, as this-worldly psychological truth of a transcendent order and as "promise" of a redeemed future. The Creed is not appropriated as invocation of and trust in present power, ready to come into our consciousness. The church's thought has been fashioned by theology seen as history, theology molded by anthropology or theology presented as a promise of a glory to come, with no links to the task of present channels, the *angeloi,* and the saints, divine deputies on earth, as the Book of Revelation and the early church speak of them, messengers working some of God's will into the destiny and consciousness of mankind.

In lifting out Martin Luther's ways of communicating his experiences of the invisible, and especially the present power of the mystical Christ, we are doing three things. First, we are pointing out the essentialness of the mystical in the Reformer's justification experience. Second, it is noted that this mystical element has been almost eclipsed by too much objective ratiocination in the past. Third, we submit that Luther's spiritual experience is likely to be better understood and meet with more sympathetic response in contemporary revolts against the aridity of mere intellectualism.

\* \* \* \* \* \*

Experiential piety has of course sometimes turned into legalism. But we tend to toss out the baby with the bath water by speaking pejoratively of piety-grounded religion. "Pietism," derived from "piety," has become a heresy in mainstream theology and practically every seminary graduate leaves his alma mater with the adjective "pietistic" in his bag of bad words. Yet, let us not forget that no faith and no true Christian ethics exists without a measure of prayer-borne spirituality, i.e., piety. Arndt, Spener and Francke— persons of piety in the history of Lutheranism—correctly counted themselves partakers of the kind of experienced grace which Luther had called *sapientia experimentalis.* Their piety and the piety of many later Lutheran "pietists" lie within, not outside, Luther's perception of faith. If mystical theology according to Luther is experience, that is to say felt presence of the gracious God, then the tradition of piety—the nucleus of "pietism"—no doubt coincided with Luther's thought about life in God. But, alas, alienated by its outgrowths of judgmental legalism, the church has rather opted for the descriptions of faith which turn revelation into dogmatic intellectualism.

\*  \*  \*  \*  \*  \*

Placing Luther's spirituality in relief—as we have done in this book—does not imply advocacy of "emotionalism." Luther used the word "feeling" when he wrote of the necessary accompaniment to the historical faith called true or inner faith. To him the feeling component of faith did not spell emotionalism, if this term be taken to imply mandatory emotional states of excitement in an order of salvation. Feeling-in-faith was rather an experience of God's comforting presence. This experience was logically unregistrable just as love is unregistrable. Yet the inner "knowing" made the difference between a true theologian and an unauthentic one. In this sense the *Schwärmer*, those who enjoyed the psychological emotions of their God-immersions, embraced a false spirituality. They *relied* on emotions and knew little about the feeling which accompanies the use of external spiritual symbols in the church. This feeling engenders humility; the emotional states tend to become self-serving and create self-righteousness.

The mystical life of the soul in God is in Luther's view the subjective, other side of the objective symbols. There are theologies which insist that the story they recount is a story strictly confined to the objective, the ordinary and the public. Our discourse suggests that this teaching should be amended to include the mystical dimension without which little justice is done to Luther's theological thought. This is to say, the story of Christ is by no means merely a drama relatable in objective terms; nor does it deal solely with ordinary conditions; nor is it so public that everyone apprehends it. When the gospel penetrates man's objective consciousness through a spiritual Presence hitherto unsuspected, it transmits a joy and an awe which are subjectively appropriated, contain intimations of the extraordinary and belong to the personal-private realm. To put it differently, Martin Luther's thought cannot be reduced to purely objective verbalizations inside ordinary commonsense frameworks, intelligible to all and in that sense "public."

The objective and the public dimension is doubtless a part of any theology of incarnation. We have seen how important the external symbols were for Martin Luther. But, we repeat, Luther's reflections on the condition of a justified sinner reckon with a world beyond the historical and the objective, experienced as the Presence of the "mystical Christ." To Luther, the *promise* of freedom makes no spiritual sense without the *presence* of the Lord. In every prayer to God and in every response from God the objective is vivified by the subjective, the ordinary world touched by extraordinary revelation and the public surface of the kerygma given life and meaning by a personal-private impulse. Through the mystical experience—prayer included—the non-rational is infused into the rational. Systematizing the kerygma is a necessary theological-logical enterprise. But the inspiration for such reflection is mystical and therefore trans-logical. In this sense the criteria of scientific knowledge must be inadequate for theological reflection and we are mistaken if we let them become the sole arbiters in our explications of revelation. Luther keeps on reminding us of this by placing such emphasis on "mystical incarnation" and by constantly reminding readers of the limited value of "historical faith."

Martin Luther's thought about God's grace was inspired by mystical intimations. Numinous reality informed his reflection even in periods when his main preoccupation had to be dogmatic controversy. "The supernatural" was inseparable from "the natural" in his world, not as a name for a "God-out-there" but as an experienced dimension not comprehendible by senses and logic alone.

\*   \*   \*   \*   \*   \*

It has been argued on these pages that Luther's terms for numinous intimations and his obvious acceptance of the supernatural cannot be removed from theology with impunity, as contemporary thought about Luther largely does. Many Luther interpreters suggest, as we have seen, that the Reformer's claims regarding the supernatural and its mystical work on man's psyche were time-bound and mirrored the lore of his era, now rendered obsolete by man's increasing mastery of the natural world.

True, Luther shared with his time that lack of knowledge about our physical existence which is sometimes translated into "superstition," i.e., the abject, irrational, magic-producing attitude to a supernatural dimension. But we "moderns" have been tutored by scientific materialism to classify as "superstition" *all* claims of visionary and clairaudial information or dreams and poetic or prophetic inspiration. Since such phenomena are beyond measurement in the conventional sense they have been rejected as sources of "knowledge." The result is that *all* manifestations of supernatural life in Luther's thought have been ignored as time-bound superstition. Exceptions are made, however. It is generally recognized that Christ in some sense "lives," at least in the sacraments, and that his resurrection did in some manner occur. The two latter propositions are of course essential for any respectable treatment of the gospel. Yet, none of these concessions is germane to a theological framework which rules out mystical theology as a part of true evangelical theology. For whatever drawbacks there are to the use of the adjective "supernatural," it does convey transcendental overtones without which the interpretation of faith becomes locked up in scientific materialism. In the last analysis the supernatural and the natural may indeed coincide. But for pedagogical reasons we shall have to restore the word "supernatural" to theological legitimacy. It does betoken the fact that biblical revelation is in part an invasion from the para-normal. The mystic has always known that his feeling of God's presence and power is instilled by a Holy Spirit who

exists *for* and *in* the natural world but, because of this, also
*beyond* the human and the natural world. Martin Luther's
statements concerning mystical incarnation, about the feeling
of God's closeness, and about the healing power of the mystical Christ should not therefore be excised as references
to superstitious medieval lore. For these statements echo biblical reality and are consonant with prophetic mystical experience throughout the ages.

*   *   *   *   *   *

Was Luther's language about the mystical really in an essential sense the same as that of the medieval mystics? Are
not those theologians right who assert that Luther's use of
mystical terminology reflected only an apparent dependence on
otherwise unbiblical and unevangelical symbols of God's self-
disclosure? The point of our argument has been that such a
theological reading of Luther ignores two facts. First, Luther's
language about mysticism did not only consist of assaults
against the Schwärmer. This is to say, theological analyses
based on this supposition misinterpret Luther's attitude to the
mystical. Second, Luther assessed mystical experience from
within his own spiritual knowledge of how man becomes justified by faith. The gauge was God's take-over in a person who
ceases to seek after self-righteousness. By this standard some
of the medieval mystics Luther read were congenial, others
not. Luther openly declared his inner kinship with those who
had tasted the bitterness of the inner reduction and enjoyed
the rapture of justification. He shared with them the feeling
of God's presence. He sensed the absence of this feeling in
scholasticism. He pointed out that justification is more than
a forensic declaration of forgiveness. To Luther God-in-Christ
was present so that in some way the forgiven sinner could
feel it.

Luther's inner *sensorium* for kinship with some writers
who preceded him by more than a century should be taken
seriously. It seems inappropriate to censor his positive verdicts
about mystics on the grounds that modern scholarship can
assess his judgments in this regard better than he could.

We have discussed attempts at placing mystics congenial to Luther's inner experience in theological frameworks which supposedly violate biblical truth about God's grace and man's sin. On this reading the two mystics Luther cherished in a special way as spiritual brothers fall short of the mark. Consequently Luther is assigned to one theological world, these mystics to another. The word for the one is "salvation," for the other "self-salvation." However, instead of letting our peculiar intellectualistic standard determine that Luther's positive appraisal of mystical companions depended on a limited theological perspective, which modernity can correct on the Reformer's behalf, the time has come to acknowledge that Luther indeed knew whereof he spoke.

Just a few sentences from Johann Tauler about the relationship between the Savior and the saved render this plain. Not all mystics will receive their due by being consigned to one major category of systematic thought, in this case the one which Protestant Reformation interpreters regard as self-salvation theology. Tauler wrote (and we quote from pages 45 and 94 in the Georg Hofmann edition):

> The Father of the house is our Lord Jesus Christ. His house is heaven and earth, purgatory and hell. He saw that all of nature was confused and his lovely vineyard was lying fallow. Human nature, created to possess this vineyard, had gone astray. . . . Jesus Christ is his Father's inheritor. We are co-inheritors. The Son has received all from the Father. The Father has given all things into His hands. . . . Whenever you ascribe the divine to yourself, you change the divine into the creaturely and obscure the divine. . . .

Here we find both appreciation of the objective deed of God-in-Christ and knowledge of man's waywardness. It was against such a background that both Luther and Tauler (as well as other mystics) waxed eloquent about the joy-filled Presence, about the nearness of God, closer than your clothes, yes, closer than your skin, as Luther once expressed it.

In his appreciation of Tauler Luther implicitly agrees with the mystic's basic paradox (expressed on pages 567 and 594 in the above work) : that conformation to God moves between our nature as created by God, and thus good, and our nature as rebellious will, and thus evil. The consonance between Luther and his mystical soul-mates lies in the *experience* of justification, not primarily in *cognition* about an old biblical truth revisited.

\* \* \* \* \* \*

We have argued that Luther's mystical theology pervaded his entire life. His later use of the term "trustlike faith" in lieu of the medieval "synteresis" and his attacks against mystical Schwärmer are in the nature of changing tactics rather than reversed strategy. Even after having become an "institution," and after much disillusionment about God's possibilities with man, Luther was aware of the power-filled Presence. The impingement of angelic and demonic powers upon a Christian and Christ's mystical presence in holy communion, in baptism and in intercessory prayer for healing were potentialities of faith that Luther integrated with his theological considerations throughout his life. In other words, it is questionable whether changes in his terminology can serve as corroboration of the theory that Luther left the mystical-experimental behind him as he moved deeper into his Reformation task. In fact, Luther as a man of spirituality gives us little reason to hold this theory at all.

\* \* \* \* \* \*

The objection might be raised that mystical intimation, although doubtless part of the phenomenon of religion, is not only subjective but also non-observable according to scientific yardsticks of repeatability, hence it should be excluded from theological quests. This view of the task of theology ignores the undeniable fact that all true revelation is based on extraordinary, non-repeatable data. The revelatory event as supernatural occurrence is at the center of the dogma which develops around it. We preach and do our Bible study on the basis of paranormal activity, that which may be termed invasions into the determinate and natural. If we think about it a little further we shall find that the reason why we are drawn to the gospel of and about Christ is precisely these links between the natural and the supernatural. Something exceeding the purely human is communicated. The attraction of Jesus and Peter and Paul and many other spiritual leaders, including Martin Luther, grows out of the message "from abroad," from dimensions that existed before, exist simultaneously with and will exist after the material dispensation in the world of five senses. If the gospel of Christ were a mere account of observations that may be fully accommodated by our common sense, both adventure and comfort would evaporate from it. But because of the extra-ordinary, the numinous and the miraculous, our imagination and longing are constantly stirred. If ordinary spiritual curiosity were the driving factor in this attraction, this in itself would be evidence of the validity of our contention that the extra-ordinary, the supersensible, and the para-psychic are bells that chime the spiritual summons in the gospel.

Therefore, in our thinking about revelation we do injustice to the subject by excluding mystical stirrings. They may not be repeatable, thus not fitting objects for exact scientific accounts. However, for the theological quest, they make all the difference. They are like lightning in a dark night, suddenly illuminating the landscape and quickly gone, but the illumination has let the wanderer see the lay of the land and the run of the road. The experience is fleeting and isolated yet decisive for the total view and the direction of the course.

As noted, Martin Luther evidently had experiences of a mystical nature, which not only engendered a feeling of Christ's presence but also at times communicated a sense of being wrought up into an out-of-the-body state. Although he never made experiences of the ineffable a *conditio sine qua non* for the faithful, nor included them in his didactic instructions about Christian faith, they permeated his belief about

the reality of the grace of God. It was not just words when
he assured his readers that he did not merely propound theological *loci* but conveyed experience of the living God. Because
of the latter the former took on life.

In much the same manner, yet in less intense forms, each
praying Christian has become acquainted with the mystical
life which lends spiritual meaning and power to the external
symbols, and miraculously carries us through seemingly impossible quandaries. Most of the time we do not consciously
register the new knowledge. Indeed, we, as true western rationalists, may brush off intimations of a mystical presence.
But there are indications in this latter half of the 20th century that human consciousness is awakening to the call of a
still small voice and prepared to recognize that knowledge is
also acquired through various forms of non-rational intimation.

A new look at Martin Luther's experiences as a person of
spirituality (present in the midst of his often earthy ways)
will perhaps meet with a more sensitive understanding in this
age than in the mechanistic one out of which we are moving.
The new age embraces more people who are prepared to listen
to the overtones of the gospel and extend the adventure of faith
into "the knowledge of the mystery of God, Christ, in whom
all the treasures of knowledge are hidden." For there is, as
St. Paul pointed out, a "knowledge" which grows out of faith
and mystery and surpasses the "knowledge" of logical argumentation.

*   *   *   *   *   *

Deep within modern man a rebellion is taking place against
the all-pervasive rationality of his existence. We see the revolt
in many fields of secular search for truth. We have evidence
of it in the charismatic renewal within the churches. The other
side of this revolution could be a contact with the Holy Spirit,
or at least a potential prolegomenon of this advent. Not that
Christian evangelism and Christian preaching would have to
rely on a change in the scientific climate. After all, a "parapsychological" extension of man's knowledge can be, as it

were, sequestered by materialism, as evidenced by much modern research into the para-normal. Yet it is of considerable moment and a challenge to Christian evangelism that psychological, sociological and philosophical enquiries into the nature of man are abandoning the exclusively rationalistic creed of our Enlightenment tradition. According to this creed man's rationality will progressively gain ground from the so-called primitive, until our existence is harnessed by logic and common sense.

But, says "modern man" in his revolt, perhaps our wholeness as human beings implies an advance toward the primitive, a revival of forces the conquest of which we thought was the prerequisite for true humanity. These forces express themselves through intuition, inspiration, intimation from transrational and paranormal dimensions. They lead us to the belief that human wholeness includes suggestions from the unconscious and the divine. Poetic, artistic and prophetic insight has of course always suggested that knowledge is more than rational summaries of external observations. But western man considered this proposal a threat to his world of what Luther referred to as merely "gefasste Gedanken," rationally circumscribed thought. Modern man—or should we say "post-modern man"—questions the suppositions of rationalism. Yet this does not mean that our attitude to the extraordinary should be irrational. The non-rational flows into the rational. It is when rational dealings with the non-rational become dogmatism that we must speak critically of rationalistic thinking.

Psychologist Carl Jung has opened doors into the coming age by his examination of the unconscious and the role of universal symbolism in dreams. Jung proposed that some intuitive knowledge is likely to originate in worlds beyond the conscious and the unconscious. His quest points toward a scientific psychology freed from Freudian naturalism. Jung said that the only and central drive is not sexually colored libido (Freud), nor the drive for power (Adler), but that the religious urge is, in addition to the others, an essential, autonomous force. We find in Jung's psychology a "modern man" who lives in a symbiosis of objective, sophisticated rationality and subjective, primitive religious feeling. The latter is not passé and never can be.

In the field of parapsychology observations are being made which nullify concepts of "reality" hitherto determinative for assessment of the parasensible. Extrasensory perception and manifestations of the Divine Spirit are being explored as areas which add to knowledge. In his work *The Roots of Coincidence,* Arthur Koestler presents evidence to support his thesis that parapsychology is growing increasingly "scientific" and at the same time theoretical physics is becoming increasingly "occult." The mechanical metaphor of our existence, the clockwork image, does not serve us well any more. Physicist Jeans is quoted by Koestler as saying that the universe is not a machine but a thought. A physical reality resting on thought—such a view may in part illumine long-embraced traditional persuasions about the force of prayer and about unity inside one global and cosmic body. Indeed, the study of thought as vibration might provide pragmatic proof that there is no neutrality, ever, in our human existence, precisely as Jesus Christ proclaimed. Scientific studies of parasensible layers of life are—in part with the aid of established scientific tools, in part by recourse to new instruments—liberating western rationalism from its captivity in quantification of reality.

The contemporary revolt against reason as a tyrant extends into our view of creation. Man's impact on his surrounding is shown to be mental, not only physical. Nature proves to be pan-psychic deep into its minutest components. Thought and prayer have an impact on the shape of so-called inanimate objects and so-called soul-less beings. Only a few decades ago people would have smiled incredulously and condescendingly at Peter Tompkin's *The Secret Life of Plants.* In the latter part of the 20th century we are ready to concede the possibility that man operates on different levels simultaneously and therefore through his consciousness makes invisible imprints on nature—and fellow-men—around him. Benedict of Nursia,

St. Francis of Assisi and Pierre Teilhard de Chardin, although representing minority traditions, may prove to be the mentors of future environmentalism.

Even contemporary sociological investigations have been influenced by the sea-change within post-modern man. Sociological investigations have traditionally employed models from the natural sciences. The ideal has been a detached, value-less examination. On this accounting religious phenomena are depicted as, essentially, projections of anthropological and sociological conditions, that is to say, exclusively as emanations of the material world, crystallizations of the human self, not as partial intimations from an extra-terrestrial dimension.

But during the past decade sociologists have come to accept the need and necessity for personal value and passionate engagement on the part of the examiner. There are indeed sociological scholars who tend to ascribe extra-terrestrial influence to certain sociological phenomena. Such a scholar is Peter Berger who in his book *A Rumor of Angels* suggests that certain pervasive human postures are not only transcendent symbols but manifestations of transcendental, supernatural reality.

It is, in my opinion, essential to see the charismatic renewals in the Christian church against the background of this deeper realization of the nature of knowledge. The western world is engaged in a revolt against reason, or, better, against the monopoly of conceptualization. Western human consciousness is abandoning its proud ambition to crown reason Lord of creation. Thinking-with-the-heart is emerging as a *bona fide* activity besides the predominant ideal, thinking-with-the-head.

*      *      *      *      *      *

Charismatic experiences of our age represent the trans-human counterpoint to the new discoveries of human transcendence. These experiences are more than a fad. They herald an age when religious man to a greater extent will recognize that he is part of and channel for invisible, dynamic, ever present Spirit. It will dawn upon us that Christ uttered literal truth when he said that he would always be with those who go to the source of grace in his name. Furthermore, the biblical experience of the Savior's presence is not limited to biblical times. His presence can always issue in works of power, gifts of grace ("charismata"), such as those described by St. Paul in 1 Corinthians 12.

When Haag's authoritative *Bible Dictionary* declares, concerning spiritual gifts, that the church is institutional, not charismatic, it describes a traditional posture rather than biblical experience. The church is no doubt called upon to serve as God's external medium and a conveyor of grace through institutional order (baptism, holy communion, and preaching of the Word). But the church is thereby committing itself to the charismatic power of the Holy Spirit, she is not confining the presence of the Holy Spirit to her institutional orders.

We are reminded of Luther's words about the life-giving presence of God-in-Christ under persecution. If a tyrant throws a Christian into a cesspool (and Luther did not choose examples like this one for unimpressive reasons; his life with God was frequently tested by threats to his earthly life), God would not be God if he could not sustain the afflicted one right there. Were this not the case, wrote Luther, we would have to assume that God could be experienced only on the institutional premises, in a stately cathedral.

The presence of Christ was (and is) consequently not dependent on a liturgical setting or institutional arrangements, however essential these may be. When Luther was on his way to the awesome encounter with the authorities in Worms, he testified to the cheering presence of Christ which made him peculiarly dauntless. We should rest assured that Luther relied on more than an influential memory of Christ and on more than the performance of a sacramental rite. His experience was charismatic, if by this term we mean the inner knowledge of the present Christ.

\*     \*     \*     \*     \*     \*

The charismatic renewal is in essence a recovery of the New

Testament experience that the Holy Spirit bestows new forms of life in the Christian. In this sense it can also be termed mystical.

When we speak of Martin Luther's mystical theology we are no doubt aided by contemporary experiences of the presence of God which go under the names of mysticism and charismatic Christianity. But it is important to keep in mind that we are also asked to "test the spirits" under the tutelage of Christ. Teaching, wonder-working faith, healing, miracles, prophecy, the gift of distinguishing true spirits from false, the gift of speaking in tongues and the gift of interpreting what the exuberant tongue-speaker utters—all of this is more or less associated with a feeling of divine presence. Yet these gifts are worth little in themselves if they do not create humility. *Homo mendax*, man as self-aggrandizer, and therefore mendacious, can emerge in the most dedicated souls, perhaps as pride among theological proclaimers and as smug doctrinalism among experiential pentecostalists. We should not forget that when St. Paul has discussed the charismatic gifts, he advises us that the greatest of all the gifts is charity. (See the transition between 1 Cor. 12 and 13.)

This is a truth which brings proportion to the current interest in the occult (e.g., astrology and spiritism, their significance and inadequacy from the aspect of faith in Christ) and also to the various forms of charismatic life, (e.g., glossolalia, spiritual healing and exorcism, their significance and inadequacy from the aspect of faith in Christ). Charity flows out of a center which Luther called the Sun of Righteousness, Christ, who is the spiritual force behind the sun of our celestial system. "Baptism of the Holy Spirit" refers to no one single individual spiritual gift—which especially the glossolalists tend to overlook. "Baptism of the Holy Spirit" is experience of "the births" of Christ in the soul, as Luther expressed it. This view of the work of the Holy Spirit embraces the presence of Christ as dynamic force and loving support.

The mystical dimension of faith is the essence of the charismatic renewal. Unbiblical and unspiritual aberrations in this "movement" provide no adequate reason for Christian believers not to take it seriously. Martin Luther's mystical-charismatic consciousness and his practice of the presence is a reminder of the Third Article of the Creed which many of us have intellectualized and institutionalized. Luther would no doubt have recognized and greeted with joy the current evidence of the power of the Holy Spirit, both in Protestant and Roman Catholic circles. Had he known more about the Eastern Orthodox he would also have acknowledged their sacramental mysticism. In *Mysticism, Its Meaning and Message,* Georgia Harkness writes: Many are now being "touched and transformed by the vital sense of the Presence of God through the Jesus they adore." Today this ought to be welcomed by all those who, like Luther in his time, seek and find the God who is both the *tremendum* which reduces us to nought and the *fascinosum* which makes our spirit soar.

\* \* \* \* \* \*

In this book there was but little space for the relationship between mystical life in God and moral fruits, between mysticism and ethics. I submit that this relationship is paramount in Luther's thought. It is important that this be pointed out.

It is important, first, because mystics and those who, like Luther, adhere to mystical theology, have traditionally been relegated to the quietistic camp. A mystic, according to the theological slogan, is so concerned with immersion in God and flight from the senses that he or she pays no heed to social realities. The adjective "gnostic," pejoratively colored, often appears in the context.

It is important, secondly, because a good many contemporary Christian ethicists tend to describe their undertaking as "rational decision-making" delimited by sociological, anthropological and humanitarian concerns.

The slogan that a mystic is by definition a non-doer is refuted by the lives of many mystics. Even a cursory glance at the history of Lutheran pietism should correct the error. Most missionary undertakings, issuing from the "pietistic" experience of God's gracious presence, also disprove the long-lived fallacy. The pietist's mystical encounter with God has been translated into social charity in "mother lands" and practical attention to ordinary human needs in traditional "mission lands." Georgia Harkness in the above work avers that only erroneous theological and historical thinking poses a categorical distinction between mystics and practical doers. She writes:

> Mystical devotion in its best sense is found within and not in disassociation from the total stream of human events. It may appear in visions, illuminations, and even in a transitory but rapturous sense of union with deity, and still be mysticism. But when it breaks radically with the concrete world of reality, suspect it! In any case, the surest proof of its reality is what ensues in the day-by-day living of the individual within his total universe.

In order to illustrate her case Dr. Harkness devotes a chapter to "twentieth century persons" who, although mystics, in no way isolated themselves from social realities. She mentions Frank Laubach, Toyohiko Kagawa, Pierre Teilhard de Chardin and Dag Hammarskjöld. Many modern charismatics could be added to the list (although some conversions doubtless lead to social quietism). The encounter with the divine engendered a challenge "to make the world a substructure to a better world."

Our second point about the intimate links between the mystical and the moral concerns the tendency among Christian ethicists to render the enterprise a mere "rational decision-making."

In some kind of exaggerated reverence for the academic postures which we have described as scientific materialism or scientism, these ethicists shy away from strong indications in the Bible that the moral life is an effluent of the mystical life in God, and that the contemplation of the words of and about the Lord engender moral force. Instead, the ethical analyst prefers to deal with the Bible in terms of generalized themes on the supposition that the content of individual passages is well-known anyhow. There is no doubt also a certain fear that one may be accused of using biblical ethical injunctions as a kind of moral fundamentalism.

This incursion of the secular into the treatment of Christian morality eclipses the mystical character of the biblical word. Words in the Bible related to Christ vibrate the self-same Christ. Luther spoke of divine words in the Holy Writ as "sacraments." He did so precisely because he knew of their vibrancy. Distilling them into general themes removes the moral analyst from the Presence which the words of God communicate, right through form-critical and redactionistic considerations.

The tendency to consider Christian ethics solely a form of rational decision-making conceals the biblical experience that Jesus Christ is present in sacrament and personal piety. This aspect is missing in numerous Christian ethical treatments of moral issues. Jesus is described as model, paradigm, norm, teacher, principle, provider of redemption. He is all of this but he is preponderantly the mystical Christ present in and among his friends. Rather than being rooted in rational decision-making Christian ethics is based on a Lord who provides strength for moral responsibility. No doubt we have to apply scientific verifiability codes and dress our opinions in rational language. But the ultimate source of moral responsibility is the Lord's mystical presence rather than rational calculations.

Does this mystical approach make any difference as far as Christian ethical deliberation is concerned? Most decidedly so. Instead of being guided only by the calculated prudence of the humanly possible, the person mystically communing with Christ is in touch with a world which gives strength for the humanly impossible.

H. Richard Niebuhr gave his readers an often unnoticed hint of this truth when at the end of his classical *Christ and Culture* he came to the question of "the surd." The surd beyond all human calculations is the source of the humanly impossible, the heart of God himself. When everything crumbled around him and human prudence failed, Jesus Christ turned in prayer to the divine surd and received power to carry the moral burden. Only so does the impossible happen and only so do moral burdens become light burdens.

The ethics of mere cognitive considerations has little understanding for the mystery of cross-bearing, turning the other cheek, walking the second mile, aiding the thankless, in a word, vicariousness. We theorize about the cross but few of us choose the unpopular or uncomfortable ethical option in the fields of private charity and socio-moral action.

Completing the complete deed of Christ demands incessant prayer. Incessant prayer is a mystical enterprise. New vision emerges from it. Through incessant prayer one may receive ever renewed strength to work in moral tasks which transcend the summations of the possible submitted by social sciences. Why do so many sessions among Christian ethicists in the western world begin without a prayer? Does the fact mirror our secret assumption that the invisible should and can have nothing to do with cognitive pursuits? Would a public prayer compromise our stated desire to be academically acceptable?

Not from an intellectual supposition of imputed grace, not from a conceptual schema of the meaning of revelation, but from Living Presence in sacrament and personal communion with God comes the strength for cross-bearing moral life.

Against the background of this realization Martin Luther spoke of moral fruits growing out of the justified life. Justified man's hiddenness-in-God is the wellspring of ethics, according to Luther. The outward way in which Christians and non-Christians do their daily round is likely to be similar, he thought. But the real difference is tremendous. By his communion with God in prayer the Christian is a transmitter of moral force from God, we read in Luther's comments on Galatians. This force is no less potent because it is invisible.

Here we touch upon the mystery of the grain of wheat which must die for life's sake. The meditations and supplications of a person in communion with God are so essential that, wrote the Reformer in his book on John 14-16, "no city or country would enjoy peace," grain would not grow in the fields, people would not recover from illness, the world would indeed be unprotected without the hidden life of Christians in the mystical Christ. This means that no one can shoulder the Christian moral commitment without recourse to the mystical surd behind the ordinary logic of things.

Others rightly speak of Luther as a theological renewer, as a reshaper of language, as a poet and musician, as a politician, as a person of commonsensical modernity, or as an earthy, vituperative anti-saint. He was a crystal with many facets. In this book we have met Luther as a person of spirituality, living in Christ, yearning for Christ's entry into the soul, knowing about God's presence, experiencing healing grace. Our focus on "the mystical Christ" and "the mystical incarnation" in Luther's testimony has brought us to the center and the secret of his battle. Perhaps we recognize here our own longing for wholeness in God and usefulness among men. Moreover, our intimations may be confirmed to the effect that God is not far from any of us.

# Notes

## Introduction

1. *D. Martin Luthers Werke*, Weimarausgabe (Weimar: Böhlaus), 1; 341, 3. This work will be cited hereafter as *W*. Martin Luther's letters in the same Weimarausgabe will be cited as *WB* and the Table Talks in the Weimarausgabe as *WT*. Available English translations: *Luther's Works* (St. Louis and Philadelphia: Concordia Publishing House & Fortress Press, 1955- ), abbre. *LW*. On Luther's expression, "mystical theology" see *W* 9; 98, 20, also *W* 7; 546, 27 and 9: "Experience" is "the school of the Holy Spirit" where we can "taste and experience." The Word of God must be understood as a medium for such experience. Erich Vogelsang deals with Luther's Bernard-influenced definition of "mysticism" in "Luther und die Mystik," *Luther-Jahrbuch 1937* (Amsterdam: John Benjamins N.V., 1967), pp. 32-54.

The problem treated in this Introduction is also discussed in two articles I have recently published: "Luther and the Mystical," *The Lutheran Quarterly*, XXVI, Number 3, August 1974, pp. 316-329, and "On the Relationship between Mystical Faith and Moral Life in Luther's Thought," *Bulletin*, Lutheran Theological Seminary, Gettysburg, vol. 55, Number 1, February 1975, pp. 21-35.

2. On Melanchthon's "intellectualism" see for instance Holsten Fagerberg, *A New Look at the Lutheran Confessions* (St. Louis: Concordia Publishing House, 1972), pp. 47-48. Cf. Robert Stupperich, *Melanchthon* (Philadelphia: Westminster Press, 1960), p. 13: Luther was moved by the mystical inwardness of Tauler and *Theologia Germanica* but "we hear of nothing similar from Melanchthon." Cf. also Michael Rogness, *Reformer without Honor* (Minneapolis: Augsburg Publishing House, 1969), p. 138: Melanchthon stressed "imputed righteousness," made justification abstract and separated justification from sanctification.

Erich Vogelsang maintains that what the church lost through Melanchthonian intellectualism was in a sense recovered by the nature-mysticism of Goethe and romanticism. In the 20th century the realities of "mystery" as direct experience of the divine "again knock at the doors of the church. Will we receive power both to conquer the mystical errors and the Melanchthonian onesidedness . . . ?" See Erich Vogelsang, "Die Unio mystica bei Luther," *Archiv für Religionsgeschichte*, Vol. XXXV, 1938 (Leipzig: Karl W. Hiersemann), p. 80.

3. The philosopher-physicist James Jeans has written: "Today there is a wide measure of agreement . . . that the stream of knowledge is heading toward a non-mechanical reality; the universe begins to look more like a great thought than a great machine. Mind no longer appears as an accidental intruder into the realm of matter; we are beginning to suspect that we ought rather to hail it as the creator and governor of the realm of matter." James Jeans, *The Mysterious Universe* (New York: Macmillan Co., 1932), p. 186.

4. Rudolf Otto, *The Idea of the Holy* (New York: Oxford University Press, 1960), p. 108 *et passim*.

# Chapter 1

1. Abraham Calovius, *Hypomnemata* (Wittenborg, 1664), Section III, "episagma."

2. The allusion made here to a divergence between Lutheran and Calvinistic concepts of law does not imply that Calvinistic orthodoxy was more open to mystical modes than Lutheran orthodoxy. The sole intention is to illustrate the conceptual-propositional character of "the Lutheran school" which prevented a genuine appreciation of Luther's mystical interest.

3. In his works on the Reformation Karl Holl frequently indicated that he saw no fundamental difference between the medieval mystics and the medieval scholastics. As we shall see, the evidence in many cases leads to the opposite conclusion. Medieval mystics often openly looked askance at scholastics.

4. Let it be reemphasized, however, that this fact did not imply a more open attitude to mystical experience on the part of Calvinism.

5. *Grundtlicher Beweis, dass die Calvinische Irthumb* . . . (Wittenberg, 1664), p. 109.

6. *Ibid.*, pp. 674-675.

7. *Ibid.*, pp. 712, 715. "Is it not enough then that they . . . know their faith in Christ from the inner testimony of the Holy Spirit or within themselves?" The answer: "No right, firm, persuasion" can be based on such individualism.

8. *Ibid.*, pp. 721-722.

9. *Die Religion in Geschichte und Gegenwart* (hereafter referred to as *RGG*), (Wittenberg: J. C. B. Mohr, 1957), 1, 1587. "Calovius equated faith and the doctrinal formula."

10. Heinrich Schmid, *Die Dogmatik der evangelisch-lutherischen Kirche*, 3rd ed. (Frankfurt am Main: Herder and Zimmer, 1853), p. xvi. ET: *The Doctrinal Theology of the Evangelical Lutheran Church*, trans. and ed. from the 6th German edition by Charles A. Hay and Henry E. Jacobs (Minneapolis: Augsburg Publishing House, reprint 1961), p. 12.

11. *Ibid.*, pp. 374-375. ET: 480-486.

12. For a discussion of Lutheran orthodoxy's notion of *unio mystica* including Quenstedt's part in it, see Vogelsang, "Luther und die Mystik," pp. 63-64.

13. Schmid, p. 355. Schmid's use of the terms *ecstasis* and *raptus* reveals no acquaintance with Luther's employment of them. Especially in the second part of this book we shall return to the question of "raptus" as it is related by Luther to justification by faith.

14. Ernst Luthardt, *Kompendium i dogmatik*, Swed. trans., (Stockholm: A. V. Carlson, 1879), p. 40.

15. *Ibid.*, pp. 260, 266. "Knowledge . . . precedes will . . . in contradistinction to mysticism which lets purification precede illumination."

16. Franz Pieper and J. T. Mueller, *Christliche Dogmatik* (St. Louis: Missouri Synod, 1946), pp. 60-61. The quotation from Luther is taken from his "Reply to the libellous pamphlet of the King of England," *W* 23; 28, 12-14, 1527: "For the sake of the doctrine no one is so great that I cannot consider him less than a water bubble."

17. *Ibid.*, reference to *W* 34, 2; 527, 1531.

18. Pieper and Mueller, p. 62. "Modern theology must draw a line right through itself should it again wish to be in touch with real Christian certainty."

# Chapter 2-A

1. The nomenclature for categorization of different theological schools can never be wholly accurate. The last century saw the birth of a great many theological proposals which mediated between Christ and culture, spoke of Christianity as incentive toward human potentiality and in more or less qualified terms reckoned with man's goodness. One of these movements was "mediation theology" which rose to an apogee through Schleiermacher and whose later exponents were Dorner, Rothe, Neander and Martensen, among others. Ritschl belongs in part to this school. These thinkers had little understanding for "mysticism," although one might have thought that Schleiermacher would have shown interest. That was not the case. His rationalistic and secular audience presumably molded his language about mysticism. See Friedrich Schleiermacher, *Der christliche Glaube*, Vols. I & II (Berlin: W. de Gruyter & Co., 1960), Vol. I, pp. 204-211; Vol. II, pp. 93-97. ET: *The Christian Faith*, ed. by H. R. Mackintosh and J. S. Stewart (Edinburgh: T & T Clark, 1960), Vol. I; 170-184, Vol. II; 425-431.

2. Robert F. Davidson, *Rudolf Otto's Interpretation of Religion* (Princeton University Press, 1947), p. 42.

3. Albrecht Ritschl, *Geschichte des Pietismus in der reformierten Kirche* (Bonn: Adolph Marcus, 1880), pp. 36-61. See also Albrecht Ritschl, *Die christliche Lehre von der Rechtfertigung und Versöhnung* (Bonn: Adolph Marcus, 1882), p. 195. ET: *The Christian Doctrine of Justification and Reconciliation*, ed. by H. R. Mackintosh and A. B. Macaulay (Clifton, N.J.: Reference Book Publishers, Inc., 1966), p. 180.

4. *RGG*, III, 433. Holl rendered Luther "more modern or consistent than he was."

5. Karl Holl, *Was verstand Luther unter Religion?* (Tübingen: J. C. B. Mohr, 1917), p. 5.

6. *Ibid.*

7. *Ibid.*, pp. 21-22.

8. Karl Holl, *Gesammelte Aufsätze zur Kirchengeschichte, I, Luther*, 2nd, 3rd ed. (Tübingen: J. C. B. Mohr, 1923), pp. 10-11. "Romanic mysticism comes into the picture only as a counter-position to the Reformation." "In German mysticism one observes the same tenor . . . as in Duns Scotus," i.e., mysticism is scholasticism. The validity of this assertion (mysticism and scholasticism are identical) will be discussed in Chap. 5. It is also mentioned in connection with Ebeling's view of mysticism.

9. *Ibid.*, p. 12. Holl did not substantiate these assertions by reference to specific documentation. It is conceivable that Holl's picture of Tauler was somewhat dependent on the idea that different forms of mysticism comprised the same basic fallacies, from a Protestant point of view. Yet, as will be indicated later in the present paper, Tauler's experience and view of sin were rather similar to Luther's notion of sin.

10. *Ibid.*, p. 27.

11. On Luther and Gerson, see Hermann Hering, *Die Mystik Luthers* (Leipzig: J. L. Hinrich, 1879), p. 9. On Luther's reference to Gerson as regards *Anfechtung*, see *WT* 1; 495, 33-35, 1530's.

12. Holl, *Gesammelte* . . . , p. 40. "The reintroduction of this teaching [on God's wrath] . . . means . . . a contradistinction to mysticism, to which the world seemed only like a shadow." Holl cited Luther from *W* 40, 1; 371, 13, 1535: "Deus odit peccatum et peccatorem, et necesse, quia alioqui deus iniustus et amator peccati" ("God hates the sin and the sinner, of necessity so, since otherwise God would be unjust and a lover of sin"—author's trans.). *LW* 26; 235. Holl: Luther here "took the reality of the world seriously."

13. *W* 10, 1, 2; 388, 29-30, 1526.

14. *Johann Taulers Predigten*, ed. Georg Hofmann (Freiburg: Herder, 1961), p. 361 and p. 364.

15. *Ibid.*, p. 321.

16. Holl, *Gesammelte* . . . , p. 60. Holl: "To Luther this idea was always incomprehensible."

17. *J. Taulers* . . . , p. 329: "The righteous have gone through . . . fear of God." *Ibid.*, p. 405: "In the gigantic distance between tiny man and the great awesome God it is established that man must pronounce God with fearful trembling."

18. *Ibid.*, p. 41. Tauler: "A person who has erected an obstacle, whatever it may be, however small, that person is unable to look into this ground. . . . The mirror of his soul cannot mirror God."

19. *W* 9; 102, 10ff. Holl uttered (in *Gesammelte* . . . , p. 60) that mysticism's claim for a natural ground in man "wholly escapes Luther." Before this dictum one could place a *sic et non*. The question will be taken up again in Part II, in the discussion on man's nature.

20. *Eine deutsche Theologie*, ed. Joseph Bernhart (Leipzig: Im Insel-Verlag, 1922), p. 102. "Man's created soul has two eyes. One is the capability to look into eternity . . . the other to look into time." *Ibid.*, p. 95: "If the creature ascribes essence to itself . . . as though it would emanate from the creature, the creature goes astray. The devil does precisely that."

21. Holl, *Gesammelte* . . . , p. 21.

22. *J. Taulers* . . . , p. 403. See also *ibid.*, pp. 124, 161, 178-179, 442; *Eine deutsche Theologie*, pp. 141-142.

23. *W* 45; 535, 1538. Luther: "The very greatest works in the world—even though they are not recognized as such—are continuously performed by Christians . . . the preservation of peace . . . help, protection, and salvation in all sorts of distress and emergencies. All this, Christ says, will come to pass through Christians because they . . . derive everything from him as their head." *LW* 24; 82.

24. Holl, *Gesammelte* . . . , p. 33.

25. *J. Taulers* . . . , p. 209. Tauler: "You should sigh: O Lord, have mercy on me, a sinner." *Eyn deutsch Theologia*, Martin Luther ed. (Wit-

tenberg, 1518), chap. XXII, closing lines: "Wan nu die creature oder der mensch sein eigen und sein selbheit un sich verleusst un aussget, da get got ein mit seim eigen, das ist mit seiner selbheyt." ("When the creature or man leaves and goes out of his own and his selfdom and himself, then God goes in with his own, that is with his selfdom.")

26. Holl, *Gesammelte* . . . , p. 90. According to Holl scholasticism, monasticism and mysticism represented the same anthropological error and this error unites Luther's opponents.

27. See *J. Taulers* . . . , p. 392 where Tauler spoke out against scholasticism, and *ibid.*, p. 344 where he criticized monasticism. Similar statements are found in *Eine deutsche Theologie*, pp. 141, 166-167.

28. Holl, *Gesammelte* . . . , p. 90. Luther is cited as an example of salutary absence of indifference. Holl's reference is *W* 14; 467, 20-23, 468, 1, 1523-1524, a Luther sermon on Genesis: "Hec ideo dico, ne putemus sanctos tales, qui penitus lapides sint, ut hactenus predicavimus. Maria fuit fortis, vidit filium in cruce pendentem, attamen scriptura non silet gladius transivit per cor eius. Quod martyr mortem non timere debeat, impossibile. Sic Christus ipse timuit mortem et tamen contra deum non egit." ("So I say, we do not consider those holy, who are like stones inwardly, as we have always argued. Mary was courageous, saw her son hanging on the cross. Yet the Scripture does not hide that a sword pierced her heart. Although a martyr ought not fear death, it is impossible not to. Thus Christ himself feared death, yet he did not act against God.")

*Ibid.*, p. 96. Holl refers to but does not quote *W* 2; 754, 9-18, 1519. *LW* 35; 67. The document is a sermon about sacrament and *Bruderschaften* (1519). Luther assailed "selfish love" in connection with holy communion. Likewise referred to but not quoted by Holl is *W* 4; 401, 18, 1513-1516, where Luther wrote: "Christus est nostrum idipsum in quo omnes participamus." ("Christ is our common friend in whom we all participate.")

29. Erich Seeberg, *Grundzüge der Theologie Luthers* (Stuttgart: W. Kohlhammer Verlag, 1940), pp. 147-148. Seeberg: The fact that Luther was not a sacramental positivist is "probably attributable to mysticism." Seeberg's proposal that Luther's non-positivistic thinking about the sacramental might have been inspired by mysticism is an interesting, indirect admission of error in another area. Seeberg, like Holl and others in the liberal and neo-orthodox traditions, tended to equate mysticism and scholasticism. Scholasticism, however, theorized *positivistically* about the sacraments. Mystics took a more spiritual and personal stance with regard to the sacramental. This fact is one indication that mysticism and scholasticism did not coincide. Although at other times placing the two in the same symphony, in connection with Luther's sacramental theology, Seeberg gave mysticism a separate score.

30. *Ibid.*, p. 32.

31. *Ibid.*, p. 32. Seeberg: "Yet somehow Tauler lodges the incipience of the religious process in man, despite the fact that he tried to give honor to God."

32. *Ibid.*, pp. 31-32.

33. *Ibid.*, p. 32. The question of a differentiation between various forms of mysticism will be discussed in Chap. 3B. The Areopagite belonged to the mystics whom Luther found less congenial. Tauler was in a different class as far as Luther was concerned. See Friedrich Theophil Ruhland, *Luther und die Brautmystik nach Luthers Schrifttum bis 1521*, pp. 140-

141 (Giessen: Münchowsche Universitätsdruckerei, 1938). Ruhland questions some of Seeberg's statements about mysticism in general and about Johann Tauler in particular. In part Ruhland uses material which Seeberg may have overlooked.

34. Seeberg, p. 33.

35. Rudolf Otto, *West-östliche Mystik* (Gotha: Leopold Klotz, 1929), pp. 351-352. Luther's tract *How to Pray* (*Wie man beten soll, für Meister Peter Balbierer*. Wittenberg, 1535) insists on method in meditation and sets the goal of the soul's immersion in the Spirit. Luther's thoughts on both method and union were such that they could hardly be germane to Seeberg's tendency to spiritualize mysticism and despiritualize Luther. In *W* 38; 358-375, 1535, this tract is given the title, "A Simple Way to Pray; for a Good Friend." *LW* 43; 193-211.

36. Seeberg, p. 210.

37. *Ibid.* When our discussion reaches theologians who take into account the varieties of Christian mysticism, the question of Luther's attitude to the mystical experience reflected in the terms *gemitus* and *raptus* will be taken up. See Chap. 7C.

38. Emanuel Hirsch, *Das Wesen des reformatorischen Christentums* (Berlin: Walter de Gruyter & Co., 1963), pp. 55-56.

39. *Ibid.*, p. 53.

40. *Ibid.*, pp. 64-65.

41. *Ibid.*, p. 67.

42. *Ibid.*, p. 140.

43. *Ibid.*, p. 87.

44. Heinrich Bornkamm, *Protestantismus und Mystik* (Giessen: A. Töpfelmann, 1934), pp. 13-14.

45. *Ibid.*, p. 15.

46. *Ibid.*, p. 16.

47. Johann Tauler, *The Inner Way*, ed. Arthur Wollaston Hutton (London: Methuen & Co., n.d.), p. 147.

48. *Johann Taulers . . .*, p. 321.

49. *W* 40, 3; 738, 4ff., 1544. See also Chap. 7B.

50. *W* 40, 1; 285, 5, 1531. *LW* 26; 168. *W* 40, 3; 542, 31, 1534-1535. *LW* 13; 110. The matter of immediacy of religious experience with Luther will be discussed at other junctures in the present book. Since it seemed of importance in connection with the generalization problem in Bornkamm's interpretation it became necessary to touch upon it briefly here.

51. See *J. Taulers . . .*, pp. 403, 210, 519-520 and 489, in that order. We shall return to the problem in the discussion of man's nature and salvation. See Chaps. 6 and 7.

52. Heinrich Bornkamm, *Luthers geistige Welt* (Lüneburg: Heliand-Verlag, 1947), pp. 262-263. Bornkamm seemed preoccupied with the notion of the gospel's "virility." Not only did he think that he denigrated mysticism by implying that it typified a feminine grasp on life. In his eagerness to present Luther in heroic array he also invested two of the mystics, for whom Luther had expressed admiration, with a measure of manliness. Bornkamm spoke of "the manly Tauler" and made a point of the possibility that the author of *Theologia Germanica* was an "Ordensherr," a knight.

Heinrich Bornkamm, *Luthers World of Thought*, tr. Martin H. Bertram (St. Louis: Concordia Publishing House, 1958). This translation is not based on the original, as stated, but on the 2nd edition of the book,

*Luthers geistige Welt*, published by C. Bertelsmann, 1953. The passages referred to in our text are to be found in a chapter entitled "Luther and the German spirit" and contained in the original published by Heliand, 1947. This chapter is not found in Bertram's translation.

53. Heinrich Bornkamm, "Luther," *RGG*, IV, pp. 487-488. About the mystical enthusiasts of Luther's day, the *Prophetentum*, Bornkamm used the term "spiritualistic mysticism." Judging from his remarks about medieval mystics this term could also be applied to them.

54. Gerhard Ebeling, *Evangelische Evangelienauslegung* (München: Lempp, 1942), pp. 157-158. See also Gerhard Ebeling, *Luther, Einführung in sein Denken* (Tübingen: J. C. B. Mohr, 1964), pp. 11f., 260, 264, 296. ET: *Luther: An Introduction to His Thought*, trans. R. A. Wilson (Philadelphia: Fortress Press, 1970), pp. 21f., 226f., 230, 256. The references to mystical thought in these passages presuppose a generalized concept of mysticism, with a "Grundorientierung," a main thrust, always and essentially opposed to Luther's.

55. Ebeling, *Evangelische . . .*, p. 158. Ebeling based his assertions on "later critical considerations." The sole source quoted, however, is H. Boehmer, *Der junge Luther* (Gotha, 1929).

56. Heiko Oberman, "Simul gemitus et raptus: Luther und die Mystik," *The Church, Mysticism, Sanctification and the Natural*, ed. Ivar Asheim (Philadelphia: Fortress Press, 1967), p. 37. Cited hereafter as *CM*. Oberman quotes Bernd Moeller who provided this statistical research. Oberman adds: Tauler and the Frankfurter were and remained significant for Luther "for they showed him how it was possible to retain the mystical affect despite the break with the synergistic elements in *contemplatio acquisita* and the speculative elements in *contemplatio infusa*." *Ibid.*, pp. 37-38. Ebeling may be transmitting the view from Harnack who held an opinion similar to the one propounded by Ebeling on this matter. See Adolf Harnack, *Lehrbuch der Dogmengeschichte*, Vol. III (Tübingen: J. C. B. Mohr, 1909), p. 822. ET: *History of Dogma*, trans. from the 3rd German ed. by Neil Buchanan (London: Williams & Norgate, 1905), Vol. VII, pp. 229-231.

57. Bengt Hägglund, "Luther und die Mystik," *CM*, p. 86. Reference is made to O. Scheel who declared that Luther only erroneously expressed dependence on Tauler. The same kind of proposal was made on p. 61 in Karl Holl, *Luthers etiska åskådning*, trans. (Uppsala: SKSF, 1928), from *Gesammelte . . .* chapter "Der Neubau der Sittlichkeit," Vol. I, 5th ed. Holl wrote that as far as Luther's relationship to mysticism is concerned "his [Luther's] own opinion about the relationship, particularly the relationship with *Theologia Germanica* is not decisive."

58. *W* 1; 557, 33f., 1518. *LW* 31; 129.

59. Ebeling, *Luther . . .*, p. 264. ET: p. 230.

60. Johann Tauler, for one, made a distinction between the two approaches. The problem was mentioned briefly in the discussion of Holl's views. It will emerge in Chap. 5.

61. *W* 56; 299, 23-27, 1515-1516: "Per Christum . . . nos confidamus ad accessum Dei . . . 'Iustificati ergo ex fide' et remissis peccatis 'accessum habemus et pacem,' sed 'per Ihesum Christum Dominum nostrum.'" *LW* 25; 287.

62. Ebeling, *Luther . . .*, p. 264. ET: p. 230.

63. The passage in question is found in *W* 56; 299, 27-28 through 300, 1-3, 1515-1516: "Hinc etiam tanguntur ii, Qui secundum mysticam theologiam in tenebras interiores nituntur omissis imaginibus passionis

Christi, ipsum Verbum increatum audire et contemplari volentes, sed nondum prius Iustificatis et purgatis oculis cordis per verbum incarnatum." ("This also applies to those who follow the mystical theology and struggle in inner darkness omitting all pictures of Christ's suffering, wishing to hear and contemplate only the Uncreated Word Himself, but not having first been justified and purged in the eyes of their heart through the incarnate Word.") *LW* 25; 287.

64. *W* 40, 1; 603-604, 1531. *LW* 26; 396-397.

65. Ebeling, *Luther* . . . , p. 264. ET: p. 230.

66. Karl Barth, *Die kirchliche Dogmatik* (Zürich: EVZ, 1953-1967), Vol. IV, 4; 16. ET: *Church Dogmatics* (Edinburgh: T. & T. Clark, 1960- ), IV, 4; 15.

67. *Ibid.*, IV, 3, 2; 620. ET: IV, 3, 2; 540-541.

68. *Ibid.*, IV, 4; 12. ET: IV, 4; 11.

69. *Ibid.*, IV, 1; 372. ET: IV, 1; 337.

70. *Ibid.*, IV, 1; 702. IV, 2, 403. ET: IV, 1; 629. IV, 2; 360-361.

71. *Ibid.*, IV, 1; 316, 32, 323. ET: IV, 1; 287, 31-32, 295.

72. *Ibid.*, IV, 2; 10. ET: IV, 2; 11.

73. *Ibid.*, IV, 1; 702. ET: IV, 1; 628-629.

74. *Ibid.*, IV, 1; 112-113. Barth: "A feeling of enjoyable musing on God can—one should not be a too fanatic antimystic—be considered an element of the activity which love of God sets in motion." ET: IV, 1; 103-105.

75. Reinhold Niebuhr, *The Nature and Destiny of Man*, Vols. I and II (London: Nisbet & Co., 1941-43), I, pp. 15, 17, 84 and II, pp. 116-117.

76. *Ibid.*, I, 145 and 65.

77. *Ibid.*, I, 65; II, 195; II, 25; II, 39, 103.

78. *Ibid.*, II, 26; I, 145; II, 26.

79. Bengt Hägglund discusses the question helpfully in "Luther und die Mystik," *CM*, pp. 85-86. The problem is described as an alleged "uniformity" of all mysticism and a presumed "basic thought" behind all mystic writings.

# Chapter 2-B

1. *RGG*, III, 79.

2. Harnack, Vol. III, 433. "Scholasticism and mysticism blend. . . . Mysticism is the precondition for scholasticism."

3. *Ibid.*, III, 821.

4. *Ibid.*, III, 826.

5. *Ibid.*, III, 846. Harnack: "The question of the relationship between faith and works was thus settled. Hereby Luther conquered mysticism."

6. *Ibid.*, III, 836. Harnack: "To him in whom the Holy Spirit has awakened this faith there is no mystery and no enigma. . . ."

7. *Ibid.*, III, 823. See also *ibid.*, 822: Mysticism and "the teaching about the righteousness which God gives" are considered mutually exclusive in Harnack's appraisal of Luther's theology.

8. *Ibid.*, III, 439. Ironically, becoming a Christ is not a wholly foreign thought to Luther, as will be noted later.

9. *Ibid.*, III, 441.

10. *Ibid.*, III, 821.

11. *W* 4; 265, 18ff., 1513-1516, on ecstasy, and being beyond oneself; *W* 40, 1; 591, 31 to 592, 13, 1531. *LW* 26; 389, on the unspeakable sighs.

12. Harnack, III, 44.
13. Holl, *Gesammelte* . . . , p. 27.
14. *Ibid.*, pp. 27-28. Luther's "conscience alone remained the immovable yardstick." A "thought"—God works through pain—"became his salvation." Cf. *ibid.*, p. 33 where Holl concedes that both mystics and Luther perceived that a "yes" to God may well entail sacrifice of private happiness, and a "mystical" experience might ensue. Yet, Holl added, Luther's doctrine could test the relative validity of the mystical insight.
15. *Ibid.*, p. 150.
16. *Ibid.*, p. 27-28, 33. "This knowledge came as a surprise, as a sudden illumination. St. Paul mediated this to him." That God works through pain, "this thought became his salvation. In it he understood God."
17. In Luther's thought there was, of course, conceptualization but behind the conceptualization we find experiences of "the non-rational energy and majesty of God and his 'awefulness.' " These experiences then become "conceptualized and symbolized as 'Will.' " (Otto, *The Idea* . . . , p. 107.)
18. Karl Holl, *Was* . . . , pp. 27-30.
19. See again Seeberg, pp. 31-32. Martin Luther's *Eine einfältige Weise zu beten, für einen guten Freund* (How to Pray, A Simple Way to Pray; for a Good Friend) was written at the middle of the 1530's (far removed from "young Luther's" mysticism) and is found in *W* 38; 358-375, 1535. *LW* 43, 193-211. It was briefly cited under "Mysticism generalized," Chap. 2A.
20. *RGG*, III, 364.
21. Hirsch, pp. 29-32.
22. *Ibid.*, p. 39. "Die persönliche Vergegenwärtigung," personal actualization or realization of faith, and God's presence, here form the existential centerpiece. Against this true Christian existentialism Hirsch posed uncongenial metaphysical contentions which the *Kirchenglaube*, the church faith, illegitimately advanced as Christianity. These metaphysical ideas must be considered "contaminations," distorting the "unadulterated faith," a personal, existential relationship to God.
23. *Ibid.*, p. 47.
24. Martin Luther, *Ein Predigt von den Engeln* (Wittenberg, 1535). *W* 32; 111-121, 1530.
25. Barth, III, 3; 439. ET: III, 3, 380.
26. *Ibid.*, pp. 427, 567, 585-586, 561. ET: pp. 369, 485, 500, 479.
27. Hirsch, pp. 39-48.
28. *Ibid.*, 48-49.
29. Heinrich Bornkamm, *Mystik, Spiritualismus und die Anfänge des Pietismus im Luthertum* (Giessen: A. Töpfelmann, 1926), pp. 5-9.
30. Heinrich Bornkamm, *Luther und Böhme* (Bonn: A. Marcus & E. Webers Verlag, 1925), pp. 231-237. Bornkamm pointed out that there are "immediate lines from Böhme's Christ-mysticism to Luther." He remarked that Luther in his treatise on Christian freedom used expressions like "the soul unites with Christ like a bride with her bridegroom" *(W* 7; 25, 28) and "by faith . . . Christ is born by" us.
31. Bornkamm, *Luthers geistige* . . . , p. 263. Not translated in *Luther's World of Thought*, see Chap. 2A fn. 52. The tendency toward absolute distinction between the Catholic-mystical and the Lutheran-evangelical is visible already in *Luther und Böhme*, p. 231 where Albrecht Ritschl's verdict is accepted.
32. Bornkamm, *Protestantismus* . . . , pp. 7-10.

33. *Ibid.*, 263: "The Evangelical truth." "Protestant faith calls this [mysticism's] interpretation . . . untruth" (p. 8). "The plausible immediacy of mysticism is an untruth" (p. 15). The claim that Luther experienced the divine "immediately," "this . . . is fraud" (p. 12).
34. Bornkamm, *Luthers geistige* . . . , p. 93. ET: p. 95. Concerning Luther's remarks on Holy Communion see reference to his comments about Carlstadt's "spirituality" in Chap. 7E of the present book, the part dealing with salvation as *Erfahrung*.
35. *Ibid.*, p. 264. Not translated in *Luther's World*. . . . Cf. *Luthers geistige*, p. 96. *Luther's World* . . . , p. 99.
36. Ebeling, *Luther* . . . , p. 33. ET: p. 39. Luther's words in *W* 54; 185, 14-15, 1545. Ebeling's translation: "Ein ganz ungewöhnlich brennendes Verlangen hatte mich gepackt." Clemen's translation: "Ich war von einem wundersam glühenden Verlangen gepackt worden und es beherrschte mich noch." *LW* 34; 336.
37. Ebeling, *Luther* . . . , pp. 15-17. ET: pp. 24-26. "We wish . . . to try to push forward to the foundation from which they [the separate facts or thoughts] emerge. We must enter into Luther's *thought*, into the movement which we are helping to complete . . . understand, not just register but desire to assume responsibility. . . . For what concerned him [Luther] if not the bringing of the Word into language in the right manner?" ("Das rechte Zur-Sprache-Bringen des Wortes.")—Author's trans.
38. *Ibid.*, pp. 11-15. ET: pp. 21-24.
39. *Ibid.*, pp. 26, 27, 24. ET: pp. 33, 34, 32. No "psychological analysis" will help us to understand Luther's faith. Rather, "the spiritual outline of a person is perceived from the language event inherent in the traditions pressing in on a person and the manner of his approach to them, his dialogue with them, and how he, through mutations, comes to something of his own" so that "person . . . office, vocation blend."—Author's trans. The Luther quote on experience which makes the theologian is found in *WT* 1; 16, 12, 1531. *LW* 54; 7.
40. *Ibid.*, pp. 25-27. ET: pp. 33-34. "Luther is like a musical instrument, which combines the tenderest and the loudest registers. Only a trained ear can do justice to the tonal modulations." (p. 25).
41. *Ibid.*, p. 260. ET: pp. 226-227.
42. *W* 10, 3; 348, 9-15, 1522. *LW* 51; 112. *W* 40, 1; 280-283, esp. 283, 16-32, 1535. *LW* 26; 165-167.
43. *W* 5; 165, 21-23, 1519-1521.
44. *W* 2; 501, 34.
45. *W* 3; 117, 32, 1513-1516. *W* 7; 574, 24-32, 1521. *LW* 21; 328. See Ruhland, p. 40.
46. Ebeling, *Luther* . . . , p. 301. ET: p. 260. Cf. *ibid.*, p. 262: Luther's theology of the cross confirms any true religious experience today. "It is existential theology."
47. *W* 56; 306, 26-307, 15, 1515-1516. *LW* 25; 293-294.
48. Ebeling, *Luther* . . . , p. 296, 301. ET: 256, 260. See reference to this Aquinas dictum, *infra.* p. 117, n. 48.
49. *Ibid.*, p. 299. ET: 258-259.
50. *W* 18; 614, 22-26, 1526: "Hoc autem asserto, certe simul asseris, Dei misericordiam solam omnia agere et voluntatem nostram nihil agere sed potius pati . . ." *LW* 33; 35. ("This I assert on the contrary, and you will surely agree, that God's mercy alone moves [activates] all and that our will moves [activates] nothing but rather surrenders. . . ." Author's

trans.) Luther added that, if this were not so, "the totality" would not be ascribed to God.

51. *W* 7; 20-31 (German version), *W* 7; 49-73 (Latin version), 1520. From Section 29: "The good things we have from God should flow from one to the other and be common to all, so that everyone should 'put on' his neighbor and so conduct himself toward him as if he himself were in the other's place." *LW* 31; 371. This is to say, heartfelt trust in God transforms man into an acting person. He acts in the face of God because he is activated, moved by God.

52. Ebeling, *Luther . . . ,* p. 303. ET: p. 262. A distinction should be made between *synteresis* and *conscientia*. See Chap. 6 pp. 141-142 and note 17.

53. *Ibid.* Ebeling says that Luther's words about the conscience may suggest that he had in mind actual, inner, mental, psychological change. However, this is only apparently so, Ebeling holds. Luther is merely taking the existential pulse at the points of friction between God and world.

54. *W* 3; 479, 17ff., 1513-1516. *LW* 10; 418-419.

55. *W* 39, 1; 204, 12, 1537.

56. *W* 40, 1; 360, 5, 1531: "Fides est creatrix deitatis non in persona sed in nobis." *LW* 26; 226-227.

57. Ebeling, *Luther . . . ,* p. 303. "Gott und Welt müssen zusammengedacht werden." ET: p. 262. The English translation here lessens the force of the original's perception of Luther's theological existence as primarily a conceptualization process.

58. Steven Ozment, *Homo Spiritualis* (Leiden: E. J. Brill, 1969). "Our study will compare the anthropology of Tauler, Gerson and Luther within the full systematic context of their thought." (p. 9).

59. *Ibid.,* pp. 8-9, 45-46.

60. *Ibid.,* p. 4. Without further explanation the expression "generally accepted" remains obscure. Is something objectively right only because it is generally accepted? What percentage would qualify for the adjudication?

61. *Ibid.,* pp. 9, 33.

62. *Ibid.,* p. 4. Ozment's use of Erich Vogelsang appears one-sided. Vogelsang in his writings on Luther and the mystics was clearly swayed in different directions by the material itself. In "Luther und die Mystik," and "Die Unio mystica bei Luther," he did sometimes make a distinction between "psychologizing" moods in mysticism and "theological" postures in Luther (e.g., in Vogelsang, "Luther und . . . ," pp. 48-49). But on the same pages he also said the opposite: that the psychological and the theological converge as evidenced by Luther's remarks in *W* 7; 550, 28, 1521. *LW* 21; 303. Cf. *infra,* p. 144. There was also a more qualified statement regarding the ground of God within man, in his conscience. Luther, according to Vogelsang, did not look at the conscience as "indisputable God-ground." But, did the mystics? Ozment hears Vogelsang, one of his major mentors, answer this question in the affirmative. In my judgment that is letting the wish become the guide. For some mystics conscience was not "indisputably" a God-ground. With regard to Tauler Vogelsang noted "an inner kinship" with Luther ("Luther und . . . ," p. 43). In Tauler Luther found the judgment of man's nature, the place of the crucified Lord and the experience of the Lord in the depth of the human being (*ibid.,* p. 41). Luther, on Vogelsang's accounting, spoke of God's being and our being as part of the same piece

("Die Unio . . . ," p. 67. referring to *W* 5; 144, 20, 1520). Vogelsang's findings will be discussed in Chap. 3 of this book. Suffice it to say here that he is not as absolute in his total approach as Ozment's quotation above would lead one to believe. Vogelsang on the one hand expressed critical evolutionistic ideas (radical polarity, *one* theme exhaustively supplanted by another) and, on the other hand, a more pneumatic appreciation of the place of inwardness and the existence of pervasive spiritual motifs with Luther (continuity, less categorical views of mysticism's manwardness and Luther's "anti-psychologism"). The reason for this ambiguity is the nature of the material itself and probably the nature of spiritual life itself.

63. Luther said in Table Talks that God *potentialiter* and *substantialiter* is in each creature. *WT* 1; 101, 27-33, 1532. The question of salvation can of course not be wholly unrelated to this fact. Ozment's account seems overlogical at this point.

64. Ozment, p. 32. On Luther's spiritual friendship with Tauler, see *W* 1; 557, 29, 1518, where Luther says: "In Tauler I have found more true theology than in all the university doctors lumped together." As noted earlier, theologians have undertaken to correct Luther on this score. Vogelsang was more cautious. He simply stated that Luther saw Tauler's central concern but "did not see the differences," a deficiency which modern knowledge is purportedly remedying (Vogelsang, "Luther und . . . ," p. 43).

65. *J. Taulers . . .* , pp. 405, 321.

66. *Ibid.*, p. 542.

67. *Ibid.*, p. 110.

68. Ozment, p. 201. See further the discussion on views of man in Chap. 6 of the present book.

69. *Die Predigten Taulers aus der Freiburger Handschrift*, ed. Ferdinand Vetter (Berlin: Weidmannsche Buchhandlung, 1910), p. 172. Ozment, pp. 199-201.

70. *W* 9; 102, 10ff., 1516. Luther: *Deo statuimus modum.* Ozment, p. 199.

71. *W* 9; 102, 34-35, 1516. Luther in marginal notes to Tauler sermons: "Ut hic docet [Tauler], tota salus est resignatio voluntatis in omnibus." In other words, Luther *agrees.*

72. Ozment, p. 203. Ozment's problem is whether Tauler's stress on the resignation of the will led Luther to be "totally uncritical." Tauler's concept of "will-lessness" has been described by Ozment as "a means to achieve the full emergence of man's own substantial form," in contradistinction to Luther who, on Ozment's accounting, thought that justification means destruction of man's substantial form.

73. Philipp Strauch, "Zu Taulers Predigten," *Beiträge zur Geschichte der deutschen Sprache und Literatur* (1919), p. 19. Strauch devoted painstaking work to problems surrounding Eckhart and Tauler editions. This contribution deals with Tauler. Strauch writes: "It is generally acknowledged that the Leipzig print of 1498 contains four Eckhart sermons, namely L. No. 2, 6, 8, 9 to which should in all likelihood be added No. 1 which is Vetter No. 1." See also the same author on Eckhart, *Meister Eckhart-Probleme* (Halle: E. Karras, 1919). The material from an *Eckhart* sermon used by Ozment to prove that Tauler calculated with "a pure disposition for salvation" can be found in Ozment, pp. 204-205. As already indicated, the collection of Tauler's sermons most frequently

referred to in the present book is *Johann Taulers Predigten*, ed. Georg Hofmann.

74. It is beyond the scope of our examination to probe the evangelical orthodoxy of Eckhart's mysticism. Concerning the judgment that the idea of "inflow" (God's breakthrough into the ground of the soul) and "outflow" (man's breakthrough to the godhead behind God) is beyond the evangelical pale, one should recall Luther's allusions to the ineffable God as *absconditus*, a corollary to God as revealed.—On the double meaning of "substance" in Tauler's preaching see Johann Tauler, *The Inner Way*, pp. 117, 123, 172. Cf. Bengt Hägglund, *The Background of Luther's Doctrine of Justification in Late Medieval Theology* (Philadelphia: Fortress Press, 1971), pp. 13-14: "The *Seelengrund* with Tauler is the transcendent man, belonging to the realm of the supernatural and the divine. All working is here divine working. . . . The doctrine of redemption in Tauler's mysticism, from this point, can with perfect right be characterized by the formula *sola gratia*."

75. Ozment, p. 199.

76. *Ibid.*, p. 202 *et passim*. Ozment declares that human life is "soteriologically de-substantial." Yes, but not in absolute, cognitive fashion, rather as a religious explication of "in him we live, move and have our being—we are his offspring" (Acts 17:28).

77. *Ibid.*, Preface.

# Chapter 3

1. Ernst Benz, *Die Vision* (Stuttgart: Ernst Klett, 1971), Introduction, pp. 112-113.

2. Rudolf Otto, *Naturalistische und religiöse Weltansicht*, 2nd ed. (Tübingen: J. C. B. Mohr, 1909), pp. 11-12, 24. ET: *Naturalism and Religion*, pp. 1-16, 23-24.

3. Harry McSorley, *Luther: Right or Wrong?* An ecumenical-theological study of Luther's major work, *The Bondage of the Will* (Minneapolis: Augsburg, and New York: Newman Press, 1969).

4. *Ibid.*, pp. 217-273, a chapter entitled "Luther's early reaction: From *Liberum Arbitrium* to *Servum Arbitrium*." Note esp. p. 218: "What follows is a sketch of his evolution from a doctrine of *liberum arbitrium* to one of *servum arbitrium*."

5. *Ibid.*, p. 222. Luther is quoted as saying in his *Lectures on the Epistle to the Romans*: The gift of Christ was not due to any merits of human nature. Yet, "there had to be a preparation and disposition in order to receive him." It is rightly said that "God infallibly gives grace to the man who does what he is able to do."

6. *Ibid.*, pp. 226-227.

7. *Ibid.*, p. 229.

8. *Ibid.*, p. 250.

9. *Ibid.*, p. 221.

10. *Ibid.*

11. *Ibid.*, p. 21.

12. *Ibid.*, p. 259.

13. *Ibid.*, pp. 254-260.

14. *Ibid.*, p. 21.

15. *Ibid.*, p. 247 *et passim*. McSorley: Luther's "terminology is poor

and misleading for he does not adequately distinguish between . . . acquired freedom and natural freedom."

16. *Ibid.*, pp. 348-349.
17. *Ibid.*, p. 352.
18. *Ibid.*, p. 250.
19. McSorley quotes H. Bandt on the issue of immediate logic with respect to Luther's view of the will. Bandt: "One must remember that . . . the intention of his [Luther's] propositions frequently do not unequivocally coincide with their naked, logical-grammatical sense. Indeed he often employed such paradoxically sharpened formulations . . . that the sense of the words and the underlying intention sometimes contradicted each other. Hence one has to examine in Luther's writings whether . . . he really desires to say what on first blush he seems to be saying." McSorley attaches a program declaration: "We seek to discover Luther's genuine intention by doing more—not less—intensive historical research. . . ." As noted, the question is whether one can delve deeper into the "intention" if disregarding Luther's mystical experience of the God of the burning bush who could obliterate man and had it all prepared in advance and who was at the same time counting on a person's will to work out his purpose. In this sense the logical-grammatical does not suffice as the sole arbiter of gospel truth. *Ibid.*, pp. 14-15.
20. Otto, *The Idea* . . . , pp. 86-87. "Nothing remains so alien to the rationalist as this doctrine" (p. 86). It is not philosophical but "the result of immediate religious experience" (p. 88).
21. *Ibid.*, pp. 90-91, 98-100.
22. *Ibid.*, p. 103.
23. Harry J. McSorley, "Erasmus versus Luther—Compounding the Reformation Tragedy," in Jared Wicks, ed., *Catholic Scholars Dialogue with Luther* (Chicago: Loyola University Press, 1970), p. 115.
24. Otto, *The Idea* . . . , pp. 103-104.
25. It is customary in the field of comparative religion to distinguish between non-Christian Eastern impersonal mysticism and Christian personal mysticism. The distinction is not always tenable inasmuch as mystics in the Christian church sometimes speak of the ground of the soul in such a way that it resembles non-Christian mysticism's references to the universal mind rather than a personal God.
26. Vogelsang, "Luther und . . . ," p. 34. See *W* 56; 299, 27-300, 1-4. *LW* 25; 287. Also with respect to Psalm 91, *W* 4; 64, 27-30 and *W* 4; 65, 1-3, 1513-1516.
27. *Ibid.*, p. 35, reference to *W* 5; 163, 17-29.
28. Harnack, III, pp. 823, 826.
29. *Ibid.*, p. 826.
30. *Ibid.*, p. 846.
31. Harnack, IV, p. 435. "If you deduct mysticism from the Catholic faith . . . Catholicism becomes empty of content."
32. Holl, *Gesammelte* . . . , p. 28: "These men had after all made their peace with ordinary Catholicism . . . made a distinction between mortal and venal sin." When Paul purged Luther's thought of this fallacy the mature Luther emerged. The conquest of mysticism was the dividing line.
33. Nathan Söderblom, *Humor och melankoli och andra Lutherstudier* (Stockholm: SKSR, 1919), p. 186. In a personal friendship with mystic Sadhu Sundar Singh of India, Söderblom later came to a deeper appre-

ciation of "personality mysticism." Regarding Luther, he was, it seems, always dependent on German scholarship which at that time fashioned its judgments on mysticism in Luther's life out of studies of *Schwärmertum*.

34. Gustaf Ljunggren, *Synd och skuld i Luthers teologi* (Stockholm: SKDB: 1928), p. 45. Ljunggren, too, wrote at a time when theological-historical verdicts on the mystical in Luther almost totally issued from preoccupation with Luther's reaction to post-Reformation enthusiastic mystics, not from studies of Luther's use of medieval mystics.

35. Bornkamm, *Luthers geistige* . . . , p. 263. Not translated in *Luther's World*. . . . It is in this connection that Bornkamm brands as "dilettantes" those who would term Luther a mystic. See Chap. 2 of the present work where the same Bornkamm passage is cited.

36. Bornkamm, *Protestantismus* . . . , p. 8: "Protestantism calls [mysticism's] interpretation of nature untruth." See Chap. 2 of the present work where Bornkamm is quoted as saying: the claim of "immediacy" in the God-relation is "an untruth."

37. Ebeling, *Luther* . . . , pp. 12, 296, 303. "Still with borrowings from the language of mysticism."—"Seeming internalization and spiritualization." ET: pp. 21, 256, 262.

38. *Ibid.*, p. 260. ET: pp. 226-227. Even mysticism spoke of the theology of the cross. With Luther this means something more and deeper than with the mystics. It was more than an *Augenblicksanliegen* or "a peculiarity of young Luther." Had it *been* sheer passion-mysticism or if it *were to be regarded as* sheer passion-mysticism it would be wholly irrelevant to the mature Luther, in Ebeling's opinion.

39. *Ibid.*, pp. 14-15. ET: p. 24.

40. *Ibid.*, pp. 34-36. ET: pp. 41-42. See Luther in *W* 54; 185, 14-186, 16, 1545. Ebeling calls the spiritual illumination "a sudden, isolated intimation"; Reformation theology would be distorted, were one to concentrate on a second conversion experience. For this theology "does not depend on" isolated experience. It deals more with "process" and a substitution of thought with thought. To this argument one could object that, although "isolated," religious illumination tends toward pervasiveness, as a blessed reminder of reality and a molder of theology. Biblical experience and prophetic testimony bear out the central importance of "the isolated illumination." To insist on the application of the natural scientific criterion of "repeatability" to the reality with which theology deals, is to disregard the central importance of the extraordinary breakthrough. Young Luther's kinship with mystical theology was rooted in isolated and extraordinary inner events. Yet precisely these events, the isolated intimations, both reverberated in and were confirmed by mature Luther's experience and theology. The "sudden isolated illumination" consequently should be considered inseparable from "Luther's theological testimonies" which shaped "Reformation theology."

41. Ebeling, *Evangelische*, p. 158. Cf. pp. 53-54 in the present book where the factual error is mentioned according to which Luther after 1520 "never quoted the German theologian and Tauler."

42. Wilfried Joest, *Ontologie der Person bei Luther* (Göttingen: Vandenhoeck & Ruprecht, 1967), p. 53. Joest argues properly that Luther replaced the Aristotelian notion of substance with faith, thus abandoning the concept of substance as being which exists in and for itself (pp. 249-250). But he overlooks the fact that Luther's *fiducia* has "a greater continuity" with *synteresis* (in the medieval tradition) "than Luther re-

search has thought." Herbert Olsson, *Schöpfung, Vernunft und Gesetz in Luthers Theologie* (Uppsala: Acta Univ. Ups., 1971), pp. 561-562. In other words, the mystical presence often seems to escape the conceptualization process of Protestant theology. The contention with respect to a time border also loses its plausibility when we compare Luther's mystical Christology with the profound Christology of *Theologia Germanica*; see for instance *Eine deutsche . . .* , pp. 141, 175, 187. Do we face only concepts that supersede one another, or themes that pervade?

43. Otto, *The Idea . . .* , pp. 97-98. Mystical doctrines (in the first place *mirae speculationes* upon the unrevealed majesty of God) "stand in the most intimate connection with his own innermost religious life."

44. *Ibid.*, p. 97.

45. Vogelsang, "Luther und . . . ," p. 52. The Psalm commentaries referred to are to be found in *W* 18; 479ff. "Christ is not, as some suggest with blind words, a righteousness *causaliter*, which stays outside, for such a righteousness is dead, indeed it never was. But Christ is himself there, in the same way as the rays of the sun . . . are not . . . where the sun is not." *W* 18; 529, 12-18. Cf. Chap. 7F, note 80.

46. *Ibid.*, p. 38. Luther on Bernard: *W* 3; 640, 40, 1514 and *W* 43; 581, 11, 1542.

47. Erwin Iserloh, "Luther und die Mystik," *CM*, pp. 60-62. These are Luther's words in *W* 10, 1, 1; 728, 14-16, 1522: "Es ist ein unendlich Wort und will mit stillem Geist gefasset . . . sein . . . Es begreift auch sonst niemand, denn ein solcher stiller betrachtender Geist." ("It is a limitless word and wants to be grasped in a serene spirit. No one but such a still contemplating soul can understand it anyhow.") Iserloh's way of looking at the "young-mature"-issue in Luther's thought differs widely from that of Ebeling who illustrates the conceptualistic approach. Ebeling wishes to read Luther as only apparently propounding mystical intuitions. As mentioned, Luther regarded man as *not* acting in God's economy according to Ebeling. It was a discovery which closed the pre-Reformation stage and opened a totally new stage, Ebeling suggests *(Luther . . .* , pp. 26, 301). On the other hand, if we hear Luther say that God's mercy activates all and our own will in isolation, nothing, then man is conceived as an *agent*. An agent is not an agent if he is non-acting. Faith grows as the will of service grows (see Luther in *De Libertate*, par. 27). The continuous elements in Luther's thought are to be found in the realm of love-will.

48. See Ebeling, *Luther . . .* , p. 301: ET: p. 260. In connection with our study of preconception we saw that Ebeling found internalization unevangelical. The same observation can serve here as a counterpoint to Iserloh's findings regarding the feasibility of establishing absolute theological disparity between young Luther and mature Luther. Ebeling provides a good example of the theory of disjuncture which counterposes "faith" and "actual change in man" ("reale Veränderung des Menschen"). The latter is looked upon as fallacy and adjudged Roman Catholic. Ebeling holds that, even if "young Luther" subscribed to the notion of inner change, "mature Luther" certainly did not. The distinction between "faith" and "inner change" is, Ebeling holds, a confessional one. Thomas Aquinas' remark that "love unites with the united" in Ebeling's view becomes an illustration of "the extraordinary depths of the confessional difference."

49. Oberman, *CM*, pp. 34ff.

50. *Ibid.*, p. 33. Luther-quotes from *W* 9; 98, 20-34 and *W* 4; 650,

5-15. "Hanc Maria vitam significat, alteram vero Martha . . . prius esse cum Deo quam cum Christo."
51. *Ibid.*, pp. 34-35. Luther-quotes from *W* 43; 72, 9-14, 22-28, and 72, 31-73, 9. *LW* 3; 275-277. The disputations with the *Schwärmer* had sharpened Luther's terms in the course of 20 years.
52. *Supra*, pp. 53-54.
53. Oberman, *CM*, pp. 37-38.
54. Vogelsang, "Luther und . . . , " pp. 32-33. After the appearance of Emil Brunner's *Mysticism and the Word* in 1924 it has become fashionable to say that "faith and mysticism are mutually exclusive." But this is fallacious. "The total understanding of his [Luther's] theology" must envelop the specific utterance. And this total understanding must include the mystical experience: "to have Christ in the heart" *(ibid.,* p. 51).
55. Oberman, *CM*, p. 32. It is "not unequivocal that Gerson should belong to Roman mysticism."
56. Vogelsang, "Luther und . . . , " p. 49 where Vogelsang surmised that Luther did use the experience and language of bridal mysticism. However, on p. 40 he described Luther's faith as "the exact opposite" of bridal mysticism. Again on pp. 78-79 the marriage symbol is said to be an important element in Luther's thought. Man and wife are "one person," Luther is quoted to say, and in like manner the Christian is related to Christ *(W* 22; 337, 31). In Ruhland, *Luther und die Brautmystik* . . . we have an analysis of Luther's use of bride-bridegroom symbolism up to 1521. This mystical imagery is shown to have been an integral part of Luther's theology up to that time. In "Luther und die Mystik" in *CM*, pp. 60-83, esp. p. 73, Erwin Iserloh maintains that Luther employed the same notion of mystical unity and the same imagery throughout his life.
57. *CM*, p. 24 where Oberman by and large rejects Vogelsang's attempt to apply a strict chronology and says that, although Vogelsang's contributions to a necessary typology of mysticism are of lasting value, his chronological distinctions must be questioned, as well as his classification of individual mystics. Oberman points out that there is a *sic et non* dimension in much of Luther's treatment of mystical writings. Medieval use of authorities seldom signified the total acceptance of an earlier theologian. Aquinas used Augustine, Gerson used Bernard, Eck used Gregor of Rimini in this fashion, severally not totally. Neither negative nor positive references are therefore conclusive evidence of dependence. Luther cited medieval teachers approvingly whose general theology was foreign to him. It is indeed to render Luther extremely naive and ignorant to claim that he had misunderstood them. A chronological determination of links between Luther and the mystics is not feasible. For instance, when Luther attacked the Dionysian speculations around 1519-1520, there is no reason to speak of a development or a sudden change of temper (pp. 25-28). Although Oberman carefully avoids criticism of named theologians in the mainstream of historical-critical reflection it is obvious that he questions stances like Ebeling's. The latter holds, as noted, that "later critical judgments show . . . a temporal (chronological) borderline in Luther's development." (See Ebeling, *Evangelische* . . . , p. 158.) We shall return to this statement because it serves as an illuminating contrast to a pneumatic-dynamic notion of Luther's relationship to mysticism.
58. As noted, Heiko Oberman questions Vogelsang's differentiation. He points to passages from, for instance, Gerson which do not fit the

typology. But he does continue to use the typological principle of Vogelsang's. See *CM*, pp. 30-33.

59. *W* 9; 98, 33.

60. *W* 2; 493, 12, the Commentary to the Galatians 1519: "Nostra enim iusticia de coelo prospicit et ad nos descendit." *W* 4; 647, 19: "Omnis ascensus ad cognitionem Dei est periculosus praeter eum qui est per humanitatem Christi, quia haec est scala Jacob, in qua ascendum est." *W* 6; 562, 8-10: "In 'Theologia' vero 'mystica,' quam sic inflant ignorantissimi quidam Theologistae, etiam pernitiosissimus est, plus platonisans quam Christianisans, ita ut nollem fidelem animum his libris operam dare vel minimam. Christum ibi adeo non disces, ut, si etiam scias, amittas. Expertus loquor. Paulum potius audiamus, ut Jesum Christum et hunc crucifixum discamus. Haec enim via, vita et veritas; haec scala, per quam venitur ad patrem." In other words, one can speak of a "ladder," *scala*, but only through Christ. See also *W* 16; 144, 3: "Ipse descendit et paravit scalam." (On Exodus 9, 1524) and *W* 9; 406, 17-31, 1519-1521.

61. *W* 57, 3; 114, 15-19; *LW* 29; 124.

62. See Heiko Oberman's brief discussion of this subject in *CM*, p. 24, Vogelsang, "Luther und . . . ," pp. 49-50 and Vogelsang's "Die Unio mystica bei Luther," pp. 63-80, esp. p. 79. Vogelsang assails the notions of Ritschl, Holl, Barth (pp. 64-66), Bornkamm, Emil Brunner (pp. 74-75) with respect to their understanding of mysticism in Luther's life. Vogelsang points out that " 'the ecstatic love' of older mysticism" is replaced by "the likewise ecstatic faith which walks out of itself and goes into God's darkness" (p. 70). Again attention should be drawn to Iserloh's positive appraisal of Luther's nuptial language *(CM*, p. 70) and Ruhland's affirmation of the same, for instance on p. 136 in *Luther und die Brautmystik.* . . . Ruhland, however, clouded the issue by a generalized notion of mysticism: "But there is no regression to mystical thoughts" (p. 136). Compare the objection to Bornkamm's idea that Luther never employed Bernardian love-play images in relation to Christ. Luther does do this, said Ruhland against Bornkamm. Ruhland could not endorse Bornkamm's claim that the bridal relation was just "an exchange of Christ's goods and our guilt" *(Luther und Böhme,* p. 237). Bernard painted the bride-bridegroom relationship in more vivid colors, yet Luther also "depicts bridal mysticism." This happens not only, as Bornkamm avers, in the time of "the temptations of Romanic mysticism." Not even in the most hectic years of reformational-theological activity did the marriage and man-woman symbolism disappear (Ruhland, p. 138).

63. *W* 4; 401, 25-30.

# Chapter 4

1. See Chapter 2B, Conclusion.

2. Otto, *The Idea* . . . , pp. 206, 202, 204-205, citing Luther without specific reference.

3. Vogelsang, "Luther und . . . ," pp. 38-43. Some scholars claim that Luther had found spiritual *Anfechtung* only in Gerson among mystics (and probably none anywhere else). Vogelsang's information about Tauler and *Anfechtung* is slightly equivocal for, on the one hand, he wrote that Romanic mysticism knew only fleshly *Anfechtung*, not a spiritual

one (p. 40), on the other hand he maintained that Luther had found spiritual *Anfechtung* with Tauler who did belong to Romanic mysticism (p. 42). We note that Jared Wicks takes the view that Luther, from having spoken of *fides caritate formata*, faith formed by love, by 1517 affirmed a *fides certitudine formata*, faith formed by certitude. Wicks calls the change "a new departure," i.e., an emphasis on "felt" change was replaced with an emphasis on faith as certitude that Christ's priestly work is effective (pp. 213-215). We should remember, however, that Luther's emphasis on "certitude" in 1517 emerged from his arguments about sacramental efficiency. The motifs of mystical feeling continued to play a central role with him. On Wicks' work, see *infra.* fn. 6.

4. Otto, *The Idea*, p. 102.

5. See Chapter 3, Section A.

6. Jared Wicks, *Man Yearning for Grace, Luther's Early Spiritual Teaching* (Washington: Corpus Books, 1968), p. 8. It is outside the scope of the present book to discuss Wicks' notion that Luther's concept of faith in 1518 changed from spirituality to a mere assurance and certitude of forgiveness (pp. 11, 271-273). Some scholars of note take a line similar to Wicks' suggestion. Others, equally notable but perhaps not in the mainstream, argue that the later Luther remained substantially a transmitter of spiritual-mystical experience permeating the rational with non-rational intimations.

7. *Ibid.*, pp. xi, 152, 280. "This is to weaken Luther's point beyond recognition," Wicks writes about the rationalizing interpretation of Luther's conception of sanctification. "Luther continues this passage (W 56; 279, 22 quoted by the criticized theologian, H. Hübner, and W 56; 279, 25 and W 56; 280, 2 added by Wicks for elucidation [*LW* 25; 267] by comparing the just man to the Church . . . the real ground of praise is not the Church itself but Christ 'dwelling' in it. Luther then speaks of the saints whose good is outside themselves in Christ, who, nevertheless, is inside them through faith. Luther concludes that we are his [Christ's] kingdom and that his beauty is in us to cover our ugliness. His [Luther's] thought is fuller and more plastic than Hübner would admit" (p. 332).

8. A work by Regin Prenter, *Spiritus Creator: Luther's Concept of the Holy Spirit* (Philadelphia: Fortress Press, (1944, 1953) took the opposite view from Wicks: "The love of God . . . is not an active yearning with Luther" (p. 16). Prenter subscribed to the traditional notion that mysticism (used as a block-word) represents "the medieval piety of imitation," "ascetic technique," "spiritual exercise," "imagined hell," thinking that is "metaphysical" and "supernatural," effort that is "the work of man," movement which is "religio-psychological" and "co-extensive with the work of the Holy Spirit" and "idealistic." Martin Luther, on the other hand, spoke of "conformity" rather than *imitatio* and thought "theologically" to the virtual exclusion of the "anthropological" and was (like the purported thrust of Prenter's investigation) "biblical" and "realistic."

Prenter's "compromise" between the historico-genetic, the purely systematic, and the systematic-exegetical approach is guided by preconceptions similar to those which I discussed in greater detail with respect to other Luther interpreters. Prenter depicts Augustinianism, scholasticism and mysticism as inspired by theologies of identical bent. He places himself in the camp of those who think of Luther's faith in the real presence of the Spirit as having nothing to do with "supernatural force" and "experience of a mystic sensation of him [the Spirit]" (pp. 5-26). This is to say, Prenter subjected to scrutiny neither the individual mystics, nor Luther's words about the mystical but employed traditional generalizations.

Louis Bouyer, a Roman Catholic scholar, alludes to Luther's mysticism in *Orthodox Spirituality and Protestant and Anglican Spirituality* (London: Burns & Oates, 1969). He notes the "polemics," "tragedy" and the "vicious circle" which soon became manifest in the dogmatic polarization between a Roman Catholic teaching of grace "as a mere excitant" and the evangelical view of "salvation where everything was from God," with man having "no part in it." Bouyer's account recognizes the element of mystical piety in Luther's faith. Yet his references, Jaeger and Nygren, prompt him to accept the common proposition that "forensic justification" emptied Luther's thought of Christ's indwelling. Also, Bouyer appears not to accord full recognition to the fact that Luther in effect differentiated between various forms of medieval mysticism (pp. 66-69).

# Chapter 5

1. See Vogelsang, "Luther und . . ." where the dichotomies concerning man's views of God are described as "Luther's quandary." Vogelsang cited *W* 17, 1; 437, 31, 1525 as evidence.

2. *W* 17, 2; 192, 28, 1525. *W* 18; 709, 22, 1525. *LW* 33; 176. *W* 19; 219, 31, 1526. *W* 23; 133, 29, 1527.

3. *W* 40, 1; 287, 8ff., 1531: "Christ living in heart and conscience." *LW* 26; 170. See Vogelsang, "Die Unio mystica . . . ," p. 68.

4. *W* 18; 633, 7-8. "Ut ergo fidei locus sit, opus est, ut omnia, quae creduntur, abscondantur."

5. Otto, *The Idea* . . . , p. 102.

6. *Ibid.*, p. 103. Otto's reference is in part to an Easter sermon by Luther concerning the *feeling* of God's presence, the *experience* that God through Christ can be *felt* as a present *friend.* "Otherwise," wrote Luther, "it [faith] would be sheer hypocrisy" *W* 1, 2; 216, 4-6, 1526.

7. Rudolf Otto made incisive observations about the nature of dogmatic ideograms and thereby furthered an understanding of Luther's God-language which exceeds common-sense logic. (*Ibid.*, pp. 104, 108.) Spiritual facts cannot always be formulated but they can indeed be experienced, said Luther in his comments on Psalm 90:7, *W* 40, 3; 542, 27-543, 13. *LW* 12; 110-111. Anguished sadness, corresponding to the *tremendum* within God, that which Luther termed *gemitus*, can and should be experienced. But, Luther added, it must occur through *sanctum crucem*, the holy cross.

8. An almost contrary position is found in the allegation that mysticism considers the negative aspects of God's hiddenness as the central truth about deity. The varieties of assessment of mystical theology are numerous. In our examination of the place of mystical experience in Luther, the criterion is the meaning of justification for the various authors.

9. *Johann Taulers* . . . , p. 405.

10. Ozment, p. 42.

11. See for instance, *Johann Taulers* . . . , pp. 328, 392.

12. Söderblom writes in *Humor* . . . , p. 170: "The German theologian Johann Tauler speaks about it [melancholy] in his sermons not infre-

quently." We also found that Vogelsang cited Luther as believing that Tauler knew spiritual *Anfechtung* (*supra*, p. 124).

13. Vogelsang, "Luther und . . . ," pp. 53-54.

14. *Johann Taulers* . . . , p. 45.

15. *Eine deutsche Theologie*, p. 150. Cf. p. 141: "Through Christ" a Christian's life of obedience "is already prepared." "Christ is in all, over all"; p. 187: "No one comes to the Father but through me [Christ]."

16. *W* 5; 549, 40. *W* 3; 254, 27-29. See also the discussion of bridal imagery, pp. 155-158.

17. *W* 40, 1; 284, 2 and 6-7, 1531. *LW* 26; 167-168. *W* 40, 1; 235, 6, 1531. *LW* 26; 134. *W* 40, 1; 290, 10, 1531. *LW* 26; 172. The secret event is also depicted as "Christ becoming me and I Christ," *W* 17, 1; 187, 9, 1525. Or, the Christian can say, "I am Christ." Christ can say, "I am that sinner"—author's trans. *W* 40, 1; 285, 5, 1531. *LW* 26; 168. This coincides with the experience of a contemporary mystic, Mary C. Fullerson, who in her book *By a New and Living Way*, (London: Stuart and Watkins, 1971), writes on p. 39: "I live surrounded by his Being. I live because of it. In order to bring a whole dedication at the moment of partaking of the symbols of Bread and Wine, I must acknowledge his real Presence within and without at all times and in all things."

18. *W* 19; 492, 22-493, 28.

19. *W* 3; 479, 16-18. Cf. Ruhland, p. 47.

20. All quotations from 1527 are taken from Söderblom, *Tre Livsformer: mystik, förtröstan, vetenskap* (Stockholm: Hugo Geber, 1923), p. 63.

21. *W* 40, 1; 229, 4, 1531. *LW* 26, 130.

22. *W* 40, 1; 290, 24-31. *LW* 26; 172. Luther comments on a report from Melanchthon to the effect that a youngster, returning to consciousness after hours in a deathlike state, "began to breathe again and . . . say, with joy, that he indeed had seen Christ and that he knew that another life was in store for him after this life. . . ." Christ had shown him "the wondrous joys in the other life." Luther proposes that this experience of the living Christ should be published in print after having been properly investigated. An examination took place and the description of the Christ encounter and also of a case of obsession were published at Melanchthon's and Luther's suggestion in 1530. *WB* 5; 668-669 and *WB* 5; 684, 20-21 and 685, note 3.

23. On Christ as sacrament and example, see Iserloh in *CM*, pp. 75-83. Iserloh quotes *W* 2; 501, 34-37, 1519, consisting of a comment on Galatians 2:19. *LW* 27; 238.

24. Cf. Bengt Hägglund, "Luther und die Mystik," *CM*, pp. 89-90. In Hägglund, *The Background* . . . , pp. 14-16, the following statements confirm our contention that Luther's experience of close spiritual unity with especially Johann Tauler and *Theologia Germanica* was also, and not least, related to Christology. "It is therefore not true when it is said that mysticism knows Christ only as an example and emphasizes in this connection only the imitation of Christ." Hägglund cites W. Preger, *Geschichte der deutschen Mystik im Mittelalter* (Leipzig: Dörffling & Franke, 1874-93), Vol. III, 184ff.: "As for the redemptive act in Christ's death itself, Tauler emphasizes at times its fundamental importance in so clear and exclusive a manner that one must assume that also when he speaks of God's being born in us or when he stresses the way of discipleship of Christ as the way of salvation—and both of these, to be sure, predominate in his sermons—it constitutes the self-evident basis."

It should, however, be remembered, Hägglund adds, that the cross of Christ which Luther found so vividly and prominently held forth by some mystics represented justification in man's inner being. Tauler and *Theologia Germanica* did not see justification as, primarily, an imputation of Christ's righteousness, that is to say, something that is "done outside of me." But, as we have argued in this book, Luther, who did take recourse to the objective, declarative and imputative side of the gospel, never thought that it should or could ever be separated from the birth of God in the soul. It is here that "mystical faith" comes into play.

25. On the place of the truly devotional, see Otto, *The Idea . . .* , p. 108. The purely conceptual bars us from the truly devotional, Otto maintained.

# Chapter 6

1. *W* 7; 550, 19-551, 27. *LW* 21; 303-304.

2. *Johann Taulers . . .* , p. 41.

3. *Theologia Germanica* says about the soul that it is *capax Dei*, participating in God, in possession of God, equipped to receive God. See for instance *Eine deutsche Theologie*, p. 103. I.e., dualism within unity.

4. *Johann Taulers . . .* , p. 51.

5. I am indebted to Bengt Hägglund for most of the above thoughts on Luther's concept of *the whole man* in relation to Tauler's ideas concerning the ground of the soul. See *CM*, pp. 90-92 under the article heading "Luther und die Mystik."

6. Quoted by Otto, *The Idea . . .* , p. 138 from *WT* 5; 368, number 5820. The Luther-quote continues to expound the theme as follows: "There has never been a people so wild and savage that it did not believe that there is some divine power that created all things. And thus it is that Paul says: 'The invisible things of God from the creation of the world are clearly seen, being understood by the things that are made, even his eternal power and godhead.' . . . Although men . . . have lived just as though there were no God . . . the conscience . . . testifies . . . that God is."

7. Otto, *The Idea . . .* , p. 137. Luther is quoted as saying that theological knowledge is a posteriori. " . . . we look at God from without . . . as one looks at a castle or house from without and thereby feels *(spüret)* the lord or householder thereof. But a priori from within has no wisdom of men as yet availed to discover what and of what manner of being is God as he is in himself or in his inmost essence, nor can any man know nor say aught thereof, but they for whom it has been revealed by the Holy Ghost." Otto placed the utterance in the context of Luther's suspicion of scholastic faith in reason. He also remarked that "Luther overlooks the fact that a man must 'feel' or detect the householder a priori or not at all." Otto proceeds to Luther dicta based on the a priori concept.

8. Wicks, p. 146. Wicks cites *W* 4; 469, 7.

9. *Ibid.*, pp. 74 and 273-274, reference to *W* 4; 11, 9 and *W* 4; 10, 35. Wicks uses the quoted dictum to substantiate his assumption that the early Luther's anthropology is platonic, sharply dividing the human person into a material and a spiritual part. Should not early Luther's spirit-matter dualism rather be seen as part of his thought on faith? Those

without faith *do* live in materialistic captivity, those of faith live by and in invisible things.
10. Olsson, p. 249.
11. *W* 45; 494, 21-35. *LW* 24; 37-38.
12. *Johann Taulers* . . . , pp. 489, 390.
13. See discussion of Ozment's interpretation in Chap. 2B. I subject the reader to a repetition of this illustration, since it strikes me as particularly useful for our discussion about man's nature in Luther's and the mystics' view.
14. *W* 9; 102, 34-35. As already indicated, I can see no reason in this context for Ozment's curious remark about Luther's "explicitly critical non-explicit criticism" of Tauler. *Supra*, p. 94.
15. Oberman in *CM*, pp. 57-58. Luther: "This synteresis persistently appeals in the human will." *W* 1; 32, 1.
16. *W* 1; 36, 15-19 and 36, 37-37, 2, 1514. See Oberman, *CM*, p. 58: "This synteresis signifies the esse, not the bene esse of man."
17. Oberman, *CM*, p. 56. In scholasticism *synteresis* was the ground of moral discrimination and *conscientia* its existential application, ordered by the church and often issuing in casuistry.
18. Hägglund, *CM*, p. 92. Referring to W. Preger, Bengt Hägglund, in *The Background* . . . , pp. 7-8, maintains that Tauler's "Seelengrund, or ultimate essence of the soul" should be partly understood as "the image of God in man." Yet, "we are not simply confronted with some type of synergism."
19. *WT* 1; 101, 27-37. See Chap. 2B fn. 62, pp. 247-248.
20. The Tauler quotes are from Kurt Ruh, *Altdeutsche Mystik* (Bern: A. Francke, 1950), pp. 50, 52. The somewhat anxious uncertainty over this question in theological circles is illustrated in Vogelsang's "Die Unio mystica bei Luther," p. 76. Vogelsang first declared that he was in agreement with Holl and Bornkamm who both claim that mysticism means "extinction of the Ego" and that Luther therefore could not be essentially involved in mysticism. Vogelsang thereupon wrote, apparently maintaining that he was in agreement with the ruling opinion: the "reborn" person is the "I" as "indestructible individuality." On p. 74 Vogelsang asserted that in Luther's view "personal identity" (with its Godward inclination) is antecedent to Christ becoming one with the person. On p. 48 in "Luther und die Mystik" Vogelsang averred that with Luther the psychological and the theological are united. (Quote from *W* 7; 550, 28, 1521. *LW* 21; 303. Cf. *supra*, pp. 91-92.) Vogelsang indicated that Luther supplanted mystical psychology and theology. "Interiorization . . . became a theological consideration" *(ibid.)*. Vogelsang also cautiously suggested a middle ground between continuity and discontinuity: The ground of soul and the conscience are not to be considered "indisputable God-ground" *(ibid.)*.
21. Otto, *The Idea* . . . , pp. 139, 144-154.
22. "Si vis vivere Deo, oportet te omnino mori legi. Hanc doctrinam ratio et sapientia humana non capit." *W* 40, 1; 268, 13, 1535. Among a wealth of similar assertions: "The Christian faith must stand outside reason for the faith of the Turks, the Jews and the Tartars stands inside reason." *W* 34, 2; 152, 1.
23. "Das ist die Meinung, das ich gleuben sol, das ich Gotts geschöpffe bin, das er mir geben hat leib, seel, gesunde Augen, rationem, gute, weib, kinder." *W* 30, 1; 87, 5-7.
24. *W* 55, 2, 1; 113, 5. Concerning the necessary differentiation be-

tween Luther's critical treatment of reason from a soteriological angle and his positive evaluation in the perspective of man as a creature of divine substance, see *Luther: Sol, Ratio, Erudio, Aristoteles*, Archiv für Begriffsgeschichte, Vol. XIV, 1 and Vol. XV, 1, ed. Heiko Oberman (Bonn: Bouvier-Grundmann, 1971), p. 192.

25. *W* 18; 719, 20-26. *LW* 33; 191. Author's trans.

26. *WT* 5; 368, 20-36. Luther quoted St. Paul: "The invisible things of God from the creation of the world are clearly seen, being understood by the things that are made, even his eternal power and Godhead."

27. Ozment's *Homo Spiritualis*, for instance, follows this schematization, as noted.

28. *Johann Taulers . . .*, p. 97.

29. *W* 57, 3; 153, 9. *LW* 29; 157.

30. *W* 54; 186, 9. Cf. Sadhu Sundar Singh in Nathan Söderblom, *Sundar Sings' budskap* (Stockholm: Hugo Geber, 1923), p. 16: "It became clear to me that man's heart is God's throne and castle. When he deigns to live in the heart heaven begins, and God's kingdom is there." Cf. also Luther's translation of *entos hymon*, God's kingdom is *within*. A study of exegetical comments on this passage in Luke 17:21 leads to the conclusion that the general theology of the commentator and translator in the final analysis determines whether the two words are to be translated "among," "in the midst of" on the one hand, or "within," "inside" on the other. No particular knowledge has been added since Luther's days to warrant an "among" rather than a "within," as is sometimes alleged. A pneumatic theology with a sense for the dynamic side of faith intuitively chooses the "within" which of course also, then, means "among." Even if the words were addressed to the Pharisees the *entos hymon* confirms the belief that God and his kingdom are substantially *in* man, although hidden underneath distorting sin.

# Chapter 7

1. Bengt Hägglund, *CM*, pp. 92-93, points out that the biblical stories were more than metaphors of inner experience to Luther. These stories "in their historical objectivity were determinative for salvation." Luther moved away from the preponderantly allegorical inferences drawn from the Bible by mystics, for instance Tauler. What happened historically with Jesus and his disciples grew in importance to Luther. But did this difference touch the salvation experience? No, answers Hägglund, the frequent allegation that Luther and mysticism parted company on the justification issue is groundless. Luther felt at one with Tauler and *Theologia Germanica* on this score, despite all dissimilarities.

2. Otto, *The Idea . . .*, p. 138 quoting *W* 18; 719, 20-26. *LW* 33; 191. Luther sometimes assigned God-knowledge to the realm of "the whore reason." He said that conclusions about God come a posteriori. . . . But he also, in the same book, *The Bondage of the Will* to which the previous allusion belongs, accorded true cognitions of God to human reason.

3. *W* 39, 1; 108, 5. By *fides* you become what you are, *imago Dei*.

4. Olsson, *op. cit.*, offers some penetrating insights into Luther's view of man-in-God. The most instructive remarks on the aspect now under consideration are found on pp. 458-459 and pp. 491-492. Olsson's Luther citations lack detailed references.

5. *Johann Tauler's* . . . , p. 257. Sermon on Peter 5:6: "Consider courageously and intimately your soul's ground."
6. Olsson, *op. cit.*, p. 346. Olsson writes on Luther's views: "Also after he [man] lost it [*gratia supernaturalis*] through the fall, he is imago Dei." (p. 286.)
7. *W* 14; 19, 7, 1523-1524. *W* 22; 336, 30.
8. *W* 5; 144, 21, 1520.
9. Cf. Chapter 7E, *infra*, pp. 160-162.
10. Hering, pp. 171, 175.
11. *Ibid.*, pp. 19-21.
12. *Ibid.*, p. 206.
13. *Supra*, p. 51. Reference to *W* 40, 3; 738, 4ff. The passage in question is also an illustration of Luther's use of mystical bridal imagery, hence it will reappear in the discussion of this topic. See *infra*, Chap. 7D.
14. Otto, *The Idea* . . . , p. 206.
15. *Johann Taulers* . . . , p. 321, sermon 42.
16. *W* 10, 1, 1; 387, 5-14.
17. See Oberman, *CM*, p. 59, citing *W* 1; 196, 25-26, 1517. Luther: "The prayer is that he asks for Christ, the cry [of anguish] that he confesses his wretchedness."
18. *W* 3; 372, 23-25. *W* 5; 163, 28f., as quoted in Oberman, *CM*, p. 53.
19. *W* 3; 372, 23-25. " . . . in . . . multiloquio tractari non potest, sed in summo mentis . . . et silentio, velut in raptu et extasi." Oberman draws attention to a contrast between loquaciousness and taciturnity in Luther's descriptions of quietude in *raptus:* ordinary disputations on things theological contain many words but "training the gaze on Christ, seeing him with the eyes of the soul and by an overwhelming stupefaction wrought up into near muteness, we say . . . 'ecce homo.'" *W* 1; 336, 10-12. *CM*, p. 53.
20. "In Christum plane transformari," to be fully transformed in Christ. *W* 8; 111, 29-35, 1521. Oberman, *CM*, p. 54: "If further research would confirm my contention that Luther's idea of 'extra nos' is interconnected with 'raptus,' this would emasculate one of the major arguments in favor of a 'forensic' interpretation of Luther's teaching on justification." On the actual changes in the soul as a result of salvation, see *infra*, "Participation in God," pp. 169ff.
21. Oberman, *CM*, p. 55. "When Luther mentions *rapi* (carry away, transport) in the same breath as *duci* (lead) and *pati* (suffer, let), the sinner is not a dead tool in the hand of Almighty God, and justification by faith is not quietism." *W* 5; 144, 34-36, 1519-1521. The pertinent Luther passages: " . . . in divinis virtutibus . . . non est nisi passio, raptus, motus . . . " affect, rapture, movement. *W* 5; 176, 12. "Christiana iusticia est . . . passiva, quam tantum recipimus, ubi nihil operamur sed patimur alium operari in nobis scilicet deum," "Christian righteousness is passive, we receive it only where we do not work (for it) but suffer another to work in us, namely God." *W* 40, 1; 41, 3-5.
22. *CM*, pp. 36-37 cites *W* 56; 299, 17-300, 8. *LW* 25; 287-288 and *W* 4; 64, 24-65, 6, 1513-1516, on the meaning of *accessus* in conjunction with *raptus.*
23. *W* 9; 98, 21-22, 1516. (In marginal notes on Tauler's sermons.) See Chap. 8B.
24. *W* 11; 117, 35-36, 1523.
25. *W* 9; 100, 38-39, 1516.

26. *W* 56; 300. "But who is there who thinks that he is so pure that he dares aspire to this level [the highest mystical experience] unless he is called and led into the rapture by God, as was the case with the apostle Paul, or unless he is 'taken up with Peter, James, and John, his brother.'" *LW* 25; 287-288.

27. Karl-August Meissinger, *Der katholische Luther* (München: Leo Lehnen, 1952), p. 126 quoting *Resolutiones* on the 95 theses of 1518.

28. *Johann Taulers* ..., p. 428, sermon 55.

29. *Ibid.*, p. 408, sermon 53.

30. *W* 22; 339, 30-31. Our account of *gemitus* and *raptus* owes much to Heiko Oberman's thought-provoking contribution "Simul gemitus et raptus" in *CM*, pp. 20-59. Oberman's methodology is a conceptual one; he investigates Luther's usage of central mystical concepts and images, in this case especially *gemitus* and *raptus*. Oberman rejects the phenomenological, the dogmatic and the historical-genetic method, mentioned in the Introduction to the present study. Oberman considers the phenomenological approach deficient, since, in his opinion, one cannot determine the common denominator among the mystics to whom Luther alluded. The dogmatic method is not regarded as viable since, on Protestant ground, it lacks a receiver for Luther's experience of Christ-in-us and devotes exclusive attention to the idea of Christ-for-us and Christ-outside-us. On Roman-Catholic ground the dogmatic method distinguishes between an acquired form of mysticism and a higher, "infused" kind. Oberman finds such a division alien to Luther's thought. The historical-genetic method as applied by Vogelsang draws too definitive lines between various mystics, on Oberman's view. However, Oberman's instructive discourse does employ phenomenological viewpoints and in part utilizes the Vogelsang schema.

31. *W* 40, 3; 738, 6-20, selected passages. The citations belong to Luther's exposition of Isaiah 53 written in 1544, two years before his death. See the discussion of the mystery of faith, *supra*, pp. 148ff.

32. *W* 22; 339, 9-20. From a sermon on Matthew 22, 1-14, 1537. St. Paul and "the Prophet David," Luther wrote, complain about the anguish, sorrow and fear of this life, whereas they should "soar for sheer joy." But "the joy will be set aside for them in that other life where they will see without covers over their eyes and live eternally filled with joys. Now [in this dispensation] life remains a secret, hidden, spiritual wedding, which is not seen with eyes nor attained by reasoning. Only faith can grasp it, holding fast to the Word. That is how faith hears about it [the wedding] and faith only dimly apprehends it all, on account of the unyielding flesh."

33. *W* 22; 337, 29-34. From the sermon mentioned in the previous footnote. Luther: "You may even trustingly and joyfully claim his own self [Christ's] as your own. As a bride with cordial trust relies on her bridegroom and considers her bridegroom's heart as her own heart, in that manner you should rely on Christ's love and have no doubt that he is minded toward you as you are to your own heart."

34. *W* 7; 54, 31-32. *LW* 31; 351. This is a portion of section 12 in *The Freedom of the Christian*, the content of which has already been in part noted. See also Chap. 7F, "Participation in God," where this passage and its continuation is used to illustrate the Christian's internal involvement in Christ.

35. *W* 40, 1; 241, 13-14. *LW* 26; 137. This quote is from the commentary on the Galatians, 1531, later edition 1535. In other words, the

imagery in question was employed by the "mature" Luther, as seen in this and preceding quotations.

36. *W* 57, 3; 224, 13-15. *LW* 29; 226.

37. *W* 40, 2; 422, 23-35. *LW* 12; 378. The words quoted are found between lines 30 and 35: "Sicut autem vita nunquam ociosa . . . sic Spiritus sanctus nunquam ociosus est in piis, semper aliquid agit, quod pertinet ad regnum Dei."

38. Ruhland submits a plethora of nuptial metaphors from Luther's writings in *Luther und die Brautmystik*, already mentioned above. Ruhland accords an essential place to mystical experience in the early Luther (the scope of his examination) and disagrees in part with H. Bornkamm's treatment of Luther's mystical love-union language. In his *Luther und Böhme*, pp. 234-237, Bornkamm declared that Luther gives the bridal images "a more far-reaching meaning" than Tauler. It is difficult to see quite what this verdict implies. Inasmuch as the bridal images are metaphors they naturally carry a more far-reaching meaning than the immediate literal and natural one, else they would not be metaphors. Perhaps the clue to Bornkamm's statement lies in his allegation that Luther's term "Christ in us" should not be considered Christ mysticism. To Bernard of Clairvaux, said Bornkamm, bridal terminology was nothing but love-play. But, Bornkamm continued, Luther used nuptial language to indicate transference of Christ's spiritual gifts. The question arising from this argument is, what difference would it make to describe the intent of the imagery as transference of spiritual gifts once we have realized that Luther was employing metaphorical language and that Tauler no doubt did the same? The point of nuptial imagery was doubtless in both cases to depict an inner, mystical experience. It would seem that Bornkamm would like to avoid this conclusion by making a distinction between Tauler's "love-play" and Luther's "more far-reaching meaning" and by countering with his suggestion that Luther's internalization of faith is not Christ mysticism. Bornkamm's judgment on Luther's nuptial imagery presumably issues from his rationalistic preconception which prompts the assertion that Luther's thought contained no essential affinity with the experience and reflections of the mystics. (See *supra*, on Bornkamm's generalized picture of mysticism and the moment of his preconception.)

39. Ruhland, p. 38. On the church as the body of Christ and Christ's presence therein, see Luther in *W* 3; 212, 29ff.

40. See Wilhelm Maurer, "Luthers Anschauungen über die Kontinuität der Kirche," *CM*, pp. 94-121, esp. pp. 105-106. The Luther reference at this juncture is the lecture on Genesis, *W* 42; 174, 6ff., 1535-1545. *LW* 1; 233. Quotations from Luther's Genesis lectures (*W* 42-44) have to be considered against the background that these lectures and most other commentaries on the Bible by Luther, were edited by friends and followers. Peter Meinhold has raised the question of authenticity especially with regard to the *Lectures on Genesis*. Meinhold holds that the editor, Veit Dietrich, reads Melanchthon into Luther at several junctures and that this tendency is shared by the two who completed the commentary after Dietrich's death. Meinhold asserts that the commentary's views of history, of justification, of Christ, of immortality are often at variance with those of Luther, at least of "young Luther." Yet, Meinhold concludes, "there is much genuine [Luther] material in them [the *Lectures on Genesis*]." Peter Meinhold, *Die Genesisvorlesung Luthers und ihre Herausgeber* (Stuttgart: Kohlhammer, 1936), pp. 236-256, 370-

428. Citations in the present book from Luther's *Lectures on Genesis* and other material not edited by Luther himself, are in tune with thoughts that pervade the Reformer's total production. This is to say, the fact that an idea may appear purely Melanchthonian does not necessarily exclude it from an essential place in Luther's spiritual legacy. See the discussion on "immortality" in Chap. 10, fn. 14.

41. The second lecture series on the Psalms 1518-1521, *W* 5; 548-553, 1520, containing comments on Psalm 19. The reference by Maurer, *CM*, pp. 105-106.

42. *W* 7; 597, 13ff., 1521. *LW* 21; 351.

43. *W* 39, 1; 3, 24-29.

44. *W* 39, 1; 166, 4, 1536.

45. Maurer in "Luthers Anschauungen . . . ," *CM*, p. 105, asserts that "God sustains the church through the proclamation of the word" and also that "Christ is the indissoluble relation with his body, the church, and guarantor of her continuity." Jaroslav Pelikan in the essay "Continuity and order in Luther's view of church and ministry, A Study of the De instituendis ministris ecclesiae of 1523," *CM*, writes on pp. 152-154: to say that "the continuity of the church was provided by its character as a spiritual church made up of pure believers" would be "a vast oversimplification" for Luther spoke in addition of "the vertical dimension of continuity." Pelikan also rejects the inference sometimes drawn from Luther's treatise on the ministry of 1523, namely that "the intent of Luther's Reformation was an independentist view of church and ministry." Both Maurer and Pelikan appear to bypass the mystical element in Luther's language, or, perhaps better, the personalist and individual side of his discussions on the church. However, proclaiming is not *eo ipso* a channel of Christ's presence and "vertical continuity" does not cancel the need for and reality of the "spiritual church" and "the pure believer." "Doctrina" does not involve "just telling a story" but also "to employ, lean on and eagerly follow" a vital, life-giving, felt "knowledge." *W* 40, 3; 738, 9-20.

46. *W* 12; 186, 3. *LW* 40; 29.

47. *W* 43; 388, 7. *LW* 4; 349.

48. *W* 12; 191, 28-36. As Pelikan points out in his essay on Luther and the ministry *(CM*, pp. 143-154), this allusion to Matthew 18:19-20 was made in a cause which later proved to be a disappointment. Yet, the reminder of Christ's mystical presence is rooted in a far more pervasive motif in Luther's writings than is generally acknowledged. *LW* 40; 37.

49. *W* 3; 150, 16ff. *LW* 10; 125.

50. *W* 3; 254, 25ff. Author's trans. *LW* 10; 210 renders *Christus mysticus* as "Christ in a mystical sense." See also Chap. 7, Sec. D.

51. Luther in the Lectures to the Romans, *W* 56; 379, 1-2. *LW* 25; 368.

52. Iserloh, *CM*, 60-83. The quotation in the text is from p. 70 and the Luther passage from *W* 40, 2; 422, 3-5. Translated freely in *LW* 12; 377. In the original text Luther uses the verb "sentire" ("I begin to feel so that I . . . understand"). Perhaps it is significant that the translator chose to omit "sentire" as part of understanding.

53. Hering, p. 50. "Je mehr er [Luther] selbst innerlicher wird . . ." Hering's reference to documentation is *Luthers Briefe*, ed. de Wette, I, 288. *WB* 1; 424, 132-142. (Hereafter Hering's de Wette references will be transposed to the *Weimarausgabe* without specific mention of the de Wette source.)

54. Hering, p. 52. *WB* 1; 160, 3-28. In this moving letter to Staupitz

Luther explains why he prefers "mystics and the Bible" to "scholastic doctors," not rejecting everything these doctors say but reading them "with discrimination." Hence his, Luther's, name had "assumed a foul smell with many."

55. It has been noted repeatedly in the present study that theological systematizers of different intellectualistic hues have erroneously assumed that no difference exists between mysticism and scholastic speculation. As noted, much medieval mysticism, on the contrary, refuted speculative scholasticism.

56. Hering, pp. 54-55. Hering's words for the feeling-filled spontaneity of Christian mystical language: "anmuthig, herzlich, erbaulich."

57. *Ibid.*, 257, 259.

58. *Ibid.*, pp 259-260. The Luther quotes are found in *W* 7; 215-216, 218, 1520.

59. *Ibid.*, pp. 267-268 and p. 276. *WB* 2; 425, 22-40, 1522; *LW* 48; 366-367. Luther referred to a pronouncement in Exodus 33:20, Man shall not see God and live. "As a result God speaks through man [indirectly], because not all can endure his speaking."

60. See Iserloh, *CM*, p. 68. *W* 4; 265, 30f.

61. Quoted by Iserloh, *CM*, p. 68 from *W* 57, 3; 144, 10. *LW* 29; 149. Author's trans.

62. *W* 57, 3; 185, 1-8. *LW* 29; 185. We deal here with the experiential part of salvation about which Martin Luther obviously knew a great deal. For that reason he is perhaps more to be looked upon as a conveyor of "spirituality" than a forger of theological doctrine. The affinity between a statement like the one quoted in the text above and the experience of modern mystics is striking. In *Dorothy Kerin: Called by Christ to Heal* by Dorothy Musgrave (London: Arnold, Hodder & Stoughton, 1969), we read on p. 20: "St. John of the Cross tells us that 'the touch of God upon the soul is most real for it is the substance of God that touches the substance of the soul. The sweetness of delight which this touch occasions baffles all description.' The ecstasy normally accompanying this mystical experience was as familiar to Dorothy Kerin as to St. Teresa of Avila, St. Catherine of Siena, St. Mechtild, St. Gertrude, St. Brigit, St. Angela of Foligno, to mention a few of those who were her forerunners on the Mystic Way, a path that leads to union with God only after it has traversed the dark shadows of Gethsemane and the abysmal darkness of Golgotha."

63. *W* 40, 1; 360, 5: "Fides creatrix deitatis non in persona sed in nobis." Author's trans. *LW* 26; 226-227. See also *supra*, p. 88.

64. *W* 4; 273, 14. *W* 57, 3; 153, 9f. *LW* 29; 157.

65. *Eine deutsche Theologie* . . . , p. 170. Luther has been termed theologically naive on account of his general acceptance of *Theologia Germanica*. The question is if those who thus criticize may not reflect the lesser theological acumen.

66. A Luther quote from Söderblom, *Humor* . . . , p. 327.

67. *W* 9; 440, 2-19.

68. *Ibid.*, "Ita verba Christi sunt sacramenta, per que operatur salutem nostram. . . . " "Thus Christ's words are sacraments, through which he carries out our salvation. . . . "

69. The head of the household can have a church in his house, Luther wrote in a context which admittedly invited independentist suggestions. (The Czech problem 1523, see Pelikan in *CM*, p. 153.) But the question is if this statement does not after all represent a pervasive conviction:

the word comes first, baptism belongs closely to it, the eucharist is not necessary for a person's salvation. *W* 12; 171, 17-21. *LW* 40; 9.

70. *W* 18; 139, 13-18. *LW* 40; 149. In his treatise against "the heavenly prophets" Luther defended "the externality" of the "sign" of holy communion. Yet he also spoke of the internal side of the sacrament, however, in a way quite different from Carlstadt. He pointed out that "the killing of the old man . . . should not come first . . . but rather this: to have Christ through faith in the heart as an eternal treasure." In other words, Carlstadt's way to "entgröben," to render "the signs" less gross, was the wrong way to invite the Spirit. *W* 18; 138, 10-15; *LW* 40; 148. "In brief, this is the spirit of whom I have already said that he makes inward whatever God makes outward." [i.e. the reception of Christ's body and blood in the Holy Communion.] *W* 18; 175, 9-10; *LW* 40; 185. "For spiritual eating [i.e. in the Communion] is the right recognition and remembrance of the body of Christ." *W* 18; 175, 16; *LW* 40; 185.

71. See Wilfried Joest, "Das Heiligungsproblem nach Luthers Schrift 'Wider die himmlischen Propheten,' " *CM*, pp. 189-193. Sometimes Luther might have alluded to Zwinglians when he referred to Schwärmer. G. H. Williams suggests this in "German Mysticism in the Polarization of Ethical Behavior in Luther and the Anabaptists," *The Mennonite Quarterly Review*, Vol. XLVIII, No. 3 (July 1974), 290-291. Oberman in his contribution "Simul . . . ," *CM*, pp. 44-45, takes the allusion to Schwärmer in *W* 40, 1; 251, 9-11, 1535 to mean just enthusiasts in Carlstadt's style. Williams considers the "German mystical doctrine of vocation in the world" the only trace left of Luther's earlier mystical theology. Williams' account tends to blur the line between the categories "Germanic mystics" and "mystical Schwärmer."

72. Rudolf Otto, *Die Anschauung vom heiligen Geiste bei Luther, Eine historisch-dogmatische Untersuchung.* (Göttingen: Vandenhoeck & Ruprecht, 1898), pp. 60-61. "I bring a goblet to my mouth in which there is wine. I drink the wine but I do not press the goblet down into my throat. So it is with the *Word* that brings the *voice:* it falls down into my heart and comes alive. But the voice remains outside and wanes. Therefore it is a divine power." *W* 12; 300; *LW* 30; 45. Here we find another expression of the subtle balance between the "sign" and "the experience" in Luther's thought. On pp. 82-83 *ibid.* Luther is quoted (*W* 7; 546; *LW* 21; 299) as follows: "For no one is able to understand God or God's word accurately unless it occurs without means from the Holy Spirit. The highly praised Virgin Mary speaks from her own experience in which she had been illumined and taught through the Holy Spirit. . . . No one can receive it from the Holy Spirit except that he experiences it, tries it and feels it; and in precisely that experience the Holy Spirit teaches as a teacher in his own school." In the school of the Spirit Luther considered the law and the cross as *media*. " . . . hold fast to the Word which he [Christ] addresses to you: 'See my hands and feet.' Then your heart will again become joyful . . . and you will relish his Word within your heart and it will be sheer honey and sweet comfort." *W* 21; 250, 4-7. As we see, Luther constantly placed emphasis on personal experience and concomitant change in man.

73. Martin Luther, *Vom unfreien Willen*, O. Schumacher, ed. (Göttingen: Vandenhoeck & Ruprecht, 1937), p. 40.

74. That Luther thought in terms of a spiritual-psychological change or transformation as part of the Christ experience is evident from

numerous statements on various theological *loci*. He said, for example: "Thus the cross is the way by which God wants to work on us without overwhelming us, so that we may daily become more and more purified." *W* 40; 3; 200, 21-23, 1532-1533 (1540). Luther's *manuscript* lends further strength to the emphasis on "growth" and "sanctification." *W* 40, 3; 199, 2-13. And the counterpoint concerning the mediation offered by the church and her orders: as an institution she does not mediate salvation but it should be remembered that "the true church moves . . . in heaven." Christ, not the church, is the rock. (Hering, p. 31, with reference to Rambach's translation in Walch, *Luthers Werke*, Vol. IX, 2118, the Psalm Glosses of 1513. Cf. *W* 3; 388-389, 1513-1516 and *W* 47; 234-235, 1537-1540).

75. Vogelsang, "Luther . . . ," pp. 52-53 avers that Luther conceived of the Word both as mystical *generatio* and "the oral word of the gospel" whereas the mystics only had the former. It is difficult to see how this allegation can be substantiated as a general judgment. The references in the text are to *Eine deutsche Theologie*, pp. 95, 97 and 155, then to *J. Taulers* . . . , pp. 358-359.

76. Tauler, *The Inner Way*, p. 178.

77. Among numerous dicta on this topic: *W* 19; 219, 31-32, 1526. *W* 23; 133, 29-30, 1527. *LW* 37; 57.

78. For instance, *W* 4; 32, 3-5, 1513-1516.

79. Luther found himself in tune with Bernard of Clairvaux on the nature of Christian growth. In his tension between concupiscence and grace, a Christian knows that "stare est retrogredi," to stand still is to recede. *W* 9; 69, 36.

80. *W* 1; 219, 34-36, 1517. Cf. *W* 18; 529, 17-18, 1525. Author's trans. *LW* 14; 204. Cf. Chap. 3, note 45.

81. Vogelsang, "Die Unio . . . , " pp. 63-66. *W* 7; 25, 34.

82. In other contexts of the present essay referred to as *Of the Liberty of a Christian* and *De Libertate*.

83. Iserloh, *CM*, pp. 71-75, quoting Luther: *W* 7; 25, 26, 10.

84. *W* 56; 343, 18-23; *LW* 25; 332.

85. *W* 2; 145-152, esp. 145, 14-21.

86. *W* 40, 1; 285, 24-27, quoted by Iserloh, *CM*, p. 73. *LW* 26; 168.

87. "Sola humanitas nihil effecisset, sed divinitas humanitati coniuncta sola fecit et humanitas propter divinitatem." *W* 40, 1; 417, 12-40, 418, 11. *LW* 26; 266-267. Peter Manns in "Absolute and Incarnate Faith—Luther on Justification in the Galatians' Commentary of 1531-1535," Jared Wicks, ed., *Catholic Scholars* . . . , pp. 156-157, maintains that Luther's thought moved within a paradoxical unity which escapes "the Protestant scholars." The latter are "entangled in the confining alternative of *lex implenda* or *lex impleta*." Manns argues that Luther's "principles" pointed beyond this either-or of works and grace. The principles included a transformation of Christian man as he cooperates with God in salvation. "Along with Luther we understand the mystery of love through grace in terms of the mystery of righteousness to be advanced and revealed. . . . The specific originality of Luther's doctrine of justification is not thereby violated. We go beyond Luther—however, following his basic principles—by simply expanding the *simul* of 'sin and righteousness' by means of this other *simul:* our effort as necessary for salvation *and* pure grace. . . . Thus . . . faith truly becomes incarnate faith through active charity."

88. When Luther said, "Our invisible spirit is immersed in visible real-

ities," *W* 4; 11, 9, his idea did not reflect a Platonic world-view but perhaps a Platonic anthropology; this was at least true of earlier dicta. See Wicks, p. 75.

89. Some hold, Luther said, that the sun of which Psalm 19:4-5 speaks, is the visible sun, as an allegory of Christ's humanity manifested in the church. Luther himself, however, considered the sun the outward sign for the mystical Christ, "the Sun of righteousness who illumines, works and is all" in his followers. *W* 5; 548, 5-8, 14-17, 549, 6-9, 1519-1521. Concerning Christ as *sol*, the sun, see Oberman, ed., *Luther: Sol . . . ,* pp. 177-191.

90. "The body is visible heaven and earth, the eyes are stars, thunder and lightning are the words of wrath, darkening the forehead, i.e., heaven, and the eyes, i.e., the sun and the stars." *W* 4; 599, 21-23.

91. "Christ is formed in us and we are formed according to his image." *W* 39, 1; 204, 12-13, 1537. On being molded in the Spirit: *W* 14; 19, 7, 1523-1524. *W* 22; 336, 24-31, 1537. *W* 5; 144, 20, 1519-1521. *W* 4; 305, 31-34, 1513-1516.

92. *Die Predigten Taulers . . . ,* p. 348. *W* 9; 103, 40.

93. *W* 1; 436, 20. See Oberman, ed., *Luther: Sol . . . ,* pp. 258-259 on "homo spiritualis, rationalis, sensualis."

94. Quote from Luther in Rudolf Otto, *Aufsätze das Numinose betreffend* (F. A. Perthes, Stuttgart, 1923), p. 61. A comparison is made with Johann von Kastl's *De Adhaerendo Dei.* Von Kastl spoke of being "transformed, cleave to, become one in God." Otto: "Luther says *nothing* of the impelling power of Faith to bring to new birth, to justify and to sanctify, that is not also said" in this book.

95. Otto, *The Idea . . . ,* p. 206. Gal. 2:20: "I have been crucified with Christ; it is no longer I who live, but Christ who lives in me; and the life I now live in the flesh I live by faith in the Son of God, who loved me and gave himself for me." 1 Cor. 6:17: "But he who is united to the Lord becomes one spirit with him." See J. Arndt, *True Christianity* (Philadelphia: The Lutheran Bookstore, 1888), p. 14.

96. Otto, *The Idea . . . ,* p. 206.

97. *Ibid.,* pp. 96-97. As pointed out, "the numinous consciousness" should be seen as the background to the statements about the unfree will in *The Bondage of the Will.* See Chap. 3A, pp. 105-110.

98. "Supernatural" is used in this study only to denote a contraposition to the limited idea of Enlightenment thinking that "the natural" contains merely empirically observable, sensebound facts and that "knowledge" is derived exclusively within this framework. "Supernatural" is therefore more a pedagogical term than a theological one in this essay.

# Chapter 8

1. *W* 5; 45, 30-33 (Ps. 1). Cf. Hering, p. 94.

2. *W* 5; 504, 3-7, 506, 20-30, 1519-1521 (Ps. 18) Hering, *loc cit.*

3. Among many allusions to Heb. 11:1: *W* 3; 498, 27-36, 1513-1515; *LW* 10; 440; *W* 14; 692, 2-6, 1525; *LW* 9; 203; *W* 43; 554, 30-35, 1535-1545; *LW* 5; 183; *W* 44; 377, 33-37, 1535-1545; *LW* 7; 105-106; *W* 44; 700, 19-21, 1535-1545; *LW* 8; 166. See also *W* 33; 114, 13-16.

4. *WB* 1; 224, 13-14, 1518.

5. "I am surprised that a person can fall so far from the knowledge

of God as Erasmus has fallen. Erasmus is as certain that there is no God and no ongoing life (after death) as I am that I see." *WT* 2; 146, 16-19, 1532.

6. *WB* 2; 336, 9-10; *LW* 48; 221; *WB* 2; 357, 18-19, 359, 123-124.

7. *WB* 2; 348, 44-48, 1521; *LW* 48; 232 (Letter to Melanchthon).

8. Lapaeus, Johannes, *Doctor Martin Luthers Prophetior* (Söderhamn: Hamberg, 1851), pp. 27-28. In this Swedish translation of Lapaeus the Swedish translator reveals his cautious Orthodox Lutheran *Sitz im Leben* by footnoting to the Lutheran public's comfort: "The intention is naturally not to claim that Luther, like the Prophets, had immediate inspiration from God's Spirit; he was only mediately inspired and guided by the same Spirit, even as a Prophet."

9. "Satan began to dispute with me . . . he said, we condemned spirits have no faith in his [Christ's] mercy. . . ." Quote from Luther of 1521 in M. Michelet, *The Life of Luther* (London: George Bell & Sons, 1878). On obsession and possession by demonic spirits Luther spoke in his Table Talks, *WT* 1; 403-404. The relative power of "the bad angels" is described, for instance, in *WT* 2; 386 and *WT* 6; 120-121 (where the liberated will is depicted as liberation from captivity under extra-terrestrial demonic power).

10. Hering, p. 225. *W* 8; 177, 13-17, 1521. On Christ's power over Satan see, e.g., *WT* 2; 503, 20-24, 1532. *WT* 6; 83, 13-19. On Christ's angels, "given to each person," see *W* 4; 597, 26.

11. Lapaeus, p. 119. Luther's letter of the 17th of January 1546.

12. *Supra,* pp. 68-71. Luther's *Sermon on the Angels (Ein Predigt . . .)* in *W* 32; 111-121.

13. Luther, *Ein Predigt* . . . See Hirsch, pp. 47-48, a discussion on the difference between "a spiritually clear, thinking mind" and "the simple mind" which is in need of concrete guarantees and the palpableness of the divine. Luther is classed with the former, in an attempt to show that the Reformer placed no essential value on the thought of "invisibles." The mystics closest to Luther spoke about angels with the same meaning as Luther. *Eine deutsche Theologie,* p. 3: The angels exist, they are "spirits," devils are "evil angels." *J. Taulers* . . . , pp. 519-520: We are united with them by our every deed and thought.

14. Otto, *West-östliche* . . . , pp. 348-352. Luther's tract on prayer is also mentioned on p. 47 in the present book.

15. From Luther's tract *How to Pray,* translations by author. The original text is found in *W* 38; 358-375. There have been several English translations; one is found in *LW* 43; 193-211.

16. *WT* 6; 209, 20-34, Table Talk from 1546. Similarly, *WT* 5; 87, 16-22, 88, 1-3, 1540. See also *WB* 2; 397, 17-21, 1521: "Believe me, I am subjected to a thousand devils ("Satanibus") in this uneventful solitude. It is so much easier to combat the incarnated devil, that is to say, people, than evil spirit creatures in celestial realms" ("coelestibus") Eph. 6:12. On Luther's remarks in *Table Talks* concerning the diabolical, see *WT* 6; 204-222. Luther made it clear that Eph. 6:12-13 and Col. 2:15 deal with invisible but real demonic power. *W* 10, 3; 15-20, 1522; *LW* 51:73.

17. The positive salients of the invisible, described in Eph. 3:10 received Luther's attention, as seen in his words about angels. On Luther's remarks in the *Table Talks* concerning the angelic, see *WT* 1; 399, 25-400, 23. *WT* 3; 9; 35-10; 6. *WT* 4; 254, 36-39. *WT* 5; 444, 1-2. *WT* 6; 203, 32-204, 11 (angels as guardians). *WT* 4; 85, 8-86, 16. *WT* 4; 668, 9-10.

*WT* 5; 63, 21-25. *WT* 5; 211, 27-28. *WT* 5; 552, 1-7 (teaching about angels). *WT* 6; 69, 1-12 (relation to Christ). Other similar passages: *W* 32; 117. *W* 34, 2; 280f. *W* 34, 2; 277. *W* 43; 228. *W* 52; 720.
18. Söderblom, *Humor* . . . , p. 81.
19. *W* 11; 117, 35-36, 1523. See *supra*, Chap. 7C.
20. From Söderblom, *Humor* . . . , p. 306.
21. John Gottlieb Morris, *Quaint Sayings and Doings concerning Luther* (Philadelphia: Lindsay & Blakiston, 1859), p. 260.
In *WT* 1; 74, No. 157 *(LW* 54; 23) we read: "In January, 1532, he [Martin Luther] foretold that he would be sick, that in March he would be overtaken by a grave illness." Actually the ailment struck him already in January.
22. *LW* 8; ix-x with reference to the Latin section of the Wittenberg edition of Luther's Works, Vol. VI. See also *W* 40, 3; 1594; *LW* 13; 141.
23. Eph. 3:1-6.

# Chapter 9

1. *W* 9; 98, 33-34. *W* 9; 100, 28-30.
2. *WT* 1; 302, 30-35.
3. In relation to Gal. 5:20: "The works of the flesh are . . . idolatry, sorcery. . . ." *W* 2; 589, 37-590, 9. *LW* 27; 369.
4. *W* 45; 529-530.
5. *WT* 1; 419-420.
6. *Supra*, p. 191.
7. William Ralph Inge, *Christian Ethics and Modern Problems* (London: G. P. Putnam's Sons, 1932), p. 230. See note 1.
8. Matthew 10:7-8: "Preach as you go, saying, 'The kingdom of heaven is at hand.' Heal the sick, raise the dead . . . cast out demons . . . You received without pay, give without pay." Luther wrote about sacramental healing: "Similarly, we too [like the stricken man in the story of the Good Samaritan] are not entirely cured by baptism or repentance, but a beginning is made in us and the bandage of the first grace binds our wounds so that our healing may proceed from day to day until we are cured." *W* 7; 337, 14-20. *LW* 32; 24. The remark is consonant with other assertions by Luther to the effect that a change of direction through God-given faith begins when a person is "righted with God." Then an integrating force sets in which engenders greater unity between body, soul and spirit, as noted in Chapter 7 of the present essay. (7 F: "Participation in God.")
9. Luther's references to Christ as "sun" can be found in Oberman, ed., *Sol* . . . , pp. 179-191.
10. *W* 5; 549, 2, 6. Comment on Psalm 18:6: "We have received the sun allegorically from the mystical Christ, proclaimed through the apostles." *W* 5; 549, 38-40.
11. Söderblom, *Tre livsformer* . . . , p. 64. The Luther letter quoted is of 1528, *WB* 4; 319, 7-11. Luther indirectly raises the question whether the prayer for healing must be followed by the removal of the ill in order to be termed efficacious. I think Luther's answer is in the negative. The "point" lies in the turning to Christ, the sharing with Christ. The same problem is discussed by Bishop Lloyd in Dorothy Kerin's *Fulfilling* (Hodder & Stoughton, London, 1969), p. 52: "Undoubtedly we are here up against the mystery of suffering and pain which none of

us can understand. But here again the thought of sharing may help us. Our blessed Lord did not come to take away all pain from the earth but he did come to share it, *all* of it, whenever he can get to it."

12. Theophilus Stork, *The Life of Martin Luther and the Reformation in Germany* (Philadelphia: Lindsay and Blakiston, 1854), pp. 74-75. August Nebe, *Luther as a Spiritual Adviser*, trans. Charles A. Hay and Charles E. Hay (Philadelphia: Lutheran Pub. Soc., 1894), pp. 54-55.

13. Luther quoted in Michelet, p. 437.

14. Luther quoted in Morris, p. 262. James 5:14-15. "Is any among you sick? Let him call for the elders of the church, and let them pray over him, anointing him with oil in the name of the Lord; and the prayer of faith will save the sick man, and the Lord will raise him up; and if he has committed sins he will be forgiven."

15. Lapaeus, pp. 20-23.

16. *WB* 11; 112, 1545.

17. See *supra* the discussion of Luther's sermon on the angels, Chap. 2, Sec. B. Also, Chap. 8 and footnotes 16 and 17.

18. Luke 20:38, Matthew 22:31-32. See Luther's elaboration in the next chapter.

# Chapter 10

1. The Revised Standard Version has the following translation of 2 Samuel 7:12: ". . . you lie down with your fathers."

2. *WB* 2; 422, 4-17. Luther added that he felt the same would apply to the damned: some feel their punishments immediately upon death, others are "separated until that day." *WB* 2; 422, 18-19. Luther's reference: Luke 16:24.

3. *W* 10, 1, 2; 388, 30-31, 1526, sermon by Luther on the 16th Sunday after Trinity, text Luke 7:11-17. The previous Luther quote, reflecting an Old Testament concept of life after death as shadowy darkness and complete amnesia, is found in Osmo Tiililä, *Döden och odödligheten* (Helsingfors: Församlingsförbundets Bokförlag, 1964), p. 122. Tiililä writes about the suggestion that the soul in the predominant NT view is not only consciously living after death but in fact perhaps also in the process of decision-making, hence negative or positive evolution: "There are theologians who shy away from the latter assumption, as this would bring evolutionism into theology. But can on the whole conscious life exist without development? . . . Since sin basically consists of a spiritual attitude of wicked will, the liberation from a body of flesh and blood can hardly mean definitive purification. What should we say about all the individual shadings and grades of sin? Paul le Seur remarks that the penitent robber and the apostle John had hardly attained the same degree of maturity at the time of their deaths. Should not God deal with them severally considering their different needs?" Cf. *supra*, p. 41.

4. *W* 45; 494, 21-35. *LW* 24; 37-38.

5. *W* 45; 19-27. *LW* 24; 42-43.

6. Luther on Magdalen's death: *WT* 5; 190-191. The account is partially translated in *LW* 54; 430-431. On participation in divine life and immortal life: "Man is a unique creature and made to participate in divinity and immortality." *W* 42; 87, 17-18, 1535-1545.

7. *W* 57, 3; 215, 8-14, 1517. Heb. 9:23-24. *LW* 29; 216-217. See also *W* 56; 324-328, 1515-1516. *LW* 25; 312-315.

8. *W* 57, 3; 231, 13-20, 1517. Heb. 11:4. *LW* 29; 233.
9. *W* 47; 434, 36-41. *W* 47; 435, 1537-1540.
10. *W* 42; 556, 1-7, 1535-1545. *LW* 3; 10-11. It should be noted that Luther in other contexts terms "the conclusion that man is an extraordinary animal created for immortality . . . almost useless." *W* 42; 93, 38-39, 1535-1545. *LW* 1; 124-125.
11. *W* 40, 1; 428, 29-30; 429, 1-3, 1535. Galatians 3:12. *LW* 26; 274.
12. *W* 45; 499, 1-8. John 14:5-6. *LW* 24; 42-43.
13. *W* 45; 501, 19-21, 1538. *LW* 24; 45. *W* 45; 502, 1-4, 1538. *LW* 24; 45. John 14:5-6.
14. Peter Meinhold suggests in *Die Genesisvorlesung* . . . that Luther's Genesis lectures *(W* 42-44), having been published in transcribed form, may contain ideas not germane to Luther, especially views on "natural immortality." However, there is sufficient evidence in other contexts to support the suggestion that belief in immortality was an important component in the Reformer's thought, but a component which derived its meaning from "eternal life." In the tradition of Erich Seeberg, his mentor, Meinhold makes a sharp distinction between what he understands to be Luther's "transcendental theological notions" and "the psychological," the latter considered an aberration of faith perpetrated in Melanchthon circles. Similarly Meinhold submits that Luther believed in a "resurrection of body and soul" whereas the Melanchthon circle embraced the thought of "the immortality of the soul." The distinctions thus made are rather the outcomes of a special way of theologizing about Luther's legacy than expressions of evidence at hand. See Meinhold, pp. 100-103 and 392-393. See Chap. 7 of the present work, fn. 40.
15. *W* 2; 695, 16-38, 1519.
16. *W* 2; 696, 11-19, 1519. "Foll machen mit Ewigkeit," is Luther's expression, "fill to the brim with eternity."
17. *W* 2; 696, 24-27, 1519.
18. *W* 2; 697, 22-24, 1519.
19. *W* 51; 194, 4-30, 1546. *LW* 51; 391-392.

# Bibliography

## BOOKS

Aland, Kurt. *Hilfsbuch zum Lutherstudium.* Gütersloh: Bertelsmann, 1957.
*Archiv für Reformationsgeschichte.* Gütersloh: Berthelsmann, 1951—.
Arndt, Johannes. *Förklaring över Catechismum.* Åbo, 1728.
―――. *True Christianity.* Philadelphia: Lutheran Bookstore, 1888.
―――. *Vier Bücher vom wahren Christentum.* Berlin: Trowitsch & Sohn, 1831.
Asheim, Ivar (ed.). *The Church, Mysticism, Sanctification and the Natural in Luther's Thought.* Philadelphia: Fortress, 1967. *(CM)*
Barth, Karl. *Church Dogmatics.* Vols. I-IV. Edinburgh: T. & T. Clark, 1960-1969.
―――. *Die Kirchliche Dogmatik.* Vols. I-IV. Zürich: EvZ, 1953-1967.
Benz, Ernst. *Der Heilige Geist in Amerika.* Düsseldorf-Köln: Eugen Diederichs, 1970.
―――. *Die Vision, Erfahrungsformen und Bilderwert.* Stuttgart: Ernst Klett, 1971.
Benz, Ernst and L. A. Zander. *Evangelisches und orthodoxes in Begegnung und Auseinandersetzung.* Hamburg: Agentur des Rauhen Hauses, 1952.
Billing, Einar. *Ett bidrag till frågan om Luthers religiösa och teologiska utvecklingsgång.* Uppsala: Akad. Bokhandeln, 1917.
Boeke, R. *Divinatie, met name bij Rudolf Otto.* Leiden: F. Dijkstra, 1957.
Bornkamm, Heinrich. *Luthers geistige Welt.* Lüneburg: Heliand-Verlag, 1947.
―――. *Luther's World of Thought.* St. Louis: Concordia, 1958.
―――. *Luther und Böhme.* Bonn: A. Marcus & E. Webers Verlag, 1925.
―――. *Mystik, Spiritualismus und die Anfänge des Pietismus im Luthertum.* Giessen: A. Töpfelmann, 1926.
―――. *Protestantismus und Mystik.* Giessen: A. Töpfelmann, 1934.
―――. (ed.). *Imago Dei. Beiträge zur theologischen Antropologie.* Giessen: A. Töpfelmann, 1932.
Bouyer, Louis. *Orthodox Spirituality and Protestant and Anglican Spirituality.* London: Burns & Oates, 1969.

273

Calovius, Abraham. *Hypomnemata.* Wittenberg, 1664.

Davidson, Robert F. *Rudolf Otto's Interpretation of Religion.* Princeton: Princeton University Press, 1947.

*Eine deutsche Theologie.* Joseph Bernhart, ed. Leipzig: Im Insel-Verlag, 1922.

*Eyn deutsch Theologia.* Martin Luther, ed. Wittenberg, 1518.

Ebeling, Gerhard. *Evangelische Evangelienauslegung.* München: Lempp, 1942.

————. *Luther, Einführung in sein Denken.* Tübingen: J. C. B. Mohr, 1964. ET: *Luther: An Introduction to His Thought.* Philadelphia: Fortress, 1970.

Eckhart, Meister. *Deutsche Predigten und Traktate.* Joseph Quint, ed. München: Hauser, 1955.

Fagerberg, Holsten. *A New Look at the Lutheran Confessions.* St. Louis: Concordia, 1972.

Filthaut, E. (ed.). *Johannes Tauler: ein deutscher Mystiker.* Essen: Hans Driewer, 1961.

Forster, Karl. (ed.). *Wandlungen des Lutherbildes.* Würzburg: Echter-Verlag, 1966.

Förster, Th. *Luthers Wartburgsjahr. Schriften für das deutsche Volk,* XXV. Halle: Max Niemeyer, 1895.

Franzen, August (ed.). *Um Reform und Reformation.* Münster: Aschendorff, 1968.

Fullerson, Mary C. *By a New and Living Way.* London: Stuart & Watkins, 1971.

Goertz, H.-J. *Innere und äussere Ordnung in der Theologie Thomas Müntzers.* Leiden: Brill, 1967.

*Grundtlicher Beweis, dass die Calvinische Irthumb. . . .* Wittenberg, 1664.

Haag, Herbert (ed.). *Bibel-Lexikon.* Zürich: Benziger Verlag Einsiedeln, 1956.

Haas, Alois. *Nim din Selbes war,* Zum Selbstverständnis der Mystiker. Freiburg: Universitätsverlag, 1971.

Hägglund, Bengt. *The Background of Luther's Doctrine of Justification in Late Medieval Theology.* Philadelphia: Fortress, 1971.

Harkness, Georgia. *Mysticism: its meaning and message.* Nashville: Abingdon, 1973.

Harnack, Adolf. *Lehrbuch der Dogmengeschichte.* Vols. I-III. 4th ed. Tübingen: J. C. B. Mohr, 1909. ET: *History of Dogma.* Vols. I-VII. London: Williams & Norgate, 1896-1899. Translated from the 2nd and 3rd German ed.

Hering, Hermann. *Die Mystik Luthers.* Leipzig: J. L. Hinrich, 1879.

Hirsch, Emanuel. *Das Wesen des reformatorischen Christentums.* Berlin: Walter de Gruyter & Co., 1963.

Holl, Karl. *Gesammelte Aufsätze zur Kirchengeschichte,* Vol. I: *Luther,* 2nd and 3rd eds. Tübingen: J. C. B. Mohr, 1923.

————. *Luthers etiska åskådning.* Stockholm: SKS, 1928.

————. *Was verstand Luther unter Religion?* Tübingen: J. C. B. Mohr, 1917.

Inge, William Ralph. *Christian Ethics and Modern Problems.* London: G. P. Putnam's Sons, 1932.

Jeans, James. *The Mysterious Universe.* New York: Macmillan, 1932.

Joest, Wilfried. *Ontologie der Person bei Luther.* Göttingen: Vandenhoeck & Ruprecht, 1967.

Kerin, Dorothy. *Fulfilling.* London: Hodder & Stoughton, 1969.

Lapaeus, Johannes. *Doctor Martin Luthers Prophetior.* Söderhamn: Hamberg, 1851.

Ljunggren, Gustaf. *Synd och skuld i Luthers teologi.* Stockholm: SKDB, 1928.

Löfgren, David. *Die Theologie der Schöpfung bei Luther.* Göttingen: Vandenhoeck & Ruprecht, 1960.

Luthardt, Ernst. *Kompendium i dogmatik.* Stockholm: A. V. Carlson, 1879.

*Luther-Jahrbuch.* Amsterdam: John Benjamins N.V., 1966- .

Luther, Martin. *D. Martin Luthers Werke.* Kritische Gesamtausgabe. Weimarausgabe, Vols. 1-58. Weimar: Hermann Böhlaus, 1883-. *(W)*

―――. *D. Martin Luthers Werke.* Weimarausgabe, Briefwechsel. Vol. 1-14. Weimar: Hermann Böhlaus, 1930-1970. *(WB)*

―――. *D. Martin Luthers Werke.* Weimarausgabe. Tischreden. Vols. 1-6. Weimar: Hermann Böhlaus, 1912-1921. *(WT)*

―――. *Luther's Works.* Ed. by H. T. Lehmann and J. Pelikan. Vols. 1-54. St. Louis and Philadelphia: Concordia and Fortress, 1955-.

―――. *Ein Predigt von den Engeln.* Wittenberg: University of Uppsala, 1535.

―――. *Ob man vor dem Sterben fliehen möge.* Wittenberg, 1527.

―――. *Om en kristen människas frihet.* Swed. transl. Stockholm: SKDB, 1964.

―――. *Vom unfreien Willen.* Edited by O. Schumacher. Göttingen: Vandenhoeck & Ruprecht, 1937.

―――. *Wie man beten soll; für Meister Peter Balbierer.* Wittenberg, 1535.

McSorley, Harry J. *Luther: Right or Wrong?* An ecumenical-theological study of Luther's major work, *The Bondage of the Will.* Minneapolis and New York: Augsburg and Newman, 1969.

Martin, Alfred v. (ed.). *Luther in ökumenischer Sicht.* Von evangelischen und katolischen Mitarbeitern. Stuttgart: Fr. Frommanns Verlag, 1929.

Meinhold, Peter. *Die Genesisvorlesung Luthers und ihre Herausgeber.* Stuttgart: Verlag von W. Kohlhammer, 1936.

Meissinger, Karl-August. *Der katholische Luther.* München: Leo Lehnen, 1952.

Michelet, M. *The Life of Luther,* 2nd ed. London: George Bell and Sons, 1878.

Mieth, Dietmar. *Die einheit von Vita Activa und Vita Contemplativa in den deutschen Predigten und Traktaten Meister Eckharts und bei Johannes Tauler.* Regensburg: Friedrich Pustet, 1969.

Morris, John Gottlieb. *Quaint Sayings and Doings concerning Luther.* Philadelphia: Lindsay & Blakiston, 1859.

Muschig, Walter. *Die Mystik in der Schweiz.* Frauenfeld: Huber & Co., 1935.

Nebe, August. *Luther as Spiritual Adviser.* Translated by Charles A. Hay & Charles E. Hay. Philadelphia: Lutheran Publication Society, 1894.

Niebuhr, Reinhold. *The Nature and Destiny of Man,* Vols. I & II. London: Nisbet & Co., 1941-1943.

Oberman, Heiko (ed.). *Luther: sol, ratio, erudio, Aristoteles.* Archiv für Begriffsgeschichte, Vol. XV, 1. Bonn: Bouvier-Grundmann, 1971.

Olsson, Herbert. *Schöpfung, Vernunft und Gesetz in Luthers Theologie.* Uppsala: Acta Universitatis, 1971.

Osiander, Andreas. *Ein Disputation von der Rechtfertigung.* Königs-
    berg, 1551.
Otto, Rudolf. *Aufsätze das Numinose betreffend.* Stuttgart: F. A.
    Perthes, 1923.
————. *Die Anschauung vom Heiligen Geiste bei Luther.* Göttingen:
    Vandenhoeck & Ruprecht, 1898.
————. *The Idea of the Holy,* 2nd ed. New York: Oxford U. Press,
    (1923), 1960.
————. *Naturalistische und religiöse Weltansicht,* 2nd ed. Tübingen:
    J. C. B. Mohr, 1909.
————. *West-östliche Mystik.* Gotha: Leopold Klotz, 1929.
Ozment, Steven E. *Homo Spiritualis.* A comparative study of the an-
    thropology of Johannes Tauler, Jean Gerson and Martin Luther (1509-
    16) in the context of their theological thought. Leiden: E. J. Brill,
    1969.
Pieper, Franz & Mueller, J. T. *Christliche Dogmatik.* St. Louis, Mo.:
    Missouri Synod, 1946.
Preger, Wilhelm, *Geschichte der deutschen Mystik im Mittelalter.* Vols.
    I-III Leipzig: Dörffling & Franke, 1874-1893.
————. (ed.) *Luthers Tischreden aus den Jahren 1531 und 1532 nach
    den Aufzeichnungen von Johann Schlaginhaufen.* Leipzig: Dörffling
    & Franke, 1888.
Prenter, Regin. *Spiritus Creator.* Philadelphia: Fortress, 1953.
*Die Religion in Geschichte und Gegenwart.* Tübingen: J. C. B. Mohr,
    1957-1965 *(RGG)*
*The Revised Standard Version of the Bible*
Ritschl, Albrecht. *Die christliche Lehre von der Rechtfertigung und
    Versöhnung.* Bonn: Adolph Marcus, 1882. ET: *The Christian Doctrine
    of Justification and Reconciliation.* Clifton, N.J.: Reference Book Pub-
    lishers, 1966.
————. *Geschichte des Pietismus in der reformierten Kirche.* Bonn:
    Adolph Marcus, 1880.
Rogness, Michael. *Philip Melanchthon: Reformer Without Honor.* Min-
    neapolis: Augsburg, 1969.
Ruh, Kurt. *Altdeutsche Mystik.* Bern: A. Francke, 1950.
Ruhland, Friedrich Theophil. *Luther und die Brautmystik nach Luthers
    Schrifttum bis 1521.* Giessen: Münchowsche Universitätsdruckerei,
    1938.
Schleiermacher, Friedrich. *Der christliche Glaube.* Vols. I & II. Berlin:
    W. de Gruyter & Co., 1960. ET: *The Christian Faith.* Edinburgh:
    T. & T. Clark, 1960.
Schloenbach, Manfred. *Heiligung als Fortschreiten und Wachstum des
    Glaubens in Luthers Theologie.* Kuopio: Savon Sanomain Kirjapaino,
    1963.
Schmid, Heinrich. *Die Dogmatik der evangelisch-lutherischen Kirche.*
    3rd ed. Frankfurt am Main: Heyder & Zimmer, 1853. ET: *The Doc-
    trinal Theology of the Evangelical Lutheran Church.* Trans. from 6th
    German ed. Minneapolis: Augsburg, reprint 1961.
Schütte, Hans-Walter. *Religion und Christentum in der Theologie Ru-
    dolf Ottos.* Berlin: W. de Gruyter & Co., 1869.
Seeberg, Erich. *Grundzüge der Theologie Luthers.* Stuttgart: W. Kohl-
    hammer Verlag, 1940.
Söderblom, Nathan. *Humor och melankoli och andra Lutherstudier.*
    Stockholm: SKSR, 1919.

————. *Sundar Singhs budskap.* Stockholm: Hugo Geber, 1923.
————. *Tre livsformer: mystik, förtröstan, vetenskap.* Stockholm: Hugo Geber, 1922.
Stork, Theophilus. *The Life of Martin Luther and the Reformation in Germany.* Philadelphia: Lindsay & Blakiston, 1854.
Strauch, Philipp. *Meister Eckhart-Probleme.* Halle: E. Karras, 1919.
Stupperich, Robert. *Melanchthon.* Philadelphia: Westminster, 1960.
Tauler, Johann. *The Inner Way,* being thirty-six sermons for festivals by John Tauler. Edited by A. W. Hutton. London: Methuen & Co., n.d.
————. *Johann Taulers Predigten.* Edited by Georg Hofmann. Freiburg: Herder, 1961.
————. *Die Predigten Taulers aus der Engelberger und der Freiburger Handschrift.* Edited by Ferdinand Vetter. Berlin: Weidmannsche Buchhandlung, 1910.
*Theologia Germanica.* See *Eine deutsche Theologie.*
Tiililä, Osmo. *Döden och odödligheten.* Helsingfors: Församlingsförbundets Bokförlag, 1964.
Underhill, Evelyn. *The Mystics of the Church.* London: J. Clarke, 1925.
Vogelsang, Erich. *Der angefochtene Christus bei Luther.* Berlin: Verlag von Walter de Gruyter & Co., 1932.
Wicks, Jared. *Man Yearning for Grace.* Washington: Corpus Books, 1968.
————. (ed.). *Catholic Scholars Dialogue with Luther.* Chicago: Loyola Univ. Press, 1970.
Wolf, Ernst. *Staupitz und Luther.* Leipzig: Heinsius Nachf., 1927.


ARTICLES

Bigelmaier, Andreas, "Zum Verhältnis Luthers zur Mystik," *Luther in ökumenischer Sicht.* Von evangelischen und katholischen Mitarbeitern. Alfred v. Martin, ed. Stuttgart: Frommann, 1929.
Beyer, Hermann Wolfgang. "Gott und die Geschichte nach Luthers Auslegung des Magnificat," *Luther-Jahrbuch 1939.* Amsterdam: J. Benjamins, 1967, pp. 110-134.
Bornkamm, Heinrich. "Luther," *Die Religion in Geschichte und Gegenwart.* Tübingen: J. C. B. Mohr, 1957-1965, pp. 480-495.
Hägglund, Bengt. "Luther und die Mystik," *The Church, Mysticism, Sanctification and the Natural in Luther's Thought.* Ivar Asheim, ed. Philadelphia: Fortress, 1967, pp. 84-94 *(CM)*
Hoffman, Bengt. "Luther and the Mystical," *The Lutheran Quarterly* XXVI, No. 3 (August 1974), 316-329.
————. "On the Relationship between Mystical Faith and Moral Life in Luther's Thought," *Bulletin,* Lutheran Theological Seminary, Gettysburg, Vol. 55, No. 1 (Feb. 1975), 21-35.
Holsten, W. "Hirsch, Emmanuel," *RGG,* pp. 363-364.
Iserloh, Erwin. "Luther und die Mystik," *CM,* pp. 60-83.
Joest, Wilfried. "Das Heiligungsproblem nach Luthers Schrift 'Wider die himmlischen Propheten'," *CM,* pp. 189-193.
Lau, F. "Calov, Abraham," *RGG,* I, col. 1587.
McSorley, Harry J. "Erasmus versus Luther—Compounding the Reformation Tragedy," *Catholic Scholars Dialogue with Luther,* Jared Wicks, ed. Chicago: Loyola University Press, 1970, pp. 107-120.

Manns, Peter. "Absolute and Incarnate Faith—Luther on Justification in the Galatians Commentary of 1531-1535," *Catholic Scholars Dialogue with Luther*, pp. 121-156.

Maurer, Wilhelm. "Luthers Anschauungen über die Kontinuität der Kirche," *CM*, pp. 95-121.

Oberman, Heiko. "Simul gemitus et raptus: Luther und die Mystik," *CM*, pp. 20-59.

Pelikan, Jaroslav. "Continuity and Order in Luther's View of Church and Ministry: A Study of De instituendis ministris ecclesiae of 1523," *CM*, pp. 143-155.

Ruh, Kurt. "Die trinitarische Spekulation in deutscher Mystik und Scholastik," *Zeitschrift für deutsche Philologie*. LXXII, 24-53.

Söderblom, Nathan. "Fadern i det fördolda," *Svensk Teologisk Kvartalskrift*. I:1, 1925, 8-19; I:2, 1925, 117-134.

Strauch, Philipp. "Zu Taulers Predigten," *Beiträge zur Geschichte der deutschen Sprache und Literatur*. Tübingen: Max Niemeyer, 1919.

Vogelsang, Erich. "Luther und die Mystik," *Luther-Jahrbuch 1937*, pp. 32-54.

———. "Die Unio mystica bei Luther," *Archiv für Reformationsgeschichte*. XXXV 1938, 63-80.

von Walter, Johannes. "Luthers Christusbild," *Luther-Jahrbuch 1939*, pp. 1-27.

Williams, G. H. "German Mysticism in the Polarization of Ethical Behavior in Luther and the Anabaptists," *The Mennonite Quarterly Review*, XLVIII, No. 3 (July 1974), 275-304.

Wolf, Ernst. "Holl, Karl," *RGG*, pp. 432-433.

# Index of Subjects

279

# Index of Names

283